GREAT WRITERS STUDENT LIBRARY

RENAISSANCE
DRAMA

GREAT WRITERS STUDENT LIBRARY

1. The Beginnings to 1558
2. The Renaissance Excluding Drama
3. Renaissance Drama
4. Restoration and 18th-Century Prose and Poetry
   Excluding Drama and the Novel
5. Restoration and 18th-Century Drama
6. The Romantic Period Excluding the Novel
7. The Victorian Period Excluding the Novel
8. The Novel to 1900
9. 20th-Century Poetry
10. 20th-Century Fiction
11. 20th-Century Drama
12. American Literature to 1900
13. 20th-Century American Literature
14. Commonwealth Literature

Editor: James Vinson
Associate Editor: D. L. Kirkpatrick

GREAT WRITERS STUDENT LIBRARY

RENAISSANCE DRAMA

INTRODUCTION BY
DEREK TRAVERSI

First published 1980 by
THE MACMILLAN PRESS LIMITED
London and Basingstoke
Associated companies in New York, Dublin
Melbourne, Johannesburg and Madras

ISBN 0333 28351 1

CONTENTS

EDITOR'S NOTE

The entry for each writer consists of a biography, a complete list of his published books, a selected list of published bibliographies and critical studies on the writer, and a signed critical essay on his work.

In the biographies, details of education, military service, and marriage(s) are generally given before the usual chronological summary of the life of the writer; awards and honours are given last.

The Publications section is meant to include all book publications, though as a rule broadsheets, single sermons and lectures, minor pamphlets, exhibition catalogues, etc. are omitted. Under the heading Collections, we have listed the most recent collections of the complete works and those of individual genres (verse, plays, novels, stories, and letters); only those collections which have some editorial authority and were issued after the writer's death are listed; on-going editions are indicated by a dash after the date of publication; often a general selection from the writer's works or a selection from the works in the individual genres listed above is included.

Titles are given in modern spelling, though the essayists were allowed to use original spelling for titles and quotations; often the titles are "short." The date given is that of the first book publication, which often followed the first periodical or anthology publication by some time; we have listed the actual year of publication, often different from that given on the title-page. No attempt has been made to indicate which works were published anonymously or pseudonymously, or which works of fiction were published in more than one volume. We have listed plays which were produced but not published, but only since 1700; librettos and musical plays are listed along with the other plays; no attempt has been made to list lost or unverified plays. Reprints of books (including facsimile editions) and revivals of plays are not listed unless a revision or change of title is involved. The most recent edited version of individual works is included if it supersedes the collected edition cited.

In the essays, short references to critical remarks refer to items cited in the Publications section or in the Reading List. Introductions, memoirs, editorial matter, etc. in works cited in the Publications section are not repeated in the Reading List.

INTRODUCTION

Like other outstanding creative achievements, the English theatre of the Renaissance was the product of a confluence of diverse elements held in fruitful tension. Elements, both popular and intellectual, inherited from the Middle Ages survived to play an important part in the outlook of the dramatists and in their understanding of their craft. They existed side by side with the new attitudes promoted by continental Humanism and, beyond these, with a growing sense that the traditional world view developed through a thousand years of medieval development and expressed in a majestic conception of universal law was being largely undermined by new attitudes and new discoveries: that, in the words of Shakespeare's contemporary, the poet John Donne, "New philosophy calls all in doubt," and that the traditional foundations of certainty no longer stood unchallenged in the face of a world subjected to rapid and disconcerting change.

The reality of this intermediate position was reflected in the physical form of the theatres for which the dramatists wrote. This form underwent considerable changes during the period under consideration and there is a good deal of uncertainty concerning the details of the picture which contemporary accounts and drawings have left us; but the principal points remain, from the point of view which now concerns us, sufficiently clear. The stage for which Shakespeare wrote most of his major plays at the Globe Theatre was a platform set up in the open air, in a courtyard annexed to the tavern of the same name in the London suburb of Southwark. The platform was surrounded on three of its sides by spectators of varied social standing who stood in close proximity to the action. It has been calculated that, of an audience of up to 2000 spectators, none was more than some 85 feet from the central platform.

This stage was evidently a successor of the platforms which were set up at strategic points in medieval towns, or which alternatively moved on wheels from one point to another on festive occasions and which must have attracted a heterogeneous audience not altogether unlike that which frequented the Globe and which was regarded throughout this period with some measure of disfavour by the authorities of the city of London and by the respectable interests which they represented. The "platform," however, in the process of evolving into a "theatre," had grown considerably in complexity to answer to the more varied needs of the new secular dramatists. The general picture which emerges is of a notably flexible structure existing on various levels and offering a variety of perspectives. To the main stage, so conceived as to allow an individual actor to detach himself, where necessary, from the general action and to address himself more directly to the audience (a matter of some importance in dealing, for example, with the soliloquies which play so considerable a part in many Elizabethan plays), there was added an inner stage at the back, normally curtained off but capable of being used where required, and an upper balcony above it. Entry and exits to the "tiring" (attiring) space existed on either side of the principal platform and there seem to have been windows at the higher levels which were also available for use, as well as a musicians' gallery on the highest level of all. A trapdoor afforded access to spaces beneath the stage which could be used for representations of "hell," or other demonic interventions, and the whole stage space seems to have been covered by a canopy representing "the heavens" in their reflection of the majestic divine order which was traditionally assumed to govern the universe and in which man, on his earthly "stage," occupied a central role as he acted out his temporal drama by exercising his unique faculty of responsible choice to ends alternatively of eternal salvation or damnation.

Much in these arrangements may strike an unreflecting modern playgoer as intolerably makeshift and primitive: an impression which may be strengthened in him when he reflects that there was practically no provision for "lighting" in the open theatre, and little beyond a number of conventional "props" in the way of scenery. Such a playgoer would do well, however, to restrain his sense of superiority. It is possible to hold that the stage we have just described in outline offered the dramatist who wrote for it certain advantages, the loss of which may have been conducive at least in part to the decline of any living conception of the theatre at later times. It was, in the first place, an *intimate* theatre in which the contact between actor and public was to a high degree direct and close. The public, which practically surrounded the stage platform, was intimately present, participating in the unfolding of the action as a whole. The stage arrangements offered, moreover, a superior degree of *flexibility*. The divisions of the platform stage, complex but not rigid, together with the absence of the isolating drop-curtain, enabled a continuous and uninterrupted action to be maintained and so assured the maintenance of a tension necessary to the dramatic illusion.

These inestimable advantages were enhanced by what might seem, on a superficial view, an intolerable disadvantage: the almost total absence, already mentioned, of scenery and stage properties as we commonly understand them. Once again, we should not be over-hasty in imposing any narrowly "realistic" point of view. In the last century, and even in conservative circles to-day, there existed a real danger of confusing the conception of dramatic action with either the "realistic" representation of life or with mere spectacle. It must be stressed against this view that a play − and more especially an Elizabethan play − is not in any primary sense a spectacle, and still less a direct imitation of "real" life. It is rather a spoken and visual *action,* essentially *unrealistic* and *conventional* in kind, which calls for public participation. If we believe, as we may, that the art of the theatre is essentially "poetic" in nature and that "realism," if narrowly conceived, destroys it we shall find this view amply confirmed by three centuries of Shakespearean theatrical production.

The "poetic" nature of the Elizabethan dramatic illusion was supported by a language which to a large degree maintained the rhythms of common English speech unmodified by the abstracting influence of the printed word. As in the case of the theatre, the outstanding qualities of the language had been created in the course of several centuries. The source of English linguistic vitality, as conditioned by social, economic, and intellectual developments in medieval England, were to a high degree local, closely connected with the self-contained society of the village and the country town. It was this reality that enabled Shakespeare to introduce colloquial expressions in situations where a continental writer, more accustomed to think in terms of a distinctive "literary," cultivated idiom, would have found them intolerable. This continuity of popular linguistic tradition, however, represents only part of the situation. During the course of the sixteenth century, the new forces of the Renaissance reached England and combined with the natural mental agility of the Elizabethans to bring into circulation a great new body of words and phrases. This intensely creative development was not without its dangers for lesser writers. Words, followed for their own sake, often lacked the necessary minimum of logical connection and overreached the limits imposed by the structure of the sentence. Some of Shakespeare's writing, especially in his youth, has connections with this type of excess, the conditions of which, however, he eventually converted from a danger into an opportunity (e.g., *Love's Labour's Lost*). The speeches of such characters as Macbeth and Lear derive their effect from a vast vocabulary, and sometimes twist the sense of poetic rhythm to their own ends; but their words are characteristically charged with meaning, rarely empty or merely rhetorical. Language and emotion, which may derive equally from the most direct and popular speech or from the most abstract and intellectual sources, are fused by the action of the poet's creative power. To believe that so perfect an instrument for the recording of states of thought and feeling can be described adequately in terms of "baroque" fantasy or rhetorical excess is to misinterpret the writer who developed farther than any other the possibilities of English speech as an instrument of dramatic expression.

The foregoing discussion can be summed up in a few conclusions. In the first place, the Elizabethan dramatist, like his medieval predecessor, based his work on a popular and social conception of his art. It is true that, by the sixteenth century, the participation of the craft guilds, essential to the old "miracle" plays, had given way to a more individual spirit. The new age is marked by the rise of the capitalist *entrepreneur*: its hero, Drake, was a patriotic pirate. However, the tradition that dramatic representation was a *collective* act, from which no member of the audience, however illiterate or lacking in social standing he might be, need be excluded, was still alive. *Hamlet* is, besides a profound analysis of spiritual motives and issues, a blood-thirsty revenge story of eminently popular content. *Macbeth* deals with the protagonist's choices against a universal background of redemption and damnation, but is also a simple story of crime and punishment, of the spiritual death which evil brings upon itself. Shakespeare's greatest plays, and those of his more interesting contemporaries, are more than representations, more or less "realistically" conceived, of personal destinies. They are certainly most powerfully all that this would imply; but they are also actions of *universal* content, offering some of the appeal of *myth*, expressive of a consciousness deeply implanted in the popular mind and accessible, in varying degree, to different levels of understanding, related but not identical.

Further, the situation of the theatre was such as to concentrate attention on the action, in which the actors appeared on their raised and central platform as intermediaries between the author and the public, requiring the audience not only to watch and listen, but to *participate* in the development taking place before it. In the Middle Ages, as in the Greek theatre, this sense of *participation* had been part of a frankly religious manifestation; it survived in the sixteenth century in a form akin to myth, legend, or even fairy-tale. There is a powerful sense in most of the greater plays of the period that a stage action has, beyond its immediate content, a representative quality: that the stage on which the actors perform their roles is a microcosm of the world and that the choices which they enact, the destinies which overtake them, reflect a universal human drama in relation to which each individual life acquires its measure of meaning.

Finally, this public action is to be conceived as essentially *poetic* in nature, though not necessarily tied to any form of verse. In the best Elizabethan plays poetry and dramatic action constitute a unity, which is that of what we call *poetic drama*. The poet's personal emotions extend themselves to the public emotions of the theatre, establishing contact with society through the highly *conventional* and unrealistic medium of the stage. The possibilities of the theatre, properly understood, lie neither in detailed psychological analysis nor in "realistic" truth to the surfaces of life. Of all artistic forms the drama is perhaps the most *conventional*, requiring from the author the highest degree of identification with the special conditions which its existence implies. Properly considered, its seeming limitations constitute a source of life, because they require the poetic impulse to flower with the greatest intensity and provide the poet with a field of action that, unequalled in emotional depth, transcends the expression of purely personal sentiment. The dramatic poet does not speak with his own voice, but through that of an actor. This means that he has to objectify his emotion, to see it, as it were, as standing *over there,* in independence of himself. He is as fully poetic, as intense in his expression of emotion, as any writer of verse; but, in addition, his chosen form obliges him to aim at the creation of a world that, in so far as it is outside himself, is beyond the accidents and projections of his own experience. The theatrical conventions of our day have changed in many ways from those of the sixteenth century, and no one would wish to recreate them in a spirit of mere historical accuracy; but the lessons of the Elizabethan theatre are, in a larger sense, still available, actual, and waiting to be reapplied.

The earliest dramatists who, in the period that saw Elizabeth's ascent to the throne (1558), began to explore the possibilities of a secular drama, derived their inspiration largely from the humanist tendencies encouraged by education in grammar schools and universities. The translations of Seneca's tragedies, brought together in 1581 in the form of *Ten Tragedies,* proved powerfully influential in providing the model for a neo-classical form of tragedy in English. The first play to develop this vein, Sackville and Norton's *Gorboduc,* was presented as early as 1561 for an audience of lawyers in the Inner Temple, and was followed by a small number of academic tragedies by other authors. From the first, however, these plays existed side by side with comedies of more directly popular inspiration, such as Nicholas Udall's school play *Ralph Roister Doister*, with strong elements of popular song and rural farce that suggest a derivation from such folk entertainments as the May dances or the traditional celebrations of Misrule. These were the only forms of living dramatic entertainment which offered themselves to a writer of plays at this time and it is not easy to see how the influence of their example could have been avoided.

Only, however, with the rise of the so-called "University wits," men who chose to make their living by writing for the public theatre after following a course of study at one of the traditional centres of learning and gaining a certain notoriety as literary bohemians, did the possibilities of the new theatre begin to take shape. Robert Greene and George Peele were among the first to appeal consciously to a wider theatre-going public and to introduce new conceptions of dramatic form. Some of Greene's plays, such as *A Looking Glass for London* (1590?), are exposures of social evils which reveal their connection with the medieval "morality" plays which preceded them, and some seem to be intended as responses to the alleged "atheism" of his contemporary Christopher Marlowe. More interesting are such works as *Friar Bacon and Friar Bungay* (1589?) and *James the Fourth* (1591?), which make use of contrasted plots in ways which anticipate, however imperfectly, the effects obtained by Shakespeare and others in works of greater complexity and wider human content. The weaving together of plots reflecting different levels of life in town and country, court and tavern come to have in Elizabethan drama a function notably exceeding that of comic relief originally assigned to it. That function certainly exists in these early plays, as it continues to do in the work of the later dramatists; but the more essential purpose of this device, as it came to be developed, was to explore a moral situation, enabling it to be seen from various points of view and grasped in its full human complexity.

Peele, unlike Greene, was himself an actor and, as such, closely connected with the new theatre. Some of his plays, like the early *Arraignment of Paris* (1584?), are courtly entertainments which combine the praise of Elizabeth with the retelling of the classical story of the Apple of Discord, interweaving songs in Latin and Italian with elements of folk tradition. Such plays, bringing together elements of popular "sport" and public pageantry, were intended to find their unifying principle in the celebration of the universal harmony of "Nature," symbolized in the human order by the unity of peasant and courtier in their common devotion to the Virgin Queen. It is noteworthy, however, that in *The Old Wives Tale* (1591–94?), perhaps the most attractive of his plays, Peele returns to pure folk-tale, thus giving testimony to the continuing strength of the element of popular tradition at this relatively late date in the development of the drama.

What the new theatre needed at this stage was a figure of outstanding genius capable of firing the imagination of audiences in the process of creating fresh dramatic worlds. Such a figure was provided, in a short and meteoric career, by Christopher Marlowe whose first plays, the two parts of *Tamburlaine the Great* (1587), introduced a new order of imaginative power to the stage. This power, both intellectual and emotional in its impact, made itself felt at once in the prologue to the First Part, which has the effect of a manifesto, a declaration of intent, in relation to what follows:

> From jigging veins of rhyming mother wits,
> And such conceits as clownage keeps in pay,
> We'll lead you to the stately tent of War,
> Where you shall hear the Scythian Tamburlaine
> Threatening the world with high astounding terms
> And scourging kingdoms with his conquering sword.

In his scornful dismissal of "rhyming mother wits" and "clownage" Marlowe is evidently rejecting the theatre as he found it and declaring his determination to follow paths of his own making. This purpose finds its most immediate expression in the creation of what amounts to a new conception of dramatic verse. The Marlovian "mighty line" opened to dramatists possibilities hitherto unimagined, and echoes of it continued to permeate the work of following writers – not excluding Shakespeare – for many years. Part at least of the fascination was connected with a sense of the overweening and the precarious which these "high astounding terms" insinuated in a way that was also deeply characteristic of Marlowe's intuition of life. Something of this is implied in Tamburlaine's claim near the opening of the first play:

> I hold the Fates fast bound in iron chains,
> And with my hand turn Fortune's wheel about,
> And sooner shall the sun fall from his sphere
> Than Tamburlaine be slain or overcome.

From a public accustomed to Elizabethan ideas on rhetoric, words such as these, developed with a power and control hitherto unparalleled, must have drawn a strong emotional response. There is much in Tamburlaine's aspirations to which Marlowe's audiences must have thrilled; but such audiences were still close enough to traditional medieval notions on Fate and Fortune to perceive the danger implied in seeking to maintain human life on this level. Marlowe himself certainly recognized this danger as he developed his plays. In Part Two, particularly, the reality of death interposes, bringing with it a descending curve to set against the hero's vaulting aspirations. Tamburlaine's desire to immortalize his love for the "divine Zenocrate" is powerless to prevent her death, and his own limitless conquests are contrasted at the end with the unadorned reality of his mortal situation: "For Tamburlaine the scourge of God must die." It is typical of Marlowe's genius that this conclusion, which might have been the occasion in a lesser writer for a moralizing "lesson," is presented with detachment, as a simple fact which no rhetorical assertion can either overcome or, in the last analysis, disguise.

Marlowe's *The Jew of Malta* (1589?) presents a hero who recovers from initial disaster to achieve the wealth and power which he covets, but who in the process overreaches himself and falls a victim to the forces which he aspired to control. Barabbas, besides being a Jew, is a Machiavellian, in the Elizabethan sense of the term: one who conceives of the world in terms of effective power and who, being excluded by his race and religion from a supposedly Christian society, sees wealth as the instrument through which that power may be exercised. In this he does not differ from the world around him: the Christians who reject him and profess to live by superior standards are no better than himself, and no edifying "moral" conclusion emerges from a story which combines theatrical melodrama with what T. S. Eliot called a note of "savage comic humour."

Doctor Faustus (1588? or 1592?), without doubt the greatest of Marlowe's plays, may have been written either before or after *The Jew of Malta* and may, in the opinion of some scholars, contain material, especially in the comic scenes, not from his hand. The theme as he found it in his source, the English version of a German story, has strong medieval and moral overtones which Marlowe may have viewed with detachment, but which – contrary to what is sometimes asserted – he had no interest in evading. Faustus's aspirations are those of Tamburlaine translated from the world of conquest to that of intellectual achievement and self-gratification. They are expressed in a tone which is not dissimilar in its craving for "infinity":

> O, what a world of profit and delight,
> Of power, of honour, of omnipotence,
> Is promis'd to the studious artisan!
> All things that move between the quiet poles
> Shall be at my command: emperors and kings
> Are but obey'd in their several provinces,
> Nor can they raise the wind, or rend the clouds;
> But his dominion that exceeds in this,

> Stretcheth as far as doth the mind of man;
> A sound magician is a mighty god.
> Here, Faustus, tire thy brains to gain a deity.

The rhetorical tone in these lines is not essentially different from that expressed by Tamburlaine. Marlowe's contemporary reputation as an "atheist" should not prevent us from seeing that, whatever his own beliefs may have been, he is both here and throughout the play attuned to the moral spirit of his source. Like Tamburlaine, Faustus overreaches himself. He sells his soul to Mephistopheles in the desire to obtain "profit" and to exercise "power," to make for himself, in other words, a caricature of "omnipotence." To obtain these ends, which amount to an "infinite" extension of what is of its nature passing and transient, he deceives and dramatizes himself until he is left at the end with nothing but despair: that absence of the Christian gift of "hope" which is, in the strictest sense, "damnation." Faustus, who began by expressing confidence in his power to manipulate time, ends by expressing his desire to hold up its inexorable course: "Stand still, you ever-moving spheres of heaven,/ That time may cease, and midnight never come." The desire is, of course, vain, as it must in the nature of things be: and Faustus, having sought his "immortality" in an impossible extension of the trivial and the temporal, is left at the last with the wish to see annihilated that same soul in the unending temporal extension of which he originally conceived his "bliss":

> O soul, be changed into little water drops,
> And fall into the ocean, ne'er be found:
> My God, my God, look not so fierce on me!

To believe, as some have done, that Marlowe wishes us to identify with his hero, is to ignore the contrary evidence which the action provides. This is not to say that he necessarily wrote it in an avowed Christian spirit or meant his audience to understand it so. The prevailing tone, as in his other plays, is one of notable detachment, and what the play seems to "state" is not any moral doctrine, or any assertion about the providential nature of the real, but simply the price of following illusion in an attempt to raise trivial and self-deceiving aspirations to the level of governing obsessions in the conduct of human life.

A contemporary observer, viewing the state of the English stage in 1593, the year of Marlowe's early death, and comparing him with the emerging figure of William Shakespeare, might well have concluded that Marlowe was the more impressive and powerful figure. He would, however, have been mistaken in his estimate of the final stature of these two great writers. Shakespeare, whose earliest work might well have seemed less striking in its individuality than the products of Marlowe's meteoric genius, developed more slowly but, as time would show, on a wider front and with more varied possibilities for development. Showing from the first a consistent and, for his time, unique interest in the implications of the dramatic illusion, he began by experimenting in various styles and different varieties of play, largely creating his own forms in the process of writing. From first to last every play of Shakespeare's represents, not only a development from what has gone before, but a new beginning, a fresh attack on problems involved in the very decision to write a particular kind of play. These creative experiments were carried out on a variety of material, and developed with a refusal to be confined by limiting conceptions of genre, which answer to his uniquely self-conscious conception of his art.

The plays with which Shakespeare embarked upon his career show him variously concerned with perfecting the mastery of his craft. Almost the earliest works attributed to him, the three plays on the reign of Henry VI (1591–92?), can be seen as attempts to discover what a "history play," built upon certain coherent and dramatically viable ideas as distinct from an episodic pageant, might be. The three plays show, indeed, by the end if not at the beginning, a remarkable continuity of purpose in weaving together two contrasted ideas. (The date of *Henry VI* Part I, and the extent to which Shakespeare's hand is to be detected in it, have been the subject of much discussion. Most scholars are now inclined to recognize

Shakespeare's authorship and to propose a date which may be as early as 1591. In this case the play is likely to have preceded Marlowe's *Edward II*, and Shakespeare can be thought of as the *creator* of the history play as a serious dramatic form.) The first is the notion, derived from a great body of medieval thought, that sin is eventually repaid in the form of retribution upon the sinner; the second, more "modern" in its implications and supremely reflected in the writings of Machiavelli, relates the existence of disorder in the body politic to elements of weakness in the ruler. Both elements are developed consistently and side by side. The first finds expression in the unhappy fate of nearly all the principal contendants as they become involved in the consequences of their blood-thirsty and short-sighted appetite for power; and the unhappy figure of Henry VI serves to join the two, in so far as he is at once a good man against whom sin is almost continually committed, and a feeble ruler who is at times disposed to admit that his claim to the throne is in some respects uncertain.

By the end of the series, in the more accomplished play of *Richard III* (1592?) to which it led, the implications of the drive for power are revealed in their related intensity and limitation. The villainous royal hunchback whose presence dominates the action (it is, after Hamlet, the most extended role in all Shakespeare's work) is a character so far without precedent in English drama. He is presented as a man constrained by his awareness of being excluded from the forms and fictions of polite society and indeed from the sources of "love" itself to make the pursuit of power his exclusive and obsessive aim. In following it he shows a combination of intense passion and ironic clear-sightedness which causes him to stand out against the world of shallow, time-serving politicians and helpless moralists in which he moves; but in the very act of attaining the golden crown which is his goal, the cost of success is also revealed as he reflects, before his final overthrow, upon the inevitability of his isolated doom. "Richard loves Richard; that is, I am I." The result of a lifelong dedication to the egoist's drive for power is seen to be the impossibility of self-evasion, escape from what at the last emerges, with dreadful clarity, as the limits of the isolated self. The realization will be taken up, in various and infinitely more complex forms, in the great tragedies to come.

These early experiments in the chronicle play bore fruit, a few years later, in a second and greater series of historical dramas, running from *Richard II* (1595–96?) to the Two Parts of *Henry IV* (1596–98?) and *Henry V* (1599). The broad conception underlying these plays answers to the current political notions, intensely nationalistic and monarchical, of the age. All four plays are conceived as successive stages of a study in kingship. The power of the king is assumed to be conferred upon him by God as a guarantee of order and of that hierarchical structure of society which cannot be rejected, according to this line of thought, without plunging society itself into anarchy and chaos.

The interest of these plays lies, however, less in these traditional conceptions than in their implications in terms of human behaviour. Already in *Richard II* the pattern of feudal loyalty has been broken by an act of murder; the play turns upon the contrast between a king, lawfully enthroned but personally irresponsible, and a born politician, Bolingbroke, who achieves his ends through what is, in the traditional terms to which his victim appeals, an act of sacrilegious rebellion. In the next two plays the new king calls his followers to unite in a Crusade which is intended to provide a focus for the national unity which he now sincerely desires, but finds that his original crime fatally engenders the strife which he aims at ending. The political success which eludes him is finally achieved, in the last play of the series, by his son. In describing the achievement, and in the process of giving it full value, Shakespeare brings out what has become for him a chief meaning of the whole story: a conviction, tragic in some of its implications, that political capacity and moral sensibility tend necessarily to diverge. The public vocation, upon the exercise of which depends order in the kingdom and success in its foreign wars, demands from the monarch an impersonality that borders on the inhuman. The king, as one of his soldiers says to him in a scene particularly searching in its implications, "is but a man as I am"; and just because he is so like them, and can share their thoughts and feelings at moments of stress, there is something precarious in the iron self-control which his vocation imposes upon him and in the absolute claim he is required to make on the allegiance of his subjects.

It is as a reaction against this precariousness that Shakespeare's greatest comic creation, Falstaff, appears in these plays as both the embodiment of all that the king must repudiate and as a reminder of the human loss which this necessary repudiation implies. In Part I of *Henry IV*, where the comic aspect prevails, Falstaff is a connecting link between two realities, the tavern world of broad if corrupt humanity in which he is at home and that of political rhetoric and intrigue to which he also has access. Thus situated in two worlds, and not entirely limited by either, he is used by Shakespeare to throw a detached light on the heroic sentiments to which the more respectable characters are given in their weaker moments and to comment, bitingly if irresponsibly, on the "honour" which they so freely invoke on the battlefield, often to urge others to die in their cause.

The Falstaff of *Henry IV*, Part II, is in many ways a different person in a very different kind of play. Age has replaced youth in the main action, fear and calculation assert themselves openly, and success is sought without illusion and without disguise. Falstaff himself, no longer engaged in an exuberant attempt to ignore the reality of time, is subdued to this changed spirit. Finding his companions among aging dotards, and himself haunted by disease and the premonitory thought of death, he strips them of their pitiful pretensions. The repudiation of verbal "honour" in the preceding play is reinforced by a more sombre evaluation of the human condition. Whereas in Part I his attitude on the battlefield at Shrewsbury had implied an affirmation of life beyond the selfish calculations of politicians, the Falstaff of Part II is content to allow those of his enforced soldiers who have the means to buy release from service and to accept the resignation of the helpless to their fate: for such, and no other, is the nature of things. The "young dace is a bait for the old pike," and "necessity," the law of nature, justifies all.

This growing conviction that the moral and political orders are barely to be reconciled finds its final expression in the scene in which Prince Henry, newly crowned, rejects the dissolute companion of his younger days. Here, as so often in Shakespeare, we must not simplify the issues. Henry, with the responsibilities he has just shouldered and which, as he has said in his first soliloquy, he "never promised," never asked to assume, *must* abandon Falstaff; but there is a sense that his judgments, just and inevitable as they are in a king, strike us as impositions, rigidly and almost violently asserted, upon his normal humanity. It is significant that in *Henry V* Falstaff is only remembered in the account of his death which is by general consent the most moving moment in the play. In an action where the touchstone of conduct has become success, and in which humanity has to accommodate itself to expediency, there is no place for him. Shakespeare has prepared us for the necessary change in the later stages of *Henry IV*, and now his death affects us as the last glimpse of a more human if flawed world. No doubt the dramatist drew his Henry V with a sense of necessary public vocation in mind. One aim does not, in Shakespeare, exclude another, and the fact is that, as we follow the uncompromising study of achieved success which rounds off the trilogy, a certain coldness takes possession of our feelings as it took possession, step by step, of the limbs of the dying Falstaff; and we too find ourselves, like him, in our own way disposed to "babble of green fields."

Side by side with his early experiments in the chronicle play, we find Shakespeare in the early 1590's engaged in exploring the possibilities of the comic convention, shaping it by a process which initially resembled trial and error into an instrument for expressing the finished statements about life – and more especially about love and the human need to live imaginatively – that he was already, beneath the obvious desire to entertain, concerned to make. The early stages of this exploration from the early *Comedy of Errors* (1593?) to *Love's Labour's Lost* (1594?), involving in each play a new approach, a fresh beginning, are too various to describe in the space available; but a brief consideration of two assured successes from different periods may give some idea of what Shakespeare was able to achieve through what turned out to be a life-long interest in the comic form.

The earlier of the two plays, *A Midsummer Night's Dream* (1595), can be thought of as a comic counterpoise to the "romantic" tragedy of *Romeo and Juliet* which equally engaged Shakespeare's attention at this time. Within the frame-work of a rational and social attitude to marriage, expressed in the opening scene through the preparations for the union of Theseus and Hippolyta, the action transports two pairs of young lovers – Lysander and Hermia, Demetrius and Helena, who feel that they cannot achieve their largely wilful purposes in the "real" daylight world – from civilized life in Athens to nocturnal wandering in the mysterious woods. There the irrational but potent impulses which "love" normally covers are released and the capacity of the young lovers to master them tested. The woods, in fact, are the scene of jealous rivalry between Oberon and Titania, respectively king and queen of the fairies; and the spell which Oberon, acting through his elusive servant Puck, casts upon Titania, obliging her to dote on the "translated" figure of Bottom the weaver with his ass's head, is evidently a central symbol of the irrationality and potential destructiveness which form part of the reality of love.

With Titania thus alienated from her true self, the love of the human pairs is turned to misapprehension and hatred until, having followed their fanciful purposes to a sorry end, they are ready to express themselves as thoroughly chastened. Their delivery depends on that of Titania, whom Oberon is at length ready to release from what he calls "the hateful imperfection" of her eyes. He accordingly declares that everything that he has caused to happen in the woods shall be remembered as "the fierce vexation of a dream" once the dreamers have been restored to their true selves, awakened from the following of desire in the night of error to the light of day and the truth of reason.

On the heels of these declarations Titania awakes and Theseus and Hippolyta re-enter the action as the sound of hunting horns greets the morning. The stress is now on daylight and harmony, the bringing together of "discord" into music, the uniting of the sounds of nature to those of human sociability in "one mutual cry." Lysander and Demetrius confess that their recent behaviour during the night has reflected an unreasonable fury, and even Bottom, in the act of standing confirmed as an object of ridicule, asserts after his own fashion the power of the vision which he too has been afforded:

> I have had a most rare vision. I have had a dream, past the wit of man to say what
> dream it was. Man is but an ass if he go about to expound this dream. Methought I
> was – there is no man can tell me what. Methought I was, and methought I had –
> But man is but a patched fool if he will offer to say what methought I had. The eye
> of man hath not heard, the ear of man hath not seen, man's hand is not able to
> taste, his tongue to conceive, nor his heart to report what my dream was.

The substance of Bottom's dream turns out to be nothing less than an echo, comically confused but none the less compacted of reality, of St. Paul's celebration of love as a transforming power in human life. From his attempt to describe what he has experienced we may gather that Bottom too has his contribution to make to the play's variations upon its central theme. For love, as it is here conceived, is seen to be at once a folly and to carry within itself, obscured indeed and subject to absurdity, but none the less real, a glimpse of the divine element in human life. At this point the ridiculous and the sublime meet in what is perhaps the play's most profound moment.

In the conclusion the various elements of the action are drawn together under the renewed control of Theseus in a social and civilizing vision of love. The marriage union is presented as life-giving, joining body and soul, reason and feeling, imagination and fancy in its assertion, qualified indeed but none the less humanly potent, of essential "truth." It is this "truth" which Hippolyta, hinting at the limitation of her husband's rational distrust of poetry and the imagination – the domain, as he somewhat sceptically dismisses it, of "the lunatic, the lover, and the poet" – celebrates in her comment on the outcome of the action just witnessed:

> ... all the story of the night told over,
> And all their minds transfigured so together,
> More witnesseth than fancy's images
> And grows to something of great constancy,
> But howsoever, strange and admirable.

Against this assertion of imaginative truth Theseus, as he looks forward to the entry of Bottom and his "mechanicals" with their Pyramus play, can still speak feelingly of "the anguish of a torturing hour." In easement of this "anguish" the lovers, whom we have watched in the woods following their absurd impulses of passion to "preposterous" conclusions, are to witness an action in which romantic love is exposed to ridicule. Their reactions to what they see – their charity or lack of it – will throw light upon what kind of men and women they are. To accept this "lesson," balancing truth against the ever-present possibility of illusion, is to affirm the faith in life and its ongoing processes which comes readily to the simple-hearted and which the arrogant and the sophisticated ignore at their mortal peril.

Some six years after *A Midsummer Night's Dream*, Shakespeare wrote *Twelfth Night*, a play which replaces the "framework" structure of the earlier work by one which turns upon the interplay and contrast between two plots conceived on different levels and significantly interrelated. The play, written at a time when dramatist's mind was already turning to tragedy, seems to have been intended to mark the festivity which the title recalls. It adds to many of the qualities of an aristocratic entertainment those of a children's merry-making, an occasion for dressing-up to mock the absurdities committed in all seriousness by their elders. In so doing it gives comic recognition to that sense of the incongruous, and to the need for providing it with a salutary outlet in the interests of continued social and personal harmony, which is one of the most persistent aspects of the comic impulse. Very roughly, one could say that the element of "masque" prevails in the "poetic" part of the action, and that the sentiments and situations developed in this are given a comic reflection in the prose underplot which is interwoven with it. The result is a comedy notably different in kind from *As You Like It,* which must have been written not long before and which also represents a high point in Shakespeare's comic achievement, and one perhaps even more closely knit in its interplay of contrasted levels of meaning.

The "serious" part of *Twelfth Night* deals principally with conventions of romantic love derived from the literary taste, aristocratic and sophisticated, of the day. Orsino's passion for the unresponsive Olivia is a blend of sentiment and artifice, true dedication and elaborate self-centredness. We might say of him to a large degree that he is in love with love, with his awareness of himself as an uncorresponded lover, just as Olivia is enamoured of her own grief for her dead brother. Precisely because they are capable of *real* feelings, because their human potentiality, as revealed in the intense poetic quality of their sentiments, so exceeds the common measure, they will have to learn to go in each case beyond their initial attitudes, to accept the experience which life offers, as it always does in these comedies, on terms not exclusively of their own making.

The primary instrument of this transformation is Viola, whose readiness to rely on her own resources in the moment of trial and to allow the currents of life to move and sustain her contrasts with the tensely self-conscious and finally restricting attitudes that prevail at Orsino's court. In her male disguise as "Cesario," and obliged by circumstances beyond her control to carry to another the message of the man she loves, she becomes the instrument by which each of the loves in which she has become so unpredictably involved find their proper object. Both Orsino and Olivia are brought to a recognition that the compulsive force of their passions is such as to draw them finally beyond themselves, demanding from each the acceptance of a fuller, more natural and spontaneous way of living.

This "lesson" is reinforced and diversified by the more avowedly comic underplot. In particular it is conveyed through the exposure of Olivia's impenetrably self-centred steward Malvolio when he finds himself, through the devices of Sir Toby Belch and Maria, imprisoned in darkness and visited by Feste the Clown in his disguise as a "curate." The comedy at this point is, indeed, not devoid of a disturbing quality. Its essence lies in the fact that Malvolio, though impenetrably deceived as to his own nature – and therefore plunged in "darkness" – clings to what he recognizes as solid reality against the illusions to which he is so mercilessly subjected: "I am no more mad than you are." In so far as it is a matter of distinguishing truly between external realities, Malvolio's protest answers to the truth; he is no more – and no less – "mad" than the rest of the characters in the play, or – we might add – the members of the audience who are finding their amusement in his predicament. The comedy of his situation – if comedy we can call it – lies in the fact that, lucid as he is in his attitude to his physical surroundings, he is yet – like any of those around him, but to a less curable degree – the "prisoner" of his own self-estimate.

Malvolio, accordingly, is excluded from the final restoration of harmony, much as the finally self-deceiving "philosopher" Jaques had been at the end of *As You Like It*. It is characteristic of Shakespeare's comedies that, when the time comes to work out the final "dance" of married harmonies to which they tend and which is in some respects a faint reflection in the human order of the greater dance of cosmic harmonies in which nature itself is involved, some character should be excluded or some situation left deliberately unresolved. So is it here with Malvolio, who responds to the Duke's invitation to forgive and be forgiven with a bitter protest against his treatment and a cry – "I'll be revenged on the whole pack of you" – which constitutes his last word.

It only remains to say that Feste, the most individual and enigmatic, so far, of Shakespeare's clowns, stands equally somewhat apart from the prevailing mood of reconciliation. The spirit of his comedy responds to constantly shifting attitudes, moods more complex and varied in their implications than may at once appear. He answers, perhaps, even better than most to the constant tendency of Shakespearean comedy to qualify its imaginative harmonies with a profound sense of relativity, of a final uniqueness and autonomy in human experience. Illyria too, in spite of all the beauty of imaginative fancy which has gone to its creation, is a dream; and it is of the essence of Shakespeare's mature comedy to touch the poignant and to extract from its sense of the passing and the insubstantial some of its deepest dramatic effects.

The closing years of Elizabeth's long reign, and the first years of that of James I (1603–25) were notably different from those that had gone before. The unity between court and people, personified in earlier years by the figure of Gloriana, the Virgin Queen, was giving way to a sense of separation which was not without its literary consequences. The fruitful interplay between sophisticated Humanism and popular vigour, upon which so much of the preceding achievement had been built, was in the process of being replaced by a more fragmented, even hostile perception of the social world. The Queen was an old woman who would die without leaving an heir; the possibility of a disputed succession was associated, in the minds of Englishmen, with the threat of an extension to their country of the religious civil wars which were tearing Europe apart and which it had been Elizabeth's greatest achievement to keep away from her shores. The war against Spain, pursued in the past with immense patriotic fervour, seemed to be prolonging itself in an apparently unending and increasingly pointless drain on human lives and resources. Economic depression at home was reflected in extensive poverty balanced by the growing rapacity, as it was increasingly felt to be, of the "new men" who were held to use the resources of public power for their private enrichment. Public lands, which had long played an important part in the traditional economy, were being subjected to enclosure, and the attempts of the authorities to finance the proliferating needs of government led to a dangerous granting of monopolies for trade in the recently discovered territories of the New World, to the growth of what presented itself to many as a new and greedy capitalism, and to a spreading corruption which became a principal theme of denunciation by writers and dramatists. Many of these developments can now be seen as reflecting the birth pangs of a new social and economic order; but they did not present themselves under that light to most of those involved in the process of transformation, and much of what was written in the first decade of the century reflects a sense of disorientation and rejection which contrasts strikingly with what had gone before.

The drama of the new decade is marked, under these circumstances, by a notable turn towards tragedy and satire. It is true that relatively minor dramatists, such as Thomas Dekker, contrived to think of their craft in terms of popular entertainment of an undemanding kind; but the titles of Dekker's most popular plays – *The Shoemaker's Holiday* (1599) and *The Honest Whore* (1604) – indicate sufficiently his intention to appeal to an increasingly "middle-class" audience by tending alternately to dramatic realism and to the skilful exploitation of sentiment. More interestingly, if less coherently, John Marston, in such plays as the two parts of *Antonio and Mellida* (1599) and *The Malcontent* (1604), makes use of the currently fashionable preoccupation with melancholy and turns the revenge theme popularized by such earlier writers as Thomas Kyd in his powerfully melodramatic *Spanish Tragedy* (1589?) and presumably in his lost play on *Hamlet* into an occasion for railing against the "world" and exposing the evils of a decadent and corrupt society. None of Marston's plays achieves success as a coherent work of art, but his dark view of reality expresses itself, at least intermittently, in verse which reflects a powerful if twisted concern with moral issues and which exercised a good deal of influence of his fellow dramatists. It is indicative of the nature of his work and of the spirit of the times that, like his greater contemporary John Donne, he was ordained an Anglican priest in 1609.

More impressive, because the product of a more reflective and consistently philosophical turn of mind, is the work of George Chapman, who is best remembered for his translations of Homer, but who was also an interesting dramatist in his own right. Chapman's principal dramatic work, written between 1603 and 1613, consists for the most part of tragedies based on characters and events of nearly contemporary French history: the two parts of *Bussy D'Ambois* (1604 and 1610?), and *The Conspiracy and Tragedy of Charles, Duke of Byron* (1608). In spite of these topical themes the plays have a curiously distancing effect upon the reader. Dramatic incidents are few and often far-fetched and characters are conceived less in terms of motive or psychological development than as a mouthpiece for Chapman's own brand of Stoic philosophy and for his conception of the relationship between the individual and a world which presents itself alternately as a temptation to which he succumbs or as an occasion for achieving inner fortitude and self-sufficiency. Chapman's ideal is expressed by the character Clermont D'Ambois in a typically magniloquent and "philosophical" passage:

> know ye all (though far from all your aims,
> Yet worth them all, and all men's endless studies)
> That in this one thing, all the discipline
> Of manners and of manhood is contain'd;
> A man to join himself with th' Universe
> In his main sway, and make in all things fit,
> One with that All, and go on, round as it;
> Not plucking from the whole his wretched part,
> And into straits, or into nought revert,
> Wishing the complete Universe might be
> Subject to such a rag of it as he;
> But to consider great Necessity....

Chapman's characters attempt, with varying degrees of success, to achieve this kind of Stoic detachment in the face of what his plays present as a corrupt and dangerous world. His most profound theme is the difference which separates the ideal from the reality of things, what in human nature *is* from what, almost in their own despite, men recognize *should* be.

The tendencies of the new age, however, are better exemplified, in as much as they affected the drama, in the work of Ben Jonson. Jonson prided himself on his considerable classical learning which enabled him, in his view, to produce work free from the excess and the absurdity that he found in most of his contemporaries, not excluding at times his friend and rival Shakespeare. It would be very wrong, nevertheless, to see in him nothing more than a scholarly author applying the fruits of his study in his own work. Jonson's learning proceeded from and reflected a keen sense of living tradition, which had a transforming effect upon what might have been in its absence arid and pedantic. The example of his first important comedy, *Every Man in His Humour* (1598), is significant in this respect. Jonson wrote it under the influence of a theory, which had "scientific" support in his own time, that the character of a man was the result of a blend or conflict of physical "humours" – moist and dry, hot and cold – in his body; where one or other of the humours predominated to the extent of imposing itself upon the rest the human being in question was dominated by the corresponding quality to an extent that determined his prevailing motivation and conditioned what we think of as his character.

The result of applying this theory was to produce, in Jonson's plays, characters more simply conceived, more consistently of a piece, than those we find in the work of Shakespeare. We may agree that this represents a limitation but should understand that it becomes, as used by Jonson, the occasion for writing a different kind of play. Jonson's theories were conditioned and modified by his access to the tradition which found dramatic expression in the old morality plays, producing characters deliberately simplified so as to embody one or other of the absorbing personal drives which condition human behaviour. In the medieval dramas these characters were used to give life to familiar moral abstractions: the Seven Deadly Sins or the corresponding Virtues. The names of some of Jonson's outstanding comic characters – Volpone (the Fox), Sir Epicure Mammon in *The Alchemist* – indicate sufficiently the continuing strength of this connection. Jonson, unlike Shakespeare, worked deliberately to simplify his characters until they stand for a single dominating impulse presented, through a dramatic action splendidly conceived and controlled, as at once consuming and finally destructive.

Jonson's greater plays are marked – to put the matter in another way – by the presence of a single overriding theme: the theme of human "desire," its inordinate pursuit, and the disaster in which that pursuit fatally concludes. His dramatic structures, whether tragic, as in the Roman play of *Sejanus* (1603) or, less successfully, in *Catiline* (1611), or comic, as in the great plays already mentioned, move with an impressive inevitability through an ever-increasing accumulation of excesses to a foreseen catastrophe. What in Marlowe's plays, and especially in *Doctor Faustus,* had been a tragedy of limitless "aspiration," an impossible craving for "infinity," is now conceived in more explicit moral and social terms, reflecting the mood of a new, more "realistic" and less aspiring age; but the theme is pursued through a poetry which, though different in tone from that of Marlowe, has the same effect of transforming the impact of the moral "example." A specifically Jonsonian poetic intensity, for example, produces the mingling of the imaginative and the grotesque in Volpone's attempted seduction of Celia:

> See, behold,
> What thou art queen of; not in expectation,
> As I feed others, but possess'd and crown'd.
> See, here, a rope of pearls; and each, more orient
> Than that the brave Egyptian queen caroused:
> Dissolve and drink them. See, a carbuncle,
> May put out both the eyes of our St. Mark;
> A diamond, could have bought Lollia Paulina,
> When she came in like star-light, hid with jewels,
> That were the spoil of provinces; take these,
> And wear, and love them: yet remains an ear-ring
> To purchase them again, and this whole state.

Jonson, in creating a character derived from the theory of humours endows him with a poetry that, in the process of drawing upon his own reading of the great classical satirists, transforms the deliberately simplified conception without detracting from the moral effect at which he aims. In *Volpone* (1605) the sense of catastrophe is obtained through concentration upon a single figure, dominating and central; in Jonson's other great comedy, *The Alchemist* (1610), the tight organization of plot prevails as the web of logically connected incidents moves in a continually narrowing spiral until it is finally engulfed in the inevitable, foreseen, but always postponed disaster in which it necessarily concludes. In either case, the intention is concentrated and intensifying rather than expansive, and to this extent it is narrower than that produced by Shakespeare's work; but every considerable art requires judgment finally on its own terms, and by any other standard of comparison Jonson's greatest plays hold their own with the best that has been written for the English stage.

Shakespeare also reflected in his work the changing mood of the time, but reflected it, characteristically, in his own way and through concentration on extending the possibilities of his craft. *Hamlet* (1601?), the first of his great series of tragedies, presents a figure of unparalleled complexity whose motives touch the action at every point, seeking clarification through contact with it and illuminating it in turn by his central presence. Hamlet is, and sees himself, alternately as a tragic and a grotesquely comic figure. Always and uniquely self-conscious, he brings to light in pursuing the duty imposed upon him to avenge his father's murder a state of corruption which affects the entire field presented to his consciousness; and, in the various stages through which his action exposes the ramifications of this infection, he explores progressively the depths of his own inner disaffection.

In accordance with this conception the early part of the play is concentrated on the revelation of the Ghost. This shows Claudius not only to have supplanted Hamlet's father in his mother's bed, but to have been his murderer. As a result of this discovery the world becomes, as Hamlet sees it, infected with what proves finally to be the infirmity that preys on his own mind. His thought, embracing the universe in the process of turning in upon itself, offers him the prospect of seeing himself as "king" of a space at once "infinite" and finally empty; but in so doing it leaves him victim to the "bad dreams" to which he is led by the contrast between the "infinity" to which his thought aspires and the reality of the "prison" – Denmark, the world, his own mind – in which an inner incompatibility condemns him to live.

The intrigue to which Hamlet is exposed by his uncle's efforts to penetrate his motives has a further, more intimate consequence. His love for Ophelia, in which his nostalgia for purity – purity, nobility, and infinity represent the persistent aspirations of his thought throughout the play – might have been satisfied, becomes the occasion for the "politic" devices by which Polonius offers to discover the truth for his master. Hamlet's anger is only in part caused by his discovery of the deception to which he has been exposed. Its sources are ultimately related to his inner dilemma. Love, trapped in the "prison" of the flesh and unable to conceive other than an abstract, bodiless "infinity," is exposed to decay; and so, reacting against this fate with an asceticism based finally on resentful despair, Hamlet incorporates his intimate disgust into the "madness" which is at once a disguise, a refuge, and a manifestation of despair. At once involved in his own action and able – actor-like – to contemplate his involvement in detachment from it, Hamlet swings between poles of tragedy and farce, becomes in a very real sense his own "fool," a tragic protagonist engaged in an unending effort to evaluate, and so to distance himself from, his own predicament.

To this exposure of Hamlet's infirmity there corresponds the undermining of Claudius's appearance of regal confidence and control. The play-scene, in which he causes his father's murder to be re-enacted before the court, constitutes the centre of the entire action. It shatters the appearance of regality which his uncle has so far presented to the world – like a painted mask covering the reality beneath – and brings to the surface the division which his consciousness of guilt implies. With Claudius's crime thus confirmed, Hamlet is ready for his intimate confrontation with his mother. The reproaches he directs against her combine moral indignation with a cruelty that answers to his own moral infirmity. As he arraigns Gertrude, he at once leaves her hopelessly divided against herself and, under the guise of performing a salutary act of moral surgery, finds a certain savage satisfaction in exposing further the roots of the division in his own soul.

This distortion ends by affecting his attitude towards the action to which his father's ghost has called him. As he is stirred, in a crucial soliloquy, to enthusiasm by the sight of the Norwegian prince Fortinbras and his marching army, he is moved to affirm the necessity of action as a sign of the rational and undivided personality:

What is a man,
If his chief good and market of his time
Be but to sleep and feed? a beast, no more.

In his own inaction, Hamlet is moved initially to admire Fortinbras − "a most delicate and tender prince" − but with an admiration that turns almost imperceptibly to criticism. If the soldiers before him seem to be moved by an "ambition" that he recognizes to be "divine," he sees them nonetheless as "puffed" by its presence in themselves. The word carries a sense of vanity and inflation, so that we are ready, in Hamlet's following meditations, to coincide with him in seeing them absurdly "making mouths at the invisible event," grotesquely agitating themselves for a mere "egg-shell."

At this stage, the divisions in Hamlet's nature are amply reflected in the action of the play. Nothing in Denmark is what it seems to be, every action has an underlying content which belies its surface appearance. Claudius's final intrigues − the despatch of Hamlet to England with orders for his execution, the use of Polonius's death and Ophelia's tragic end to involve her brother Laertes in a web of plotting − are no more than attempts to cover the infirmity of his condition, from which the "rotten" state of Denmark derives, by extending the area of the disease. Something not very different can be said, in the final scenes, of Hamlet himself. His return to Elsinore is from the first involved in death − he reappears in a cemetery and struggles with Laertes in Ophelia's grave − and the final resolution which fate puts into his hands is surrounded by obscurity and misunderstanding. Claudius, intending to poison him, poisons his own wife. Laertes, hoping to avenge his father's death, is caught in the trap he has agreed to lay for his enemy; and Hamlet himself only carries out the command imposed upon him after he has realized that he is himself involved in the pattern of death which has woven itself round his person. By the end of the play he has uncovered all the evils which surround him and has shown them to be variously, if obscurely, related to the stresses in his own being.

The setting of *Hamlet* in a remote, barbaric Denmark need not obscure from us that the world of the play is that of a Renaissance court, dominated by the ruthless appetite for power and the intrigue and insecurity that went with it. Some six years later, in what is perhaps the most deliberately "universal" of all his tragedies, Shakespeare chose a story that has initially some of the marks of a fairy-tale to present what might be called a dramatic metaphor of the human condition. The central character of *King Lear* (1605) is at once father and king, head of a family and ruler of a state, and his tragedy affects us under both these aspects. Age has weakened Lear's control over his own impulses, making him the prey of an anger and resentment obscurely rooted in the passions. By wilfully banishing his youngest daughter, Cordelia, he breaks bonds which precede reason and order, but upon which the unity of the family − and, in the long run, the significance and coherence of experience itself − depend. This crime against natural paternity is balanced by his elder daughters' disregard of all natural ties. A similar division explains the parallel situation of the aged courtier Gloucester whose illegitimate son Edmund undoes the bond of nature by dispossessing his true-born half-brother Edgar and bringing his own father to blindness and death.

Under the pressures thus created, family and state in *Lear* are alike disrupted. The process of dissolution culminates in the storm in which Lear, shut out by his unnatural daughters, and Edgar, supplanted in his rights by Edmund, meet in the depth of human deprivation. The external action thus becomes a reflection of Lear's own condition. Conveyed to us through his words and those of his fellow-sufferers, the tempest becomes, as it were, an extension of the personal mood. Man and his environment are seen as organically related; natural human relationships are shattered, and the state of "unaccomodated man" is conceived in terms of subjection to the beast of prey in his own nature. By the end of the storm scenes Lear and Edgar are united in their common nakedness, and as the old man's wits collapse the Fool, whose words have so far provided a kind of crazed reflection of his master's inner stresses, finally leaves him.

At this stage the blinding of Gloucester by his enemies represents the lowest depth of man's subjection to the beast in his own nature. It is followed, first by a kind of lull as misery seems to pass into Stoic resignation, and then by a compensating moral development in Lear's own reactions. Out of his consideration, born from direct experience, of the pitiful condition of basic, unadorned humanity, there springs a fresh awareness of the failings which have brought him to his present plight: from the wounded egoism of the passion-driven animal we pass to a *moral* consciousness of the terrible wound caused by suffering in human nature. Not only is Lear's past "unkindness," in the sense of neglect of natural feeling, opposed to the sense of solicitude and paternal affection to which he is painfully feeling his way back; but many of his words at this stage suggest the cauterizing of a deep injury, as though his very grief were a necessary prelude to restoration.

In this way we are led step by step to Lear's awakening and recognition of Cordelia. Bound up to this moment on what he calls "a wheel of fire," so that his own tears "scald like molten lead," he first reacts to her presence before him as to the vision of "a soul in bliss"; and the suggested idea of resurrection ("You do me wrong to take me out of the grave") contributes to the same effect. His grief, in other words, has become such that it can at least contemplate the possibility of beatitude. Cordelia's prayer for his benediction and his answering request for forgiveness imply feeling of a kind that surpasses the possibilities of expression. This is the central reconciliation, the restoration of the natural relationship between father and child, which is seen − while it lasts − as the resolution of the ruin originally caused by passion and egoism in the most intimate and sacred of human relationships. The vision of a "bond" restored through the action of love and atonement is one which will haunt all Shakespeare's later conceptions, up to *The Winter's Tale* and *The Tempest*.

In *Lear*, it is not allowed to prevail. We are engaged in an exploration of the human reality under its tragic aspect, not elaborating the supposedly beneficial effects of suffering in promoting moral understanding. The armies of Cordelia and her husband are defeated by the "realist" Edmund who thus becomes for a brief moment undisputed master of the political action; and though he finally dies at the hands of the disguised Edgar, neither his death nor his last-minute repentance can prevent the hanging of Cordelia at his orders. As the play ends, Lear returns with her dead body in his arms and, in a world dominated by emotional petrifaction and a sense of returning darkness, the curtain falls. Lear himself dies, gaining in death the only relief conceivable in temporal terms from "the rack of this tough world" which has proved so consistently indifferent to the spiritual intuitions which suffering has brought so painfully to birth. His faithful follower, Kent, announces his readiness to follow his dead master, and Edgar, joining hands with the surviving Albany, is left with the mission of restoring the wounded state in a spirit in which exhaustion and sincerity, purged of all excessive pretension, meet in a gesture of mutual sustainment.

Shakespeare's creative energies at this time were not exhausted by his unique series of tragedies. Towards the end of the decade he returned to the Roman themes which had already engaged him in *Julius Caesar* (1599), one of his most effective and detached studies of political behaviour. The greatest of his Roman plays, *Antony and Cleopatra* (1606?), shows a dramatist who seems to be engaged in stressing all the inherent difficulties of his theme while achieving the effect of triumph at which, in part, he aimed. His Cleopatra is at once the Egyptian queen of history and something more: a woman approaching her declining years, experienced in the ways of a corrupt and cynical world and conscious of having been, not a few years before, Julius Caesar's discarded mistress. Antony's love for her is clearly, whatever else it may be, the infatuation of a man no longer young, who has chosen to give up his public responsibilities to become the dupe of an emotion that he knows to be unworthy. It is a sign of Shakespeare's confidence in his powers that he chose this apparently unpromising material for what emerges as the most triumphant and, in some sense, the most positive of all his tragedies.

A detailed study of the play would show the dramatist obtaining his effect in a series of perfectly definable steps. The first concerns his presentation of the political action of the play. This covers a vast field − vaster, perhaps, than any in Shakespeare − and imagery stressing the concept of the world or the universe is constantly in the mouths of the principal characters.

This emphasis relates in two ways to Antony's own claims. He is evidently to blame in setting aside responsibilities so great for what is, after all, an irrational and dubious impulse; but side by side with the realistic moral judgment, which the play constantly underlines, there is an implication that if he does so the measure of his passion may be, at least in his eyes and while the effect maintains itself, correspondingly compelling. Seen from this point of view, the theme of the play is the necessity, and the danger, of living by the imagination. Men live, and in some sense *need* to live, imaginatively, by a process of creating their own "reality" and imposing it upon the world around them; but the process involves an element of danger which, in the inevitable recall to what is *objectively* real and inescapable, assumes the form of tragedy.

As the action proceeds the double vision which is so characteristic of the play, and which may be said to constitute its essence, is continually underlined. The Roman world is seen to be, under many aspects, in a state of opulent decay; the outlook of its leading figures is largely cynical and the struggle for power, open or disguised, is carried on with merciless intensity. At the heart of the play lies the contrast between Antony, the political failure, and Octavius whose success in worldly and practical terms is as impressive as it is necessary. Octavius, like other exponents of the public life in Shakespeare, is the type of man whose strength lies in his dedication to the necessary ends he has set himself. His private concerns are subdued, where circumstances require it, to the achievement of these ends. When, in a moment of danger, he needs to come to terms with his rival, he arranges a political union between Antony and his own docile sister, Octavia, who is offered up for what she believes to be a contribution to peace, but is in fact no more than a calculated move in the political game. The passionate Antony is unable to play this game with any consistency. Married by a device in which personal feeling plays no part on either side, he soon returns to Egypt, where the true object of his affection lies. From this moment his public fortunes decline until the final compound of shame and self-betrayal at Actium; but with the decline the imaginative foundations are laid for his elevation to true tragic stature.

That elevation, and a corresponding exaltation in Cleopatra, are achieved in the imaginative sphere at the end of the play and under the shadow of death. Antony's end is seen, even then, to be the inevitable consequence of perverse choices and personal degradation. No play is in this sense more ruthlessly realistic in its exposure of failure. Yet, just as the folly of renouncing the responsibilities of empire was felt to be balanced, at certain moments, by the paltry nature of political domination for its own sake, so does death, which is the consequence of Antony's prodigality, come to represent, at least for certain moments and while the imagination imposes itself, a liberation from triviality. In this way his suicide, bungled and pathetic as it is to the "realistic" eye, can become in his mind the noble action of "a Roman by a Roman/Valiantly vanquished": a final act of self-affirmation which finds its counter-part in the poetry of Cleopatra's end, in which "dungy earth," the baser reality of life seen from the distancing perspective which death supplies, is imaginatively transmuted under our eyes into fire, air, and "immortality."

The end of the first decade of the seventeenth century was marked, as far as the drama is concerned, by a further notable shift in mood. It is not that anything substantially new occurred in external circumstances to account for the change. The elements of stress and disillusionment which underlay the preceding tragic development were still present, and were indeed moving towards the first signs of the crisis which would eventually produce the Civil War of the 1640's. There is, however, in the plays now under consideration a notable development in two directions. On the one hand the tragic content of the greatest plays of the preceding decade gives way to an increasingly melodramatic concern with darkness, death, and decay pursued for its own sake: on the other, we find dramatists who seem to be seeking escape from the sombre considerations of their immediate predecessors by portraying in fanciful, sentimental tones a world ruled by the conventions of pastoral romance in which the happy and reconciling ending imposes itself in ways clearly unparalleled in real life.

These developments were related in some degree to the changing social assumptions which a new age imposed upon the dramatists. There is, perhaps, a certain significance in the fact that the Globe theatre, for which so many of the greatest works of the preceding decade had been conceived, was burnt down in 1613 on the occasion of a performance of Shakespeare's *Henry VIII*. Already, in the final stages of his career, Shakespeare had been writing for a new type of covered theatre at Blackfriars: a theatre which attracted a more consciously sophisticated audience and which offered the dramatist different opportunities in the direction of spectacle and visual sensation. Throughout this late development of Jacobean drama there is a sense of something that can appropriately be called "decadence," associated with the appeal to a more narrowly based and artistically self-conscious public. The creative union of popular tradition and Humanist aspiration, on which the greatness of the Elizabethan theatre so largely rested, seemed to be in the process of breaking down, of being replaced by the demands of a new age in which finally the drama itself would prove to be, for a time, irrelevant. In this sense the closing of the theatres in 1642, on the outbreak of the Civil War, came merely as the confirmation of a reality that already existed.

This general perception of decline does not imply that powerful, even great plays, did not continue to be written. Among them was *The Revenger's Tragedy* (1606–07?), generally ascribed to the mysterious figure of Cyril Tourneur. This draws on elements from both Marston and the Ben Jonson of *Volpone* to produce what is in effect a powerful allegory of evil working itself out in a corrupt and death-obsessed society. Some of the plotting is forced and, perhaps deliberately, unreal, tending to a phantasmagoric projection of unremitting evil. The characters are conceived flatly, in the morality tradition, and there is nothing of the many-sided complexity which makes of *Hamlet*, also built on a revenge theme, the central tragedy of the age. The power of the poetry, however, is undeniable, the product of a sombre moral vision engaged in projecting a society that has lost its natural foundations in the pursuit of false appearances of wealth, power, and self-gratification. This is a central theme of the new age, already foreseen in Jonson, but raised here to another level of intensity. The play's theme is betrayal and its central image is the skull which the protagonist Vendice addresses at one point in verse which reflects unique moral urgency and expressive power:

> Does the silkworm expend her yellow labours
> For thee? for thee does she undo herself?
> Are lordships sold to maintain ladyships
> For the poor benefit of a bewitching minute?
> Why does yon fellow falsify highways
> And put his life between the judge's lips,
> To refine such a thing, keeps horse and men
> To beat their valours for her?
> Sure we are all mad people, and they
> Whom we think are, are not; we mistake these;
> 'Tis we are mad in sense, they but in clothes.

Such poetry rests on a vision that derives finally from medieval tradition, which it applies to a contemporary world presented as adrift from its moral foundations, decadent and doomed. What, in such a world, distinguishes the "mad" from the "sane"? and, beyond this, what *is* "sanity," what "madness"? The expression, which sometimes recalls that of Marston, is distinguished from that lesser writer's work by its superior energy and economy. The only other play generally ascribed to Tourneur, *The Atheist's Tragedy* (1607–11?), is a less assured success; but *The Revenger's Tragedy*, whether it is his or not, is without doubt one of the most impressive achievements of the age.

More unequivocally "decadent" in effect, but still the reflection of a powerful mind, is the work of John Webster, whose two most notable tragedies, *The White Devil* (1612?) and *The Duchess of Malfi* (1613–14?), are the work of a dramatist who has moved further away from the morality tradition in the direction, alternately, of sensationalism and sentiment. Webster's moralizing is, by comparison with that of Tourneur, rhetorical and sententious, based in great part on aphorisms in the style of Seneca and Montaigne, delivered for their own sake and failing to reflect any sustained moral attitude or any coherent conception of social values. The characters who most move us, like the Duchess of Malfi, stand out as victims against a background of unredeemed brutality and corruption which ends by destroying them. The effect, moving as it is at its most powerful dramatic moments, is sentimental rather than truly tragic. The characters face their impenetrably dark reality with a self-conscious Stoicism that is in effect a recognition of the meaningless quality of life. Once again, the inevitability of madness is the theme:

> I am not mad yet, to my cause of sorrow.
> The heaven o'er my head seems made of molten brass,
> The earth of flaming sulphur, yet I am not mad:
> I am acquainted with sad misery
> As the tann'd galley-slave is with his oar;
> Necessity makes me suffer constantly,
> And custom makes it easy.

It is typical of Webster that his character, having attained this powerful level of sententious oratory, should follow it by the question "Who do I look like now?": typical in that the tendency of his tragic victims to self-awareness, or self-presentation, falls easily into the adoption of theatrical poses and melodramatic attitudes.

The work of Thomas Middleton belongs more definitely to the late period of Jacobean drama – his two best plays, *Women Beware Women* and *The Changeling,* were written in the 1620's – and reflects a realism which is at once powerful and limiting. It is not an accident that his earlier comedies were written largely in prose, and his verse in the greater plays reads like an intensification of prose, the vehicle of a view of life to which allegory and symbolism are completely foreign, the product of a detached moral vision which, at its best, achieves an effect of its own. The characters in *Women Beware Women* are naturalistically presented: the action is handled with swift economy, and the famous seduction scene, in which a mother is seen on the lower stage engaged in a game of chess while her daughter, above, is presented to her seducer, becomes the occasion for a display of dramatic irony which is close to the author's view of the world and of human behaviour. This view finds its most powerful expression in *The Changeling,* a tragedy written in collaboration with the minor writer William Rowley, but having in its best scenes the clear mark of Middleton's own hand. The story is, once again, of intrigue and seduction, in the course of which the "heroine" Beatrice so far overcomes her loathing for her detested and evil suitor De Flores as to persuade him to murder her unwelcome fiancé in order to allow her to marry Alsemero, for whom she has conceived an irresistible passion. De Flores accepts this commission and carries it out, but with the intention of demanding payment in the form of Beatrice's surrender to his lust.

This melodramatic story becomes, in Middleton's hands, the vehicle for an exposure of the inveterate human tendency to self-deception and of the "hell" to which it leads. Beatrice's attempt to dissuade De Flores from his design stands in naked contrast to her connivance in the crime which she originally willed and which in her own despite unites them:

> Why, 'tis impossible thou canst be so wicked,
> Or shelter such a cunning cruelty,
> To make his death the murderer of my honour!
> Thy language is so bold and vicious,
> I cannot see which way I can forgive it
> With any modesty.

The appeal to "honour" and "modesty" is of course, coming from Beatrice, inappropriate, even grotesque, in its effect. "Forgiveness" on these terms is no longer in question, as De Flores makes ruthlessly clear in his reply:

You are the deed's creature; by that name
You lost your first condition, and I challenge you,
As peace and innocency has turn'd you out,
And made you one with me.

To this Beatrice replies with indignant repudiation – "With thee, foul villain? –" only to receive the unanswerable logic of his rejoinder: "Yes, my fair murderess." De Flores is not to be moved from his purpose by her appeals to his humanity, and in his rejection of them – "Can you weep Fate from its determined purpose?/So soon you may weep me" – what might have been a theatrical gesture becomes, in the complete and chilling detachment which is so characteristic of this author, a recognition of the reality of a moral situation. At the end, stabbed by De Flores who then kills himself, Beatrice's last words to her father are a recognition of the bond which unites her irrevocably to the man who has killed her:

I am of that blood was taken from you
For your better health; look no more upon't,
But cast it to the ground regardlessly.
Let the common sewer take it from distinction;
Beneath the stars, upon yon meteor,
Ever hung my fate, 'mongst things corruptible:
I ne'er could pluck it from him; my loathing
Was prophet to the rest, but ne'er believ'd:
Mine honour fell with him, and now my life.

The kind of moral vision which produced this, and which is reinforced by the directness, the unemphatic distancing of the dramatist from his creation, emerges as the last major voice in a dramatic sequence that was, at this date, already approaching its end.

It is moral conviction of this kind, together with the fruitful unity of popular tradition and cultivated aspiration, that fails in the later dramatists of the period. Philip Massinger was the last dramatist to contribute, in his most successful comedy, *A New Way to Pay Old Debts* (1621–22?), to the line of development deriving from Ben Jonson. The principal character of the play, Sir Giles Overreach, can stand the comparison at his best moments with Volpone. The intention of commenting upon the evils of an unrestrainedly acquisitive society is evidently similar; but Massinger suffers from the lack of convincing positives to set against his powerfully drawn villain, and a good deal of the verse in this and other plays is lacking in the immediate energy which was so characteristic of the greater writers who went before him.

What we sense, in other words, in these late Jacobean plays is a decline in felt, as distinct from rhetorical conviction. Much the same can be said of the productions, written largely in collaboration, by Francis Beaumont and John Fletcher: the work of a new generation of fashionable dramatists dedicated to providing theatrical entertainment for a self-consciously sophisticated public principally attracted by the exploitation of sentiment in "courtly" themes of love and honour. The prevailing tendency, in such plays as Fletcher's *Philaster* (c. 1610) was to a new blend of tragic and comic emotions, set in "pastoral" surroundings and offering theatrical "solutions" to deliberately distanced "moral" issues. In such plays as *The Maid's Tragedy* (c. 1611) we are closer to earlier conceptions of tragedy; but here too the theatrical tends to prevail over the human content, and the dramatist's purpose is less to present, still less to resolve serious conflicts, than to involve the audience in the emotional transports of the protagonists. The increasing tendency towards collaboration (Fletcher is likely to have worked with Shakespeare, and certainly joined on occasions with Massinger) is a sign of the times, as is the remarkable popularity of these plays shown in the number of their recorded performances. We sense in these later playwrights a lack of strong positive personality, only partially overcome in a writer like John Ford, whose best plays, such as *The Broken Heart* and *'Tis Pity She's a Whore* (both printed in 1633), offer muted versions of the Stoicism of earlier dramatists such as Webster, but in a more resigned and self-pitying mood. Ford, however, in spite of his limitations, represents the last individual voice of a theatrical tradition that was losing its force in relation to a new age. In the pale tragedies of James Shirley, who survived the Civil War upheaval to live under the Restoration, it is evident that the theatre has ceased to attract the living minds of a new and different age. When the events of the early 1640's caused the closing of the theatres and the removal of drama from England for 20 years what was in reality confirmed was a death that had already taken place.

Shakespeare, meanwhile, continued to write for the theatre, either alone or in collaboration, until he retired from the stage in or around 1613. Characteristically, his last plays show him following the changes in popular taste while adapting the new fashions to his own concerns and, in the process, making something new and individual of them. His last undoubted plays were a series of so-called "romances" – *Pericles* (1608?), *Cymbeline* (1609?), *The Winter's Tale* (1610?) and *The Tempest* (1611) – closely related in theme and concerned to give dramatic form, using conventions which stand in some relationship to those of writers like Fletcher, to a new content which we may call, for want of a better word, "symbolic." Near the opening of each play a father loses his daughter or is expelled from his domain, either through the machinations of evil men or through the excesses of his own passion-driven folly. The main action is devoted to the suffering and recognition which follow from this estrangement and, at the end of each play, the lost child, who is generally given a name with clear "symbolic" associations – Marina in *Pericles,* Perdita in *The Winter's Tale,* Miranda in *The Tempest* – is restored to her father's blessing and becomes an instrument of reconciliation. In these plays the harmonizing theme first approached in *King Lear* and there broken by the tragic development produces a conception of drama completely removed from common realism and scarcely paralleled in English literature.

The final outcome to which this development led was *The Tempest*. It shows Shakespeare meditating, perhaps more consciously than ever before, on the meaning of the art he seems to have been about to leave. As the play opens Prospero, master of an island which he controls through the spirits at his command, is living with his daughter Miranda in a state of idyllic simplicity. The condition, however, is a precarious one. He is only there because he has been ejected from his dukedom in Milan by the envious plotting of his brother Antonio; and, as the action opens, he knows that the time has come for a return to civilized and social life. In this reconciliation Miranda has an essential part to play. To prepare her, and at the same time to create the conditions which make reconciliation possible, he uses his magic powers to raise a tempest to bring together on his island stage all those who formerly wronged him.

The early part of the play is in effect the working out on this "stage" of Prospero's projected "drama" and the establishing of a distinction between the various degrees of responsibility of his "characters." The least reprehensible is seen to be Alonso, king of Naples, who shows himself ready to repent of the part he played in Prospero's banishment and who is overcome, moreover, by the "loss" – as he believes – of his son Ferdinand. Having shown his capacity for repentance and for natural sorrow Alonso will in due course be forgiven, included in the final pattern of reconciliation.

Not all the evil brought on the island can so easily be mastered. Evil here, as always in Shakespeare, consists in the determination of selfish men to break the bonds of unity and conscience in the following of self-interest to ends of anarchy. Antonio, more particularly, induces his companion Sebastian to plot against Alonso in the pursuit of power. As the moving spirit in this conspiracy Antonio reminds us of the illegitimate Edmund who plotted with such terrible consequences against his own blood in *King Lear*. Both are possessed of the same destructive intelligence which they use with a similar disregard of natural ties to achieve the selfish purposes which their reason proposes to them as exclusively valid in life.

Apart from these, the main actors in the conspiracy, there remain the drunken sailors, Stephano and Trinculo, whose attitudes combine gross vulgarity with a degree of venial sin and nothing more. On the island these commonplace beings are brought into touch, not with the simple, noble savage who peopled undiscovered islands in the imagination of courtly theorists, but with the true sources of energy in the natural man. Caliban, the offspring of a witch but himself untouched by civilization, is a mixture of the poetical and the grotesque, the pathetic and the savagely evil. Unlike Stephano and Trinculo he possesses true imagination, which expresses itself in the appreciation of the natural beauties of the island; but no less than they he is forced, with the break-up of the order that has hitherto depended, somewhat precariously, on Prospero's rule, to choose between his spiritual potentiality and his animal nature. From Caliban's point of view Prospero is an intruder, a usurper who has deprived him of his natural birthright. Meeting Stephano and Trinculo with their bottle, and deprived since Prospero's advent of any valid god though the primitive instinct to worship is strong in him, he salutes them as "divine" beings and becomes the servant, not of Prospero, but of the bottle-bearing drunkard whose feet he is moved to kiss. Last of all, through the release of the animal instincts which have so far been held by Prospero under uneasy restraint, Caliban becomes the prime mover in a plot to murder his master.

The true purpose of Prospero's contrivance now begins to emerge. Once more, as so often in Shakespeare, the problem of "liberty" is set at the centre of the play. The degeneration of Caliban has shown that freedom, exposed to the influences of a corrupt outer world, can lead to total enslavement to evil. The very fact of Prospero's intrusion has rendered the concept of "natural" simplicity, as applied to "his" island, unreal; the new arrivals simply confirm and aggravate an already existing state of tension. The only means, it would seem, by which the relapse into slavery can be avoided involves an acceptance of the idea of service freely given to a superior conception of good. Prospero, at a turning-point of the action, puts this conception into the mouth of Ariel, transformed for the purpose from his usual ethereal self into an avenging harpy. In the name of a shaping Destiny, Ariel calls all the assembled "characters" to repentance as a necessary prelude to salvation. Unless their sojourn on this "most desolate isle" has revealed to them their own evil, their doom is certain. For it is in the nature of uncontrolled passion, as Shakespeare had already presented it in his great tragedies, to lead its victims to self-destruction; and Prospero's action, with its insistence upon notions of penance and amendment that can only follow from a personal, spiritual conception of life, is conceived as nothing less than a counterpoise to the processes of ruin.

The Tempest, then, is no mere romantic idyll. Since Destiny is proposed to be real and since a life-giving order is sanctioned by it, reconciliation can be born from the bitterness of tragic experience. Once more, the instruments of reconciliation are the children of the parents whom passion originally divided. Miranda, awakened by her father to the realities of the world, marries Alonso's son Ferdinand, whom she first saw as a vision proceeding from a "brave new world" of her imagination, but whom she has now come to love as a man. The "brave new world" is accordingly seen as an ennobling vision of love in the light of an enriched experience. In the words of the faithful courtier Gonzalo, the "gods" are invoked to "crown" the newborn vision of humanity with a symbol of royalty. The crown that they bestow is a sign of the "second," the redeemed and "reasonable" life which has been given to the protagonists through their experience on the island. In this way the whole action − the loss no less than the finding, the separation no less than the reunion − is seen to answer to a closely woven texture of symbolic drama. For a moment it seems that here, if anywhere, the entire design presented by Shakespeare in his mature work is logically and substantially complete.

To leave matters here, however, is seriously to underestimate the scope and subtlety of Shakespeare's conception. We must always remember that what we have been following is *Prospero's* play, which is not necessarily the same thing as Shakespeare's. There are, indeed, indications in *The Tempest* that the two do not necessarily coincide. The point in which Prospero seems to celebrate the successful conclusion of his contrivances by offering a masque − a further play within a play − to mark the betrothal of Ferdinand and Miranda is also the moment in which his presentation is interrupted by a darker note that forces itself, it seems unwillingly, upon his consciousness. Caliban and his plot have been forgotten and must now be faced: and for this to be possible the shadow game of spirits has to be ended and a return made to a more real order of things. The recall to reality moves Prospero to a deep uneasiness which communicates itself to his famous words on the "insubstantial pageant" which, far from being uttered in Olympian detachment, seem to reflect the anxious mood of an aging man burdened with his weight of responsibility, conscious of the limitation of his "magic" in the face of the mysterious and always ungraspable "reality" that so insistently breaks into, and dissolves, the imaginative harmonies it has brought so painstakingly into being. In the final Epilogue, in which Prospero, stepping forward on the now empty stage to address himself to the spectators, seems to be recognizing that the dramatic illusion is the product of a marriage between the author's creative imagination and that of the audience, the implication seems to be that a play – *any* play – has *no* single meaning, of the kind that can be abstracted from the action and proposed for approval or dissent in terms of any claim to final or exclusive validity. It may be that Shakespeare finally refused to contemplate the kind of play which such an affirmation, taken to be literally "true," might have implied: that he chose to remain true to a vision which has indeed its "wonders," but "wonders" of human creation, and sharing in the limitation of all that is human. For, in the words spoken by Theseus at the end of *A Midsummer Night's Dream* in relation to another, and very "human" entertainment: "The best in this kind are but shadows; and the worst are no worse, if imagination amend them."

READING LIST

1. Bibliographies, handbooks, etc.
Chambers, E. K., *The Elizabethan Stage*, 4 vols., 1923.
Bentley, G. E., *The Jacobean and Caroline Stage*, 7 vols., 1941–68.
Greg, W. W., *A Bibliography of the English Printed Drama to the Restoration*, 4 vols., 1939–59.
Harbage, Alfred B., *Annals of English Drama 975–1700*, 1940; revised edition, edited by Samuel Schoenbaum, 1964.
Wells, H. W., *A Chronological List of Extant Plays Produced in or about London 1581–1642*, 1940.
Stratman, Carl J., *Bibliography of English Printed Tragedy 1565–1900*, 1966.
Ribner, Irving, *Tudor and Stuart Drama*, 1966.
Berquist, G. W., *Three Centuries of English and American Plays: A Checklist: England 1500–1800, United States 1714–1830*, 1963.
Wilson, F. P., *The English Drama, 1485–1585*, 1969.
Brown, Arthur, "Studies in Elizabethan and Jacobean Drama since 1900" in *Shakespeare Survey 14*, 1971.
Logan, Terence P., and Denzell S. Smith, editors, *The Predecessors of Shakespeare* [and *The Popular School*]: *A Survey and Bibliography of Recent Studies in English Renaissance Drama*, 2 vols., 1973–75.
Penninger, Frieda Elaine, *English Drama to 1660 (Excluding Shakespeare): A Guide to Information Sources*, 1976.
Fordyce, Rachel, *Caroline Drama: A Bibliographic History of Criticism*, 1978.

2. General histories
Schelling, F. E., *Elizabethan Drama 1558–1642*, 2 vols., 1908.

Brooke, C. F. T., *The Tudor Drama*, 1911.
Spens, Janet, *Elizabethan Drama*, 1922.
Chambers, E. K., *The Elizabethan Stage*, 4 vols., 1923.
Schelling, F. E., *Elizabethan Playwrights: A Short History of the English Drama to 1642*, 1925.
Sisson, C. J., *The Elizabethan Dramatists, Except Shakespeare*, 1928.
Boas, F. S., *An Introduction to Tudor Drama*, 1933.
Ellis-Fermor, Una, *The Jacobean Drama: An Interpretation*, 1936; revised edition, 1958.
Wilson, F. P., *Elizabethan and Jacobean*, 1945.
Boas, F. S., *An Introduction to Stuart Drama*, 1946.
Rossiter, A. P., *English Drama from Early Times to the Elizabethans*, 1950.
Cunningham, J. E., *Elizabethan and Early Stuart Drama*, 1966.
Wilson, F. P., *The English Drama 1485–1585*, 1969.
Leech, Clifford, and T. W. Craik, editors, *The Revels History of Drama in English: Volume III 1576–1613*, 1975.

3. Themes, topics, short periods, etc.

Schelling, F. E., *The English Chronicle Play*, 1902.
Thompson, Elbert N. S., *The Controversy Between the Puritans and the Stage*, 1903.
Henslowe, Philip, *Henslowe's Diary*, edited by W. W. Greg, 2 vols, 1904–08; edited by R. A. Foakes and R. T. Rickert, 1961.
Greg, W. W., *Pastoral Poetry and Pastoral Drama*, 1906.
Boas, F. S., *University Drama in the Tudor Age*, 1914.
Lucas, F. L., *Seneca and Elizabethan Tragedy*, 1922.
Welsford, Enid, *The Court Masque*, 1927.
Eliot, T. S. *Elizabethan Essays*, 1934.
Bradbrook, M. C., *Themes and Conventions of Elizabethan Tragedy*, 1935.
Craig, Hardin, editor, *Essays in Dramatic Literature: The Parrott Presentation Volume*, 1935.
Farnham, Willard, *The Medieval Heritage of Elizabethan Tragedy*, 1936; revised edition, 1950.
Spencer, Theodore, *Death and Elizabethan Tragedy*, 1936.
Nicoll, Allardyce, *Stuart Masques and the Renaissance Stage*, 1937.
Knights, L. C., *Drama and Society in the Age of Jonson*, 1937.
Bowers, Fredson, *Elizabethan Revenge Tragedy 1587–1642*, 1940.
Adams, John Cranford, *The Globe Playhouse: Its Design and Equipment*, 1942; revised edition, 1961.
Adams, H. H., *English Domestic or Homiletic Tragedy 1575–1642*, 1943.
Ellis-Fermor, Una, *The Frontiers of Drama*, 1945.
Charlton, H.B., *The Senecan Tradition in Renaissance Tragedy*, 1946.
Bowden, W. R., *The English Dramatic Lyric 1603–42: A Study in Stuart Dramatic Technique*, 1951.
Harbage, Alfred B., *Shakespeare and the Rival Traditions*, 1952.
Hodges, G. W., *The Globe Restored*, 1953.
Doran, Madeleine, *Endeavors of Art: A Study of Form in Elizabethan Drama*, 1954.
Simpson, Percy, *Studies in Elizabethan Drama*, 1955.
Bradbrook, M. C., *The Growth and Structure of Elizabethan Comedy*, 1955.
Curry, John V., *Deception in Elizabethan Comedy*, 1955.
Bowers, Fredson, *On Editing Shakespeare and the Elizabethan Dramatists*, 1955.
Ribner, Irving, *The English History Play in the Age of Shakespeare*, 1957; revised edition, 1965.
Craik, T. W., *The Tudor Interlude*, 1958.
Hotson, Leslie, *Shakespeare's Wooden O*, 1959.
Bennett, J. W., Oscar Cargill, and Vernon Hall, Jr., editors, *Studies in the English Renaissance Drama in Memory of Karl Julius Holzknecht*, 1959.

Ornstein, Robert, *The Moral Vision of Jacobean Tragedy*, 1960.
Galloway, David, editor, *The Elizabethan Theatre*, 4 vols., 1960–74.
Brown, John Russell, and Bernard Harris, editors, *Jacobean Theatre*, 1960; *Elizabethan Drama*, 1966.
Kaufmann, R. J., editor, *Elizabethan Drama*, 1961.
Campbell, L. B., *Divine Poetry and Drama in Sixteenth Century England*, 1961.
Clemen, Wolfgang, *English Tragedy Before Shakespeare*, translated by T. S. Dorsch, 1961.
Bluestone, Max, and Norman Rabkin, editors, *Shakespeare's Contemporaries: Modern Studies in English Renaissance Drama*, 1961.
Ribner, Irving, *Jacobean Tragedy: The Quest for Moral Order*, 1962.
Bevington, D. M., *From Mankind to Marlowe: The Growth of Structure in the Popular Drama of Tudor England*, 1962.
Hosley, Richard, editor, *Essays on Shakespeare and Elizabethan Drama in Honor of Hardin Craig*, 1962.
Beckerman, Bernard, *Shakespeare at the Globe*, 1962.
Tomlinson, T. B., *A Study of Elizabethan and Jacobean Tragedy*, 1964.
Stroup, T. B., *Microcosmus: The Shape of the Elizabethan Play*, 1965.
Bradbrook, M. C., *English Dramatic Form: A History of Its Development*, 1965.
McDonald, C. O., *The Rhetoric of Tragedy: Form in Stuart Drama*, 1966.
Margeson, J. M. R., *The Origins of English Tragedy*, 1967.
Gibbons, B., *Jacobean City Comedy*, 1967.
Roston, M., *Biblical Drama in England*, 1968.
Bentley, G. E., editor, *The Seventeenth-Century Stage: A Collection of Critical Essays*, 1968.
Blackburn, Ruth H., *Biblical Drama under the Tudors*, 1971.
Bergeron, David M., *English Civic Pageantry 1558–1642*, 1971.
Brodwin, Leonora Leet, *Elizabethan Love Tragedy 1587–1625*, 1971.
Levin, Richard, *The Multiple Plot in English Renaissance Drama*, 1971.
Lever, J. W., *The Tragedy of State*, 1971.
Waith, Eugene M., *Ideas of Greatness: Heroic Drama in England*, 1971.
Kirsch, Arthur C., *Jacobean Dramatic Perspectives*, 1972.
Leggatt, Alexander, *Citizen Comedy in the Age of Shakespeare*, 1973.
Southern, Richard, *The Staging of Plays Before Shakespeare*, 1974.
Ure, Peter, *Elizabethan and Jacobean Drama: Critical Essays*, edited by J. C. Maxwell, 1974.
Bradbrook, M. C., *The Living Monument: Shakespeare and the Theatre of His Time*, 1976.

4. Anthologies of primary works
Nichols, J., editor, *The Progresses and Public Processions of Queen Elizabeth*, 4 vols., 1788–1828.
Nichols, J., editor, *The Progresses, Processions, and Magnificent Festivities of King James I*, 4 vols., 1828.
Evans, H. A., *English Masques*, 1897.
Farmer, J. S., editor, *Early English Dramatists*, 12 vols., 1905–08.
Brooke, C. F. T., editor, *The Shakespeare Apocrypha*, 1908.
Neilson, W. A., editor, *The Chief Elizabethan Dramatists*, 1911.
Adams, J. Q., editor, *Chief Pre-Shakespearean Dramas*, 1924.
Schelling, F. E., editor, *Typical Elizabethan Plays*, 1926; revised edition, 1931.
Brooke, C. F. T., and N. B. Paradise, editors, *English Drama 1580–1642*, 1933.
Baskerville, C. R., V. B. Heltzel, and A. H. Nethercot, editors, *Elizabethan and Stuart Plays*, 1934.
Harrier, R. C., editor, *An Anthology of Jacobean and Stuart Drama*, 2 vols., 1963.
Spencer, Theodore, and S. W. Wells, editors, *A Book of Masques in Honour of Allardyce Nicoll*, 1967.

BEAUMONT, Francis. English. Born in Gracedieu, Leicestershire, in 1584 or 1585; brother of the poet Sir John Beaumont. Educated at Broadgates Hall, now Pembroke College, Oxford, 1597–98, left without taking a degree; entered Inner Temple, London, 1600, but never practised law. Married Ursula Isley in 1613; two daughters. Lived in London from 1600; a friend of Drayton and Ben Jonson; met John Fletcher in 1605, and thereafter collaborated with him in writing for the theatre until his retirement at the time of his marriage. *Died 6 March 1616.*

PUBLICATIONS

Collections

> *Comedies and Tragedies*, with Fletcher and others.   1647; revised edition, 1679.
> *The Dramatic Works in the Beaumont and Fletcher Canon*, edited by Fredson Bowers.   3 vols (of 10), 1966–76.

Plays

> *The Woman's Prize*, with Fletcher (produced after 1604).   In *Comedies and Tragedies*, 1647.
> *The Woman Hater* (produced 1605).   1607; edited by George Walton Williams, in *Dramatic Works 1*, 1966.
> *The Knight of the Burning Pestle* (produced 1607).   1613; edited by Andrew Gurr, 1968.
> *Philaster; or, Love Lies A-Bleeding*, with Fletcher (produced before 1610).   1620; edited by Dora Jean Ashe, 1974.
> *The Maid's Tragedy*, with Fletcher (produced before 1611).   1619; edited by Robert K. Turner, Jr., in *Dramatic Works 2*, 1970.
> *A King and No King*, with Fletcher (produced 1611).   1619; edited by George Walton Williams, in *Dramatic Works 2*, 1970.
> *Cupid's Revenge*, with Fletcher (produced before 1612).   1615; edited by Fredson Bowers, in *Dramatic Works 2*, 1970.
> *The Coxcomb*, with Fletcher (produced 1612).   In *Comedies and Tragedies*, 1647; edited by Irby B. Cauthen, Jr., in *Dramatic Works 1*, 1966.
> *The Masque of the Inner Temple and Gray's Inn* (produced 1613).   1613; edited by Fredson Bowers, in *Dramatic Works 1*, 1966.
> *The Scornful Lady*, with Fletcher (produced 1613–17?).   1616; edited by Cyrus Hoy, in *Dramatic Works 2*, 1970.
> *The Captain*, with Fletcher (produced 1613).   In *Comedies and Tragedies*, 1647; edited by L. A. Beaurline, in *Dramatic Works 1*, 1966.
> *Love's Pilgrimage*, with Fletcher (produced 1616?).   In *Comedies and Tragedies*, 1647; edited by L. A. Beaurline, in *Dramatic Works 2*, 1970.
> *The Wild Goose Chase*, with Fletcher (produced 1621?).   1652.
> *The Noble Gentleman*, with Fletcher (produced 1625–26?).   In *Comedies and Tragedies*, 1647; edited by L. A. Beaurline, in *Dramatic Works 3*, 1976.

Verse

> *Salmacis and Hermaphroditus.*   1602; edited by N. Alexander, in *Elizabethan Narrative Verse*, 1968.

Poems.   1640; revised edition, 1653, 1660.
Songs and Lyrics from the Plays of Beaumont and Fletcher, edited by E. H. Fellowes.   1928.

Bibliography: *Beaumont and Fletcher: A Concise Bibliography* by S. A. Tannenbaum, 1938; supplement, 1946; supplement in *Elizabethan Bibliographies Supplements 8* by C. A. Pennell and W. P. Williams, 1968.

Reading List: *Beaumont, Fletcher, and Company: Entertainers to the Jacobean Gentry* by L. B. Wallis, 1947; *The Pattern of Tragicomedy in Beaumont and Fletcher* by Eugene Waith, 1952; *Beaumont and Fletcher: A Critical Study* by W. W. Appleton, 1956; *Beaumont and Fletcher* by Ian Fletcher, 1967.

*   *   *

Francis Beaumont's career was almost a parody of the aspirations of a minor literary figure. A younger son of rural gentry, he gained notice as a poet and fame and fortune as a playwright on the London stage. At 16 he was living in London and studying law at an Inn of Court. A burlesque lecture on grammar which he gave for his fellow students at the Inner Temple survives, and he fairly certainly wrote *Salmacis and Hermaphroditus,* published in 1602. It is a fluent but routine piece of sub-erotic versifying of a story from Ovid in the fashion made popular by Shakespeare and Marlowe in the 1590's and often practised by law students. His masque, written for the Inner Temple and Gray's Inn as a contribution to the celebrations of the Palatine marriage in 1613, is a similar piece of fashionable versifying.

His lack of an inclination to study law, his preference for writing, and perhaps a need for money are indicated by the performance of his prose comedy *The Woman Hater,* by the boy company of St. Paul's. Its complex plot and strenuous wit-play owe an obvious debt to Ben Jonson's early comedies. The other boy company of the time produced his comic masterpiece, *The Knight of the Burning Pestle.* Its first performance, however, was a flop, and all of Beaumont's subsequent playwriting was in collaboration with John Fletcher, a man in a similar position and with similar ambitions. They were both members of the so-called "tribe of Ben," friends and followers of Jonson. Both Beaumont and Fletcher wrote commendatory verses for the publication of *Volpone* in 1607. Beaumont's most famous poem is his verse letter to Jonson celebrating their meetings at the Mermaid tavern, a poem which encapsulates Beaumont's vision of literary life in London in 1607.

His own greatest fame arrived when he started his collaboration with Fletcher as founder member of a writing partnership which in the end produced more than fifty plays; these works share with Shakespeare's and Jonson's the distinction of being the only corpus of Jacobean drama thought worthy of being collected in folio. Beaumont actually shared in the writing of only a few, but three of these, *Philaster, The Maid's Tragedy,* and *A King and No King,* established the distinctive style and reputation of the partnership. From 1609 they appear to have taken over Shakespeare's duties of providing his company with one serious play and one comedy each year. Beaumont retired from the partnership in 1613 when he married an heiress.

Beaumont's chief claim to artistic standing is *The Knight of the Burning Pestle.* As John Doebler notes in *Studies in English Literature* (1965), it burlesques the Prodigal Son theme of the popular merchant and apprentice plays with the story of a prodigal father, celebrating mirth above money. A witty mixture of plays within plays satirising citizen tastes and unsophisticated audiences, and laced with both popular ballads and composers' songs, it is one of the few wholly successful Jacobean comedies outside Shakespeare.

The antithesis of this sophisticated mockery of popular inanities appeared with *Philaster,* the first play written by the partnership for Shakespeare's company, and its first success. Closely related to *Cymbeline* in the time of its writing and in its genre as a tragi-comedy or romance, it was evidently designed as a vehicle for a new taste in theatrical fashion. Its ambience is the courtly world of Sidney's *Arcadia*, where honour and virtue are tested and examined in a variety of arduous situations, as J. F. Danby (*Elizabethan and Jacobean Poets*, 1952) has demonstrated. It was a taste which caught on rapidly, and the fifty or more plays which the Beaumont and Fletcher canon eventually grew into testify to its massive dominance on the Jacobean stage.

The tragicomedy which was developed as a distinctive genre in *Philaster* can be seen at its best in some of the plays written by Fletcher after Beaumont retired. Its "romance" flavour also appeared in tragedies, however, notably *The Maid's Tragedy*, the most powerful of the plays in which Beaumont had a hand. It is a tragedy in that most of its leading characters die by the end, but it shares the chief qualities of the tragi-comedies. Character is less important than moral qualities, situations are contrived to test ethics, the verse is a simple and economic vehicle for the testing situations. *The Maid's Tragedy*, for instance, canvasses the possibilities of two alternative courses of conduct when honour is at risk. A king has a secret mistress; for appearance's sake he marries her to a young man. The husband finds his honour is stained on his wedding night, but holds back from revenge because the adulterer is his king. The woman's brother, a soldier, has no such hesitation and contrives the king's death. The young husband kills himself on realising how much destruction has followed his hesitation, while the soldier lives on "accurst." This sort of patterning through parallels and contrasts is a conspicuous feature of the design of all the "Beaumont and Fletcher" plays, and a clear acknowledgement of their literary model, Sidney's *Arcadia*, as a guide to courtly ethics. The taste they created lasted on the English stage for more than a century.

—Andrew Gurr

BROME, Richard.   English.   Born in England c. 1590. Little is known about his life except that he was a servant to Ben Jonson c. 1614, and was afterwards Jonson's friend and protégé. *Died in 1652.*

PUBLICATIONS

Collections

Dramatic Works, edited by R. H. Shepherd.   3 vols., 1873.

Plays

The Northern Lass (produced 1629).   1632.
The Queen's Exchange (produced 1629–30?).   1657; as *The Royal Exchange*, 1661.
The City Wit; or, The Woman Wears the Breeches (produced 1630–31?).   In *Five New Plays*, 1653.

The Novella (produced 1632). In *Five New Plays*, 1653.

The Weeding of Covent Garden; or, The Middlesex Justice of Peace (produced 1632?). In *Five New Plays*, 1653.

The Love-Sick Court; or, The Ambitious Politique (produced 1633–34?). In *Five New Plays*, 1658.

The Late Lancashire Witches, with Thomas Heywood (produced 1634). 1634.

The Sparagus Garden (produced 1635). 1640.

The New Academy; or, The New Exchange (produced 1635?). In *Five New Plays*, 1658.

The Queen and the Concubine (produced 1635–36?). In *Five New Plays*, 1658.

The English Moor; or, The Mock Marriage (produced 1637). In *Five New Plays*, 1658.

The Antipodes (produced 1638). 1640; edited by Ann Haaker, 1966.

The Damoiselle; or, The New Ordinary (produced 1638?). In *Five New Plays*, 1653.

A Mad Couple Well Matched (produced 1639?). In *Five New Plays*, 1653; edited by A. S. Knowland, in *Six Caroline Plays*, 1962.

The Court Beggar (produced 1640). In *Five New Plays*, 1653.

A Jovial Crew; or, The Merry Beggars (produced 1641). 1652; edited by Ann Haaker, 1966.

Five New Plays. 1653.

Five New Plays, edited by Alexander Brome. 1658.

Other

Editor, *Monsieur Thomas*, by John Fletcher. 1639.

Editor, *Lachrymae Musarum: The Tears of the Muses* (elegies on the death of Henry, Lord Hastings). 1649.

Reading List: *A Study of the Comedies of Brome, Especially as Representative of Dramatic Decadence* by Herbert F. Allen, 1912; *Brome: A Study of His Life and Works* by Clarence E. Andrews, 1913; *Brome, Caroline Playwright* by R. J. Kaufmann, 1961.

*   *   *

The tradition of Jonsonian satirical comedy survived until the closing of the theatres in 1642 chiefly in the plays of Richard Brome, whom Jonson himself twice described as his servant. Between 1623, the date of his first recorded play, *A Fault of Friendship* (not extant), and 1642, when he revised a play written ten years earlier, *The Weeding of Covent Garden*, Brome was responsible for some twenty surviving plays and several others now lost. He combined a talent for satirical comedy in the Jonsonian manner with a real feeling for the more romantic comic drama of Heywood and Dekker. His two best plays, *The Northern Lass* and *A Jovial Crew*, show Brome's dramatic gifts at their happiest. Both the savage eye for the grotesque and the linguistic vitality of Jonson are lacking here, but both plays show a good deal of cheerful wit and ingenuity of plot. Another aspect of Brome's dramatic talent is displayed in *The Late Lancashire Witches*, a spirited melodrama based on topical events which he wrote in collaboration with Heywood. Among his other plays, *The Love-Sick Court* is of interest as Brome's variant on the heroic drama which held the stage in the 1630's. It is difficult to judge how far Brome intended the play as a satire on the heroic mode.

Decidedly a minor dramatist, Brome has a place in the history of English drama that is small but secure by virtue of a refreshing directness of feeling and adroitness of construction. He is the "Son of Ben" in drama to the same degree that Herrick is in lyric poetry.

—Gāmini Salgādo

CARTWRIGHT,   William. English. Born in Northway, near Tewkesbury, Gloucestershire, in September 1611. Educated at a free school in Cirencester; Westminster School, London (King's Scholar); Christ Church, Oxford, student 1628, M.A. 1635. Ordained, 1635, and became noted as an Oxford preacher; Reader in Metaphysic, Oxford University, 1642; appointed to the Council of War, 1642; Succentor of the Church in Salisbury, 1643; Junior Proctor of Oxford University, 1643. *Died 29 November 1643.*

PUBLICATIONS

Collections

Plays and Poems, edited by G. Blakemore Evans. 1951.

Plays

The Royal Slave (produced 1636). 1639.
The Ordinary (produced ?). In *Comedies...,* 1651.
The Lady-Errant (produced ?). In *Comedies...,* 1651.
The Siege; or, Love's Convert, in *Comedies....* 1651.
Comedies, Tragi-Comedies, with Other Poems. 1651.

Other

An Offspring of Mercy Issuing Out of the Womb of Cruelty (sermon). 1652.

Reading List: *The Life and Poems of Cartwright* by R. Cullis Goffin, 1918.

*   *   *

Even if William Cartwright's work had nothing else to commend it, it would provide an index to the mind and taste of Oxford in the time of Charles I. Cartwright's poetic range includes topical verse on university and court, witty songs, love lyrics (among which the ardent trochees of "A Song of Dalliance" are outstanding), deft translations and adaptations ("Lesbia on Her Sparrow" cleverly echoes both Catullus and Skelton), and choral texts on the Nativity, the Circumcision, and the Epiphany for use by the King's Music. Toward the end of his brief life he was to shine as a preacher; a surviving Passion Sermon, delivered at Christ Church, refers to the Redeemer in terms which might normally be applied to a devoted Cavalier.

Proudly claimed as a poetic "son" by Ben Jonson, he composed an Elegy on Jonson's death, and his single comedy, *The Ordinary,* is constructed on Jonsonian principles. Its array of humours, in a London setting, includes the antiquary Moth, who speaks only Chaucerian English. In *The Siege; or, Love's Convert,* a tragi-comedy based on a hint in Plutarch, a tyrant of Byzantium pursues a maid's virtue but reforms in the end ("His Flames are now as chaste, as erewhile foul"); for comic relief there is an unlovely widow who would welcome the tyrant's attentions. Another tragi-comedy, *The Lady-Errant,* which seems to have been privately produced on the occasion of a wedding, offers in the title-role a sort of female Hotspur, and there is an Aristophanic assembly of women who plan to banish all men from Cyprus; the serious plot elements involve idealized love and friendship. All these plays (even

The Siege, which Cartwright says he would have destroyed in an early draft had it not been for the intercession of the King) show ingenuity and a sense for situation, if not much depth of thought or character.

But Cartwright's undoubted triumph is *The Royal Slave*. This tragi-comedy was presented in the hall of Christ Church before the King and Queen when they visited Oxford in 1636, and it would be hard to conceive a production better fitted to the occasion. In an action enlivened by music and dance, brilliantly mounted by Inigo Jones's stagecraft, and resounding with fine speeches, the noble Cratander is, in accordance with a Persian custom, made king for three days, after which he must be slain as a sacrifice to the Sun; during this period he manifests virtues which are proof against all temptation and wins not only the eloquently Platonic love of the Persian Queen but even the admiration of the Persian King. In a final spectacular episode he is saved by a solar eclipse, along with a fall of rain which puts out the sacrificial fires. So deeply pleased were King Charles and his Queen that they expressed a desire for another performance of the play at Hampton Court. "It was the day of St. Felix," remarked Archbishop Laud, "and all things went happy."

—Rhodes Dunlap

CHAPMAN, George. English. Born near Hitchin, Hertfordshire, c. 1560. Educated possibly at Cambridge University and Oxford University. Lived on the Continent, 1585–91, and served with the forces of Sir Francis Vere in the Low Countries; returned to London and wrote for Philip Henslowe until 1599, then for the Children of St. Paul's Chapel (later known as the Children of the Queen's Revels) until 1608, and thereafter devoted himself mainly to his translations; Server-in-Ordinary to Prince Henry, 1603–12; imprisoned in the Tower of London for satirical references to James I, 1605; in later life enjoyed patronage of the Earl of Somerset. *Died 12 May 1634.*

PUBLICATIONS

Collections

Tragedies, Comedies, edited by T. M. Parrott. 2 vols., 1910–14.
Poems, edited by Phyllis Brooks Bartlett. 1941.
Plays: The Comedies, edited by Allan Holaday. 1970.

Plays

Fedele and Fortunio: The Deceits in Love, with Munday and Stephen Gosson (produced 1584?). 1585; edited by P. Simpson, 1909.
The Blind Beggar of Alexandria (produced 1596). 1598; edited by Lloyd E. Berry, in *Plays*, 1970.
An Humorous Day's Mirth (produced 1597). 1599; edited by Allan Holaday, in *Plays*, 1970.
The Gentleman Usher (produced 1602?). 1606; edited by Robert Ornstein, in *Plays*, 1970.
All Fools (produced 1604). 1605; edited by G. Blakemore Evans, in *Plays*, 1970.

Monsieur D'Olive (produced 1604). 1606; edited by Allan Holaday, in *Plays,* 1970.
Bussy D'Ambois (produced 1604). 1607; edited by M. Evans, 1965.
Eastward Ho, with Jonson and Marston (produced 1605). 1605; edited by C. G. Petter, 1973.
Sir Giles Goosecap, Knight (produced ?). 1606; edited by W. Bang and R. Brotanek, 1909.
The Conspiracy and Tragedy of Charles, Duke of Byron, Marshal of France (produced 1608). 1608; edited by W. L. Phelps, 1895.
May Day (produced 1609). 1611; edited by Robert F. Welsh, in *Plays,* 1970.
The Widow's Tears (produced before 1609). 1612; edited by Robert Ornstein, in *Plays,* 1970.
The Revenge of Bussy D'Ambois (produced 1610?). 1613; edited by F. S. Boas, 1905.
The Memorable Masque of the Middle Temple and Lincoln's Inn (produced 1613). 1613; edited by G. Blakemore Evans, in *Plays,* 1970.
The Wars of Caesar and Pompey (produced 1613?). 1631.
Chabot, Admiral of France (produced 1613?). Version revised by Shirley, published 1639; edited by Ezra Lehman, 1906.

Verse

The Shadow of Night, Containing Two Poetical Hymns. 1594.
Ovid's Banquet of Sense, a Coronet for His Mistress Philosophy, and His Amorous Zodiac. 1595; edited by Elizabeth Story Donno, in *Elizabethan Minor Epics,* 1963.
Seven Books of the Iliad of Homer. 1598; *Achilles' Shield,* 1598; *Twelve Books,* 1609(?);* complete work, 1611.
Hero and Leander, Begun by Marlowe, Finished by Chapman. 1598; edited by Louis L. Martz, 1972.
Euthymiae Raptus; or, The Tears of Peace, with Interlocutions. 1609.
An Epicede or Funeral Song on the Death of Henry Prince of Wales. 1612.
Petrarch's Seven Penitential Psalms, Paraphrastically Translated with Other Philosophical Poems and a Hymn to Christ upon the Cross. 1612.
Andromeda Liberata; or, The Nuptials of Perseus and Andromeda. 1614.
Eugenia; or, True Nobility's Trance for the Death of William Lord Russell. 1614.
Homer's Odyssey, 12 books. 1614(?); complete work, 1615(?).
The Divine Poem of Musaeus. 1616; edited by Elizabeth Story Donno, in *Elizabethan Minor Epics,* 1963.
The Georgics of Hesiod. 1618.
Pro Vere Autumni Lachrymae, Inscribed to the Memory of Sir Horatio Vere. 1622.
The Crown of All Homer's Works, Batrachomyomachia, or, The Battle of Frogs and Mice, His Hymns and Epigrams. 1624(?).
A Justification of a Strange Action of Nero, Being the Fifth Satire of Juvenal Translated. 1629.
Chapman's Homer: The Iliad, The Odyssey, and the Lesser Homerica, edited by Allardyce Nicoll. 2 vols., 1956.

Other

A Free and Offenceless Justification of Andromeda Liberata. 1614.

Bibliography: *Chapman: A Concise Bibliography* by S. A. Tannenbaum, 1938; supplement, 1946.

Reading List: *Chapman: The Effect of Stoicism upon His Tragedies* by John W. Wieler, 1949; *Chapman: Sa Vie, Sa Poésie, Son Théâtre, Sa Pensée* by Jean Jacquot, 1951; *The Tragedies of Chapman: Renaissance Ethics in Action* by Ennis Rees, 1954; *Homeric Renaissance: The Odyssey of Chapman* by George de F. Lord, 1956; *Chapman: A Critical Study* by Millar MacLure, 1966; *Chapman* by C. Spivak, 1967; *An Index to the Figurative Language of Chapman's Tragedies* by L. C. Stagg, 1970; *The Mind's Empire: Myth and Form in Chapman's Narrative Poems* by Raymond B. Waddington, 1974; *Chapman: Action and Contemplation in His Tragedies* by Peter Bement, 1974.

*   *   *

George Chapman's activities as poet, dramatist, and translator place him second only to his friend and sometimes collaborator Ben Jonson as a man of letters. While the two men shared a devotion to learning and a sense of vocation as professional writers, in other respects the differences are large. To the clarity which is Jonson's stylistic ideal, Chapman retorts that oratorically plain poetry "were the plaine way to barbarisme." His own style is so notoriously difficult that – mistakenly – he has been associated with the Metaphysicals. Instead, Chapman wrote as a Platonic mystagogue, using meaningful obscurity to conceal his truth from the many and reveal it to the worthy few. He should be seen as one in the line of visionary poets extending from Spenser through Milton and Blake.

Chapman was influenced heavily by Marsilio Ficino; and Chapman's Platonism supplies the key to his thought and poetics, as his various theoretical statements make clear. Poetry is an epiphany of Truth, always associated with wisdom and learning, attained through divine inspiration. The vatic poet accommodates this Truth to human understanding through symbolic images, fables, and myths. Although few men will undertake the intellectual and spiritual discipline necessary to comprehend such poetry, for the "understanders" it will "turne blood to soule" and "heighten [man's] transition into God." Central to Chapman's poetics is his conception of *form*: this includes conventional literary form (genre) by which the poet announces his general intentions; the inner form of the myth, fable, or story (understood via the traditions of allegorical commentary); and the indwelling form or "soul" of the Truth, a notion deriving from the Platonic Idea.

Chapman's most important poems were those published at the beginning of his career. *The Shadow of Night* consists of two hymns addressed to Night and to Cynthia, both revealed by the Orphic poet as religious mysteries, which anatomize man's condition and prescribe remedies. In the second, around the triune identity of the goddess as Cynthia – Diana – Hecate, Chapman interweaves a complex, three-level allegory – philosophical, political, and poetic. *Ovids Banquet of Sence*, an oblique riposte to the fashion of Ovidian erotic narratives, ironically presents Ovid as seducer, glibly misusing Platonic doctrine to achieve his end; deliberately ambiguous, the entire poem – as the title-page emblem suggests – is a *trompe l'oeil*, warning us not to trust our senses. Chapman's continuation of *Hero and Leander* "corrects" Marlowe's incomplete narrative (as does his editing of the Marlowe), restoring the moral balance and high seriousness in an Ovidian epic, written from the perspective of the allegorical commentaries upon *The Metamorphoses*. Of the Jacobean poems, two deserve mention: *The Teares of Peace*, oddly combining medieval dream-vision and Hermetic revelation, is Chapman's most sustained defense of learning; and *Andromeda Liberata* projects political allegory through mythological narrative in a manner reflecting the influence of court masques.

By 1598 Francis Meres could list Chapman among "the best Poets" for both comedy and tragedy; and theatrical writing in several dramatic genres dominated his activities for the next decade. M. C. Bradbrook credits *An Humorous Day's Mirth* with initiating the comedy of humours; and Jackson Cope had demonstrated that *The Gentleman Usher* and *The Widow's Tears* – tragi-comic romance and satiric comedy, respectively – are philosophic dramas, using mythic frameworks to explore positive and negative versions of the Platonic quest for absolute knowledge. In the tragedies Chapman obsessively rewrites the script of a flawed

Titan, greater by far than the surrounding society, yet contaminated and eventually destroyed by his compromises with that society and by his own hubris. It is conventional to mark the shift from the Achillean active heroes, Bussy and Byron, to the passive, Stoic virtue of Clermont, Cato, and Chabot. But, just as Platonism always informs his poetics, so Stoicism is the foundation of his ethics throughout, a personal and eclectic Stoicism that is flexible enough to encompas both Achilles's justified wrath and the encomium of Clermont as "this Senecal man." *Bussy D'Ambois* "inwardly" measures its hero's greatness and failure against the myths of Hercules, Prometheus, and Christ; "outwardly" it is heroic tragedy and sensational melodrama. This combination of dimensions has earned its modern status as the single "anthology piece" among the tragedies. An age as receptive as ours to the drama of ideas, however, might well give more attention to the interiorized tragedies of *Byron* and *The Revenge of Bussy D'Ambois*. Although only *The Memorable Maske* survives as evidence of Chapman's skill at this new form, we have Jonson's testimony "That next himself only Fletcher and Chapman could make a Mask."

Chapman launched his Homer translation with *Seven Bookes of the Iliades* and *Achilles Shield* (1598); *The Teares of Peace* (1609) announces his visionary inspiration by Homer and his renewed dedication to the task. *The Iliads* was finished in 1611, the complete *Odyssey* in 1615, the two published together as *The Whole Works* the next year, and the lesser *Homerica* followed later. Despite his unfulfilled promise to present "my Poeme of the mysteries/ Reveal'd in Homer," Chapman does not encumber the epics with Platonic exegesis; rather, he sees "naked *Vlysses* clad in eternall Fiction" as totally mythic. Disdaining "word-for-word traductions," he regarded his job as *translation*, making the universal values of Homer comprehensible and therefore relevant to his own time and culture. His English systematically renders explicit the ethical and philosophical attitudes which he perceived as implicit in the text. Chapman's famous statement that the "Proposition" of each epic is contracted in the first word (*wrath* and *man*) itself epitomizes his approach to translation: "in one, the Bodie's fervour and fashion of outward Fortitude to all possible height of Heroicall Action; in the other, the Mind's inward, constant and unconquered Empire...." The adequacy of Chapman's Greek and the degree of fidelity to the original are much mooted questions which can distract attention from his very considerable achievement. Despite the hiatus in composition, Chapman's *Iliads* is generally viewed as more successful than his *Odyssey* in its consonance to the meaning of the Homer and in its unity. Certainly Chapman's *Iliads* is a splendid poem. His other literary accomplishments notwithstanding, his description of the Homer translations as "The Worke that I was borne to doe" is one to which most readers give assent.

—Raymond B. Waddington

CHETTLE, Henry. English. Born in London c. 1560. Married; one daughter. Apprenticed to Thomas East, printer, 1577–84; Member of the Stationer's Company, 1584. Partner, with John Danter and William Hoskins, in a printing firm, 1589–91; imprisoned for debt in Marshalsea Prison, 1598–99; wrote for Philip Henslowe, 1598–1603; contracted to write for the Earl of Nottingham's Players from 1602. *Died c. 1607.*

PUBLICATIONS

Plays

> *The Downfall of Robert, Earl of Huntingdon,* with Anthony Munday (produced 1598).   1601; edited by J. C. Meagher, 1965.
> *The Death of Robert, Earl of Huntingdon,* with Anthony Munday (produced 1598).   1601; edited by J. C. Meagher, 1967.
> *Patient Grissel,* with William Haughton and Thomas Dekker (produced 1600).   1603; edited by Fredson Bowers, in *Dramatic Works of Dekker,* 1953.
> *The Blind Beggar of Bethnal Green,* with John Day (produced 1600).   1659; edited by W. Bang, 1902.
> *Hoffman; or, A Revenge for a Father* (produced after 1602).   1631; edited by H. Jenkins and C. J. Sisson, 1951.

Fiction

> *Kind-Heart's Dream.*   1593; edited by G. B. Harrison, 1923.
> *Piers Plainness' Seven-Years' Prenticeship.*   1595; edited by James Winny in *The Descent of Euphues,* 1957.

Other

> *England's Mourning Garment in Memory of Elizabeth.*   1603; edited by C. M. Ingleby, in *Shakspere Allusion-Books,* part 1, 1874.

> Editor, *Greene's Groatsworth of Wit, Bought with a Million of Repentance.*   1592.

Reading List: *The Life and Work of Chettle* by Harold Jenkins, 1934.

*   *   *

Henry Chettle, along with so many other playwrights of Shakespeare's time, has suffered from a series of disadvantages: not only is he a "candle in the sun," but also he has been badly treated by posterity (which has lost most of his work) and by fate and finances (which teamed him up with more distinguished writers and compelled him to churn out hack work for a voracious theatre). When he died in obscurity, he had already retired from a career which involved about 50 plays for the Lord Admiral's Men and Worcester's Men.

Hoffman; or, A Revenge for a Father is the only extant play he wrote unaided. It is interesting in the light of the *ur-Hamlet* and Shakespeare's own *Hamlet,* and fits into the revenge tradition by having an Ophelia character and a determined revenger. Two plays written with Munday are perhaps his best work, centering on the Earl of Huntingdon and the Robin Hood legend. Other workman-like plays were written with Haughton and Dekker (*Patient Grissel*) and with Day (*The Blind Beggar of Bethnal Green*). A play written with Dekker (*Troilus and Cressida*) does not survive, but the "plot" is described in British Museum Add. MS 10449. The titles of his other works are so varied that he was possibly a play doctor of his day, much as George Abbott is in our time.

Fate has been kinder to his non-dramatic work. Chettle was a friend of Greene, and edited his *Groatsworth of Wit* though, in the prefatory matter to *Kind Heart's Dream,* he politely dissociated himself from the wit's waspish attack on the actors ("antics garnished in our colors") and Shakespeare ("upstart crow, beautified with our feathers"). *Kind Heart's Dream* itself is a satirical dream fable; *Piers Plainness' Seven-Years' Prenticeship* is a picaresque pastoral narrative; *England's Mourning Garment* is a charming account of the end of the spacious days of Elizabeth I.

—Leonard R. N. Ashley

COKAYNE, Sir Aston. English. Born in Elvaston, Derbyshire, baptized 20 December 1608. Educated at Chenies School, Buckinghamshire; Trinity College, Cambridge (fellow commoner); entered one of the Inns of Court, London; created M.A. at Oxford c. 1642. Married Mary Knyveton c. 1633 (died, 1683); one son and two daughters. Toured France and Italy, 1632; succeeded to Pooley Hall, Warwickshire, 1638, and the family estate at Ashbourne, Derbyshire, 1664; received baronet's patent, 1642; dissipated his wealth in extravagant living and in the service of the king and church: forced to sell Ashbourne, 1671, and Pooley, 1683, and died in poverty. *Died 13 February 1684.*

PUBLICATIONS

Collections

> *Dramatic Works,* edited by James Maidment and W. H. Logan.   1874.
> *Poems,* edited by A. E. Cockayne.   1877.
> *Dramen,* edited by H. Spaemann.   1923.

Plays

> *A Masque Presented at Bretbie in Derbyshire on Twelfth Night 1639* (produced 1639).   In *Small Poems,* 1658.
> *The Obstinate Lady.*   1657.
> *Trappolin Creduto Principe; or, Trappolin Supposed a Prince* (produced ?).   In *Small Poems,* 1658.
> *The Tragedy of Ovid,* in *Poems.*   1662.

Verse

> *Small Poems of Divers Sorts.*   1658; as *A Chain of Golden Poems,* 1658; revised edition, as *Poems,* 1662.

> Translator, *Dianea,* by Giovanni F. Loredano.   1654.

*   *   *

Aston Cokayne owes his place in the annals of English drama less to his creative efforts than to his services to literary detectives. In *A Chain of Golden Poems,* an otherwise undistinguished collection of occasional verses, he revealed the existence of collaboration in the Beaumont and Fletcher cmuch wider scale than would otherwise have been supposed. He reproached the publishers of the 1647 Folio:

> In the large book of Playes you late did print
> (In *Beaumonts* and in *Fletchers* name) why in't
> Did you not justice? give to each his due?
> For *Beaumont* (of those many) writ in few:
> And *Massinger* in other few.

The work of disintegration is still not complete, but no scholar can embark upon the study of a "Fletcher" play without being mindful of Cokayne.

In other poems in the collection, Cokayne refers to his friendships with contemporary dramatists, and no doubt these friendships urged him to emulation. He had little talent. His best-known play, *The Obstinate Lady*, shows Fletcher's influence taken to absurd extremes. A fondness for the woman-page disguise is not restricted to the young girl who is in love with her "master." Cleanthe dresses as a lad, calling herself Anclethe, to wait upon Carionil, who thinks he is in love with Lucora; the situation is similar to that in Fletcher's *Philaster*, but Cokayne also introduces Rosinda, wife of Polidacre, who has reported herself to be dead and disguised herself as a man (Tandorix) in order to test her husband's fidelity:

> to know if he
> Would keep his promise to me, which with oaths
> He oft hath made, that never, if he should
> Survive me, he would take another wife.

Perhaps a touch of Marston's *The Malcontent* enters here.

The "obstinate lady" is Lucora, who first vows herself to chastity and who is then offered in marriage (by her father) to Carionil's friend, Falorus. Naturally Falorus esteems friendship with Carionil more than love for any woman, and refuses to fight: "I do not wear a weapon for such a quarrel" (I, ii; p. 36). But since Carionil cannot win Lucora's love in his own shape, he disguises himself as a negro because, as Falorus advises him, "She that cannot love a man of a better complexion,/On one of them may settle her affection." Sure enough, Lucora forgets her vow of chastity and prepares to elope with the "negro," Tucapelo. Whilst he is waiting below her window, however, Tucapelo (or Carionil) has a flash of insight into his situation: "have I cause to love/A lady that hath so neglected me/That she preferr'd a negro?" With this, he resumes his own shape, consigns Lucora to Falorus, and receives Cleanthe into his affections. Other equally confused actions complicate the plot, and the readiness of every character to assume an alias makes the play still more difficult to read; there is no evidence that it was ever performed.

Giving an account of Cokayne's life and works, Gerard Langbaine (in *An Account of the English Dramatick Poets*, 1691) reported that he was "very much addicted to Books, and the study of Poetry; spending most of his time in the Muses company." His works show every sign of this preoccupation with art – indulged, one feels, at the expense of experience of life.

—Roma Gill

DAVENANT, Sir William. English. Born in Oxford in February 1606. Educated at Oxford Grammar School; Lincoln College, Oxford, left without taking a degree. Married 1)

Mary c. 1624, two children; 2) Dame Anne Cademan in 1652 (died, 1655); 3) Henrietta Maria du Tremblay in 1655. Page to the Duchess of Richmond, then entered the household of Fulke Greville, Lord Brooke, until Brooke's death in 1628; began writing for the stage in the 1620's, presented masques at court, and succeeded Ben Jonson as Poet Laureate, 1638; managed the Cockpit Theatre in Drury Lane, 1639 until the Puritans closed the theatres; fought for the Royalists at the siege of Gloucester, and knighted by the king, 1643; negotiated numerous royal missions in the Netherlands and France, 1643–49; joined the court in exile in Paris, 1650, and was appointed Lieutenant Governor of Maryland: led a colonizing expedition to America, 1650, intercepted by the Puritans, interned at Cowes, then in the Tower of Lodon, 1651; released, 1652; pardoned by Cromwell, 1654; gave theatrical productions (which he styled as "operas" to avoid Puritan restrictions) at Rutland House, 1656, and transferred to the Cockpit Theatre, 1658; after the Restoration patented by Charles II to open the Lincoln's Inn Fields Theatre. *Died 7 April 1688.*

PUBLICATIONS

Collections

Plays, edited by James Maidment and W. H. Logan.   5 vols., 1872–74.
Selected Poems, edited by Douglas Bush.   1943.

Plays

The Cruel Brother (produced 1627).   1630.
The Siege (as *The Colonel*, produced 1629?).   In *Works*, 1673.
Albovine, King of the Lombards.   1629.
The Just Italian (produced 1629).   1630.
The Wits (produced 1634).   1636.
Love and Honour (produced 1634).   1649; edited by Harold Reinoehl Walley and J. H.
    Wilson, in *Early Seventeenth-Century Plays*, 1930.
The Platonic Lovers (produced 1635).   1636.
The Temple of Love (produced 1635).   1635.
News from Plymouth (produced 1635).   In *Works*, 1673.
The Triumphs of the Prince d'Amour, music by William Lawes (produced 1636).   1636.
The Fair Favourite (produced 1638).   In *Works*, 1673.
Britannia Triumphans (produced 1638).   1638.
The Unfortunate Lovers (produced 1638).   1643.
Luminalia; or, The Festival of Light (produced 1638).   1638; edited by Alexander B.
    Grosart, in *Miscellanies of the Fuller Worthies' Library*, 1876.
Salmacida Spolia, music by Lewis Richard (produced 1640).   1640; edited by Terence
    J. B. Spencer, in *A Book of Masques in Honor of Allardyce Nicoll*, 1967.
The Siege of Rhodes, music by Henry Lawes and others (produced 1656).   1656;
    revised version (produced 1658), 1663; edited by Ann-Mari Hedbäck, 1973.
The First Day's Entertainment at Rutland House (produced 1656).   1657.
The Preparation of the Athenians for the Reception of Phocion.   1657.
The Cruelty of the Spaniards in Peru (produced 1658).   1658.
The History of Sir Francis Drake (produced 1658).   1659.
Hamlet, from the play by Shakespeare (produced 1661).   1676 (possibly by the actor
    Betterton).
The Law Against Lovers (produced 1662).   In *Works*, 1673.

The Play House to Be Let (produced 1663). In *Works*, 1673.

The Rivals, from the play *The Two Noble Kinsmen* by Fletcher and Shakespeare (produced 1664). 1668.

The Tempest; or, The Enchanted Island, with Dryden, from the play by Shakespeare (produced 1667). 1670; edited by Vivian Summers, 1974.

The Man's the Master, from a play by Scarron (produced 1668). 1669.

Macbeth, from the play by Shakespeare (produced 1673). 1674; edited by Christopher Spencer, 1961.

The Distresses, in *Works*. 1673.

Julius Caesar, with Dryden, from the play by Shakespeare (produced before 1676). In *A Collection of Plays by Eminent Hands*, 1719.

Verse

Madagascar, with Other Poems. 1638.

London, King Charles His Augusta or City Royal. 1648.

Gondibert: An Heroic Poem. 1651; *Seventh and Last Canto*, 1685; edited by David F. Gladish, 1971.

Poem upon His Majesty's Return. 1660.

Poem to the King's Most Sacred Majesty. 1663.

Shorter Poems and Songs from the Plays and Masques, edited by Anthony M. Gibbs. 1972.

Other

A Discourse upon Gondibert. 1650; edited by J. E. Spingarn, in *Seventeenth-Century Critical Essays*, 1908.

Works. 1673.

Reading List: *Davenant, Poet, Venturer* by Alfred Harbage, 1935 (includes bibliography); *Davenant, Poet Laureate and Playwright-Manager* by Arthur H. Nethercot, 1938, revised edition, 1967; *Der Stilwandel im Dramatischen Werk Davenants* by Lothar Hoennighausen, 1965; *The Comedy of Davenant* by Howard S. Collins, 1967.

* * *

Davenant's dramatic works provide a strikingly diverse and comprehensive reflection of changing theatrical tastes in the middle years of the seventeenth century, from the reign of Charles I to the early years of the Restoration. He was an exuberant and entertaining writer whose work was both imitative and innovative. His early work was strongly influenced by Shakespeare, Jonson, Fletcher and others, but Davenant also made original contributions to the theatrical tradition of his age. He played a major part in the development of English opera and in the creation of the heroic drama, and was a lively early experimenter in burlesque and other comic forms which became popular in the Restoration period. Lurid incident and frequently strained and bombastic language mark his largely unsuccessful early attempts at tragedy, such as *Albovine, King of the Lombards* and *The Cruel Brother*, written in the manner of late Jacobean tragedies of sexual intrigue and violence in courtly settings. *The Just Italian*, with its comic ending and markedly sentimental ingredients, shows the break-up of the Jacobean tradition of tragedy and also anticipates the Restoration comedy of manners. With *The Platonic Lovers*, *News from Plimouth*, and, especially, *The Wits*, all written in the 1630's, Davenant brought to maturity his considerable gift for comedy. Set in London, *The*

Wits, his most successful and popular play, combines adroit handling of comic situation with vivacious and amusing dialogue, while *Love and Honour*, written directly afterwards and concerned with lofty themes of self-sacrificing love and manly valour, is Davenant's first essay in heroic drama. The several court masques which he produced in collaboration with Inigo Jones in the 1630's, though tediously complimentary at times, contain spirited and skilful writing in the songs and choruses.

As the first playwright to gain official approval for the staging of theatrical entertainments in the last years of the Puritan regime, Davenant produced a series of works which owe their irregular character partly to the fact that the authorities would have frowned upon the production of ordinary stage plays. *The First Day's Entertainment at Rutland House* was a presentation comprising dialogue about the opera and about the relative merits of London and Paris interspersed with songs and consort music composed by Henry Lawes and others. *The Siege of Rhodes* is a landmark in the establishment both of English opera and the heroic drama. The "heroical" story of the work, designed "to advance the characters of vertue in the shapes of valour and conjugal love," is based primarily on the account of the siege of Christian Rhodes given by Richard Knolles in his *Historie of the Turkes* (1603). The play is divided into Entries instead of Acts, and its rhymed dialogue in "stilo recitativo" and frequent songs and choruses give the work much of the character of opera. Other "operatic" works of this period were *The Cruelty of the Spaniards in Peru* and *The History of Sir Francis Drake*, in the latter of which there occur passages of dialogue in song. In the Restoration period Davenant's main energies were directed towards translation (the principal work being *The Man's the Master*, a translation, popular in the theatre for many years, of Scarron's *Le Maitre Valet*) and his notorious, but to contemporaries greatly diverting, adaptations of Shakespeare.

In non-dramatic writing Davenant's major work is the unfinished romance-epic, *Gondibert*, a poem in heroic quatrains which incorporates many of the themes and motifs of the love-and-honour drama. He was highly talented as a writer of lyrical and occasional poems, among the best of which are "The lark now leaves his watery nest," "The philosopher and the lover," "The Soldier going to the field," "For the lady, Olivia Porter," and "To the Queen, entertained at night by the Countess of Anglesey." His delightful comic songs and poems include "Wake all the dead!," "My lodging it is on the cold ground," "The long vacation in London," and "The plots."

—A. M. Gibbs

DAY, John.   English.   Born in Cawston, Norfolk, in 1574. Educated at a school in Ely; Caius College, Cambridge, 1592–93. Playwright in London for Philip Henslowe, 1598–1603, and for Worcester's Company, 1602–03. *Died in 1640.*

PUBLICATIONS

Collections

Works, edited by A. H. Bullen.   2 vols., 1881.

Plays

The Blind Beggar of Bethnal Green, with Henry Chettle (produced 1600).   1659; edited
by W. Bang, 1902.
Law Tricks; or, Who Would Have Thought It (produced 1604).   1608; edited by J.
Crow and W. W. Greg, 1950.
The Isle of Gulls, from the work Arcadia by Sidney (produced 1606).   1606; edited by
G. B. Harrison, 1936.
The Travels of the Three English Brothers, Sir Thomas, Sir Anthony, Mr. Robert Shirley,
with William Rowley and George Wilkins (produced 1607).   1607.
Humour Out of Breath (produced 1608?).   1608; edited by Arthur Symons, in Nero and
Other Plays, 1888.

Verse

The Parliament of Bees, with Their Proper Characters (pastoral dialogues).   1641;
edited by Arthur Symons, in Nero and Other Plays, 1888.

Other

Peregrinatio Scholastica; or, Learning's Pilgrimage, in Works.   1881.

*   *   *

John Day is one of the most neglected dramatists of the Elizabethan period, a distinction
which is, for the most part, justified. His dramatic talents do not include the strong lines and
"supernatural music" of Marlowe, Middleton, or Webster; and he rarely matches the
dramatic craftsmanship of Dekker or Heywood. While his surviving plays exhibit a
considerable diversity in subject matter, he pays little attention to the delineation of his
characters, who with a few exceptions remain conventional or superficial. Day's dramatic
verse is memorable for its stylistic regularity and euphuistic extravagance, though at
moments it possesses a lyrical grace and delicacy that rival the poetry of his better-known
contemporaries.
Day collaborated with at least half a dozen of Henslowe's writers on twenty-two plays
between 1598 and 1603, though only two survive: The Blind-Beggar of Bednal-Green, with
its haphazard plot construction, still maintains what Swinburne saw as "some good simple
fun"; and The Travailes of the Three English Brothers is a topical romantic adventure similar
to the early plays of Heywood. The remainder of Day's surviving plays were written for the
more sophisticated audience of the private theatres. The Ile of Guls, according to the Prologue,
is "a little spring ... drawne fro the full streame of the right worthy Gentleman Sir Phillip
Sydneys well known Archadea." The play contains some of the best of Day's verse dialogue,
but the "gulling" satire is as limp as the characterization. Law Trickes; or, Who Would Have
Thought It reveals Day's indebtedness to Marston for elements of his comic satire. The result
is an often strained but not displeasing comedy in which even the Epilogue queries, "Who
would have thought such strange euents should fall/ Into a course so smooth and comicall?"
The influence of Lyly and Shakespeare can be seen in Humour Out of Breath, a play which
shows Day at his best as a dramatic poet. The character of his heroine, Florimell, outshines
any other figure in his works, and resembles to a lesser degree Shakespeare's Rosalind. At the
same time, this well-constructed comedy contains several notable passages of lyrical value.
The Parliament of Bees, generally regarded as Day's finest work, is a series of twelve
colloquies most likely based on the Georgics of Virgil and the plethora of verse satires written

in the 1590's. The characters of the individual bees are less memorable than the abundance of pure poetry and high flights of fancy in such musical, rhymed verse as:

> When of the sudaine, listning, you shall heare
> A noise of Hornes and hunting, which shall bring
> *Acteon* to *Diana* in the spring.

Many years after his dramatic floruit, Day wrote an interesting and capable allegorical prose tract, *Peregrinatio Scholastica or Learneinges Pillgrimage*, which is divided into twenty "morall Tractates." The dedication to this piece provides an illuminating autobiographical note: Day acknowledges that he has been passed over by the "Credit" and "Opinion" bestowed on his luckier contemporaries, and yet he writes, "The day may come when *Nos quoque floruimus* may be there motto as well as myne: in the mean time, being becalmde in a fogg of necessity, I am content to ly at Anchor before the Ilands *Meliora Speramus.*"

Day's neglect, then, goes back to his own lifetime, as he presumably finished his career in "a fogg of necessity." As a hack writer in good earnest for Henslowe and the private companies, he saw moderate success on the stage, but Day will ultimately be remembered for his airy and melodious lyrics.

—Raymond C. Shady

DEKKER, Thomas.   English.   Born in London c. 1570. Nothing is known for certain about his parentage, education, or marriage(s). Playwright for Philip Henslowe, c. 1598–1602; mentioned in documents as having worked on 50 plays; after 1602 divided his time between playwriting and writing pamphlets; lived in extreme poverty: saved from debtor's prison by Henslowe, 1598, 1599; imprisoned for debt in the King's Bench Prison, London, 1613–19. *Died* (buried) *25 August 1632.*

PUBLICATIONS

Collections

> *Non-Dramatic Works,* edited by A. B. Grosart.   5 vols., 1884–86.
> *Dramatic Works,* edited by Fredson Bowers.   4 vols., 1953–61.
> *Selected Writings* (prose), edited by E. D. Pendry.   1968.

Plays

> *Old Fortunatus* (produced 1599).   1600.
> *The Shoemaker's Holiday; or, The Gentle Craft* (produced 1599).   1600; edited by R. L. Smallwood and Stanley Wells, 1978.
> *Patient Grissel,* with Henry Chettle and William Haughton (produced 1600).   1603.
> *Lust's Dominion; or, The Lascivious Queen* (as *The Spanish Moor's Tragedy,* produced 1600).   1657.

Satiromastix; or, The Untrussing of the Humorous Poet (produced 1601).   1602.
Sir Thomas Wyatt, with Thomas Heywood and Webster (produced 1602–07?).   1607.
King James His Royal and Magnificent Entertainment, with Jonson (produced 1603).   With *Entertainment of the Queen and Prince at Althorp*, by Jonson, 1604.
The Honest Whore, with Middleton (produced 1604).   1604; as *The Converted Courtesan*, 1604.
Westward Ho, with Webster (produced 1604).   1607.
The Roaring Girl; or, Moll Cut-Purse, with Middleton (produced 1604–10?).   1611; edited by Andor Gomme, 1976.
Northward Ho, with Webster (produced 1605).   1607.
The Honest Whore, part 2 (produced 1605?).   1630.
The Whore of Babylon (produced 1605–07?).   1607.
If This Be Not Good the Devil Is in It (produced 1610–12?).   1612.
Match Me in London (produced 1611–13?).   1631.
Troia-Nova Triumphans, London Triumphing (produced 1612).   1612.
The Virgin Martyr, with Massinger (produced 1620).   1622.
The Witch of Edmonton, with William Rowley and John Ford (produced 1621).   1658.
The Noble Soldier; or, A Contract Broken, Justly Revenged (as *The Noble Spanish Soldier*, produced 1622–31?).   1634.
The Wonder of a Kingdon (produced 1623–31?).   1636.
The Welsh Ambassador, with Ford (produced 1623).   Edited by H. Littledale and W. W. Greg, 1920.
The Sun's Darling: A Moral Masque, with Ford (produced 1624).   1656.
Britannia's Honour (produced 1628).   1628.
London's Tempe; or, The Field of Happiness (produced 1629).   1629.

Fiction and Prose

The Wonderful Year, Wherein Is Shown the Picture of London Lying Sick of the Plague.   1603; in *Selected Writings*, 1968.
News from Gravesend, Sent to Nobody.   1604; edited by F. P. Wilson, in *Plague Pamphlets*, 1925.
The Meeting of Gallants at an Ordinary; or, The Walks in Paul's.   1604; edited by F. P. Wilson, in *Plague Pamphlets*, 1925.
The Double PP: A Papist Encountered by the Protestant.   1606.
News from Hell.   1606; revised edition, as *A Knight's Conjuring, Done in Earnest, Discovered in Jest*, 1607; edited by Larry M. Robbins, 1974.
The Seven Deadly Sins of London.   1606; edited by H. F. B. Brett-Smith, 1922.
Jests to Make You Merry, with George Wilkins.   1607.
The Dead Term; or, Westminster's Complaint for Long Vacations and Short Terms.   1608.
The Bellman of London, Bringing to Light the Most Notorious Villainies.   1608; edited by O. Smeaton, 1904.
Lantern and Candle-Light; or, The Bellman's Second Night's Walk.   1608; revised edition, 1609; as *O Per Se O; or, A New Crier of Lantern and Candle-Light*, 1612; revised edition, as *Villainies Discovered by Lantern and Candle-Light*, 1616, 1620; revised edition, as *English Villainies*, 1638, 1648; in *Selected Writings*, 1968.
Four Birds of Noah's Ark.   1609; edited by F. P. Wilson, 1924.
The Gull's Horn-Book.   1609; in *Selected Writings*, 1968.
The Raven's Almanac Foretelling of a Plague, Famine, and Civil War.   1609.
Work for Armourers; or, The Peace Is Broken.   1609.
A Strange Horse Race.   1613.
Dekker His Dream.   1620; edited by J. O. Halliwell, 1860.

A Rod for Runaways.   1625; revised edition, 1625; edited by F. P. Wilson, in *Plague Pamphlets*, 1925.
The Black Rod and the White Rod, Justice and Mercy, Striking and Sparing London.   1630; edited by F. P. Wilson, in *Plague Pamphlets*, 1925.
Penny-Wise Pound-Foolish; or, A Bristow Diamond Set in Two Rings and Both Cracked.   1631; in *Selected Writings*, 1968.

Verse

The Artillery Garden.   1616; edited by F. P. Wilson, 1952.
Wars, Wars, Wars.   1628.

Bibliography: *Dekker: A Concise Bibliography* by S. A. Tannenbaum, 1939; supplement, 1945; supplement in *Elizabethan Bibliographies Supplements 2* by D. G. Donovan, 1967; *Dekker: A Bibliographical Catalogue (to 1700)* by Antony F. Allison, 1972.

Reading List: *Dekker: A Study in Economic and Social Backgrounds* by K. L. Gregg, 1924; *The Base String: The Underworld in Elizabethan Drama* by N. Berlin, 1968; *Dekker* by George R. Price, 1969; *Dekker: An Analysis of Dramatic Structure* by James H. Conover, 1969; *Rhetoric in the Plays of Dekker* by Suzanne K. Blow, 1972; *Serious and Tragic Elements in the Comedy of Dekker* by Peggy F. Shirley, 1975.

*   *   *

Like his predecessor Robert Greene, Thomas Dekker was both a playwright and a writer of popular didactic pamphlets. To Ben Jonson, he was merely a "dresser of plays," a debt-ridden hack in Philip Henslowe's staple of play doctors who wrote, often in collaboration, any type of play required by the Lord Admiral's Men – romantic comedy, comedy of manners, satire, tragi-comedy, or tragedy. Dekker's earliest success, performed at court by the Lord Admiral's Men in 1599, was *Old Fortunatus*, an old-fashioned play in the style of Greene and George Peele. Derived from an ancient German folk tale, it relates a rambling story of the misfortunes of an old beggar and his sons who foolishly choose riches when offered a choice of any of the world's benefits by the goddess Fortune. It represents every romantic excess the newer dramatists like Chapman and Jonson scorned: allegorical characters from the old morality plays, action that moves from Cyprus to England, farce and sentimentality, and sermonizing on the vanity of human wishes. In a fresher, more sophisticated mode is Dekker's greatest comedy, *The Shoemaker's Holiday*, also performed at court by the Lord Admiral's Men. This sprightly London Comedy Dekker based in part on Thomas Deloney's highly popular prose tale *The Gentle Craft*, the story of how a simple cobbler rose to become lord mayor of London, and on the Cinderella-like courtship in Greene's *Friar Bacon and Friar Bungay*. Like Shakespeare's Henriad plays, which were on the stage of the Globe at about the same time, *The Shoemaker's Holiday* portrays London and its environs amid the stir of Henry V's French wars, but Dekker's concerns, unlike Shakespeare's, are neither historical nor political. His story is the simple one of how Lacey, a noble's son, woos the beautiful commoner Rose in the disguise of a Dutch apprentice in the employ of the madcap shoemaker Simon Eyre and his biosterous journeymen. The comedy has all of Dekker's distinctive dramatic qualities: a tender romantic love story accompanied by a sub-plot of farce occasionally touched with realism; lyrical love scenes of unabashed sentiment contrasted with vivid colloquial prose; sweet love songs and raucous tradesmen's choruses and morris dances. *The Shoemaker's Holiday* is Dekker's sole masterpiece; in his later plays he was never able to equal this superb integration of farce, realism, and romance.

After *The Shoemaker's Holiday*, plot construction became Dekker's salient weakness, possibly because poverty compelled him to write rapidly and in collaboration with others. *Satiromastix; or, The Untrussing of the Humorous Poet* in part retaliates against Jonson for his satire against Dekker and Marston in *The Poetaster*. The rest of *Satiromastix* combines satire with tragicomedy and romanticized chronicle (England around 1100 A.D.). This indifference to form is equally evident in *Westward Ho* and *Northward Ho*, both comedies in collaboration with John Webster. Dekker worked with Thomas Middleton on Part I of *The Honest Whore* in 1604, then wrote Part II by himself the following year. Without Middleton's clever plot designing and lively characterizations, Part II is markedly inferior to Part I. Dekker collaborated with Middleton again on *The Roaring Girl*, a comedy based on the real-life story of Mary Frith, alias Moll Cutpurse, whom Dekker portrays as a tender-hearted rogue aiding lovers in distress. The characterization is typical of Dekker, who often showed bluff monarchs, stern fathers, or threatening employers to be essentially good-humored and benevolent. Never a cynic, Dekker sought out the best in human beings, and his rare moral indignation is reserved for deliberate cruelty, never simple weakness. In *The Witch of Edmonton*, written with William Rowley and John Ford, Dekker wrote those portions of the play most sympathetic to the old witch Elizabeth Sawyer, whom Dekker portrays as an ignorant and helpless woman driven to witchcraft by the persecution of her cruel neighbors.

This moral conscience, occasionally implicit in the plays, is expressed consistently and overtly in the prose pamphlets Dekker wrote during the period 1603–10, beginning with *The Wonderful Year* which opens as a commemoration of James I's succession and develops into a vivid description of the terrible sufferings of the 1602 plague. *The Seven Deadly Sins of London* excoriates contemporary economic frauds, whereas *The Bellman of London* and *Lantern and Candle-Light* resemble Robert Greene's coney-catching pamphlets in exposing the sharp practices of the Elizabethan underworld. In these and other pamphlets Dekker employs a plain, unadorned style, more didactic and exhortatory than informative. As a writer of pamphlet literature, he is far less fictive and mythic than Greene, less learned and witty than Thomas Nashe, but his occasional descriptive passages and bursts of dialogue and anecdote serve to envigorate his otherwise drab, sermonizing prose. A notable exception is *The Gull's Horn-Book*, a brilliant satire describing a typical day in the life of a London gull, or fop. Of especial interest is the chapter "How a Gull Should Conduct Himself in the Popular Playhouse," a wildly funny invective that throws considerable light on the incredibly informal and intimate theatrical conditions at public playhouses like the Globe or the Swan, where a gallant like Dekker's could sit on the stage and twit the players and playwright, and quite possibly be pulled down and beaten by the audience.

Dekker's career extends from the golden age of 1590's to the decline of the popular theatres in the 1630's, when the aged dramatist tried unsuccessfully to tailor his plays to the new, jaded tastes of the Caroline court and its coterie. What characterizes his plays and prose pamphlets throughout that lengthy period is a certain ingenuous vitality and affection for humanity, a frequent gaiety, and an occasional touch of compassion and sorrow.

—James E. Ruoff

FIELD, Nathan. English. Born in Cripplegate, London, baptized 17 October 1587. Educated at St. Paul's School, London. Married to Anne Field; had several children. Actor with the Children of the Queen's Revels from c. 1600, with Lady Elizabeth's Players, and with the King's Men from c. 1615. *Died in 1619 or 1620.*

PUBLICATIONS

Collections

Plays (includes *A Woman Is a Weathercock* and *Amends for Ladies*), edited by William Peery. 1950.

Plays

Four Plays or Moral Representations in One, with Fletcher (produced 1608–13?). In *Comedies and Tragedies*, by Beaumont and Fletcher, 1647.
A Woman Is a Weather-Cock (produced 1609–10?). 1612.
Amends for Ladies (produced 1610–11?). 1618.
The Honest Man's Fortune, with Fletcher (produced 1613). In *Comedies and Tragedies*, by Beaumont and Fletcher, 1647; edited by J. Gerritsen, 1952.
The Queen of Corinth, with Fletcher and Massinger (produced 1616–17?). In *Comedies and Tragedies*, by Beaumont and Fletcher, 1647.
The Knight of Malta, with Fletcher and Massinger (produced 1616–19?). In *Comedies and Tragedies*, by Beaumont and Fletcher, 1647.
The Fatal Dowry, with Massinger (produced 1616–19?). 1632; edited by T. A. Dunn, 1969.

Reading List: *Field, The Actor-Playwright* by R. F. Brinkley, 1928.

*   *   *

Considering that his father was a Puritan clergyman in the days when all Puritans regarded the theatre as the sink of sin, it is remarkable that Nathan Field became such a famous actor and playwright.

It began about 1600 when young Field became one of the little eyeases of whom Shakespeare complained: one of the Children of the Queen's Chapel. It may have been a fairly ordinary move for a lad educated at St. Paul's School but it meant that the chorister would also be an actor. He made a career of performing. He became one of the six principal child actors of the Queen's Revels. As a boy he starred in *Cynthia's Revels*, *The Poetaster*, and *Epicoene*, and in *Bartholomew Fair* his mentor Ben Jonson hailed him (with Richard Burbage) as the best in his profession. He stayed in the theatre as he grew up and was the leading man in Lady Elizabeth's Players when the Queen's zookeeper turned a bear-baiting pit into The Hope Theatre. When the Globe, which had burned down, reopened, Freedley and Reeves guess, he "doubtless joined with Ben Jonson, Fletcher, Massinger and others who identified themselves with the King's Men, the old Lord Chamberlain's company." So he played Shakespeare and Jonson and Beaumont and Fletcher and the leading role in *Bussy D'Ambois* with what Dryden called "grace of action" and romantic panache. In an age when competition was fierce, he was among the very greatest stars of the stage. In his day Field brought a thorough knowledge of the practical theatre when he turned his hand to plays, whether in collaboration or alone, and he made them if nothing else eminently actable. W. Bridges-Adams (*The Irresistible Theatre*) comments on this quality in the two plays Field seems to have written as vehicles for his own acting talent, *A Woman Is a Weathercocke* and *Amends for Ladies*, describing the first as "farcical comedy, salacious and second-rate but, as we should expect from Field, excellent actor's stuff."

Field also worked, as did so many other dramatists of his period, in collaboration and he had the good fortune to contribute his stage-sense to the work of more famous men. His two humour comedies were very much in the style of Jonson but his collaborations were with Beaumont, Fletcher, and Massinger. R. F. Brinkley's 1928 book and Peery's edition will give the scholar detailed information about these collaborations and related matters. Brinkley's was a fine book for its time, but after half a century Field deserves a complete modern critical study. There is more to be said than Tucker Brooke and Shaaber's terse comment in Baugh's *Literary History*: "Field naturally knew the stage, and he moulded his structure, though not his moral philosophy, upon Jonson's. He is adept at bright dialogue, brisk action, and clever disguise. His prose is lively and idiomatic; but his humour characters, though very varied, are superficial, and his verse is uninspired."

—Leonard R. N. Ashley

FLETCHER, John.   English.   Born in Rye, Sussex, in December 1579. Educated at Benet College, now Corpus Christi College, Cambridge. Met Francis Beaumont in 1605, and collaborated with him in writing for the theatre until Beaumont retired c. 1613; thereafter wrote for the King's Men, on his own and in collaboration with others, particularly Massinger and Shakespeare. *Died* (buried) *29 August 1625.*

PUBLICATIONS

Collections

    Comedies and Tragedies, with Beaumont and others, 1647; revised edition, 1679.
    Works of Beaumont and Fletcher, edited by A. Glover and A. R. Waller.   10 vols., 1905–12.
    Variorum Edition, edited by A. H. Bullen.   4 vols. (incomplete), 1904–12.
    The Dramatic Works in the Beaumont and Fletcher Canon, edited by Fredson Bowers.   3 vols. (of 10), 1966–76.

Plays

    The Woman's Prize; or, The Tamer Tamed, with Beaumont (produced after 1604).   In *Comedies and Tragedies,* 1647.
    The Woman Hater (produced 1606).   1607; edited by George Walton Williams, in *Dramatic Works 1,* 1966.
    The Faithful Shepherdess (produced 1608–09?).   1609(?); edited by Cyrus Hoy, in *Dramatic Works 3,* 1976.
    Four Plays or Moral Representations in One, with Nathan Field (produced 1608–13?).   In *Comedies and Tragedies,* 1647.
    Bonduca (produced 1609–14?).   In *Comedies and Tragedies,* 1647; edited by W. W. Greg, 1951.
    Philaster; or, Love Lies A-Bleeding, with Beaumont (produced before 1610).   1620; edited by Dora Jean Ashe, 1974.

Valentinian (produced 1610–14?).   In *Comedies and Tragedies*, 1647; edited by R. G. Martin, in *Variorum Edition 4*, 1912.

Monsieur Thomas (produced 1610–16?).   Edited by Richard Brome, 1639; as *Father's Own Son*, 1661(?); edited by R. G. Martin, in *Variorum Edition 4*, 1912.

The Maid's Tragedy, with Beaumont (produced before 1611).   1619; edited by Robert K. Turner, Jr., in *Dramatic Works 2*, 1970.

A King and No King, with Beaumont (produced 1611).   1619; edited by George Walton Williams, in *Dramatic Works 2*, 1970.

Cupid's Revenge, with Beaumont (produced before 1612).   1615; edited by Fredson Bowers, in *Dramatic Works 2*, 1970.

The Coxcomb, with Beaumont (produced 1612).   In *Comedies and Tragedies*, 1647; edited by Irby B. Cauthen, Jr., in *Dramatic Works 1*, 1966.

Henry VIII, with Shakespeare (produced 1613).   In *Comedies, Histories, and Tragedies by Shakespeare*, 1623; edited by Louis B. Wright and V. A. LaMar, 1968 (Fletcher's collaboration is questionable).

The Two Noble Kinsmen, with Shakespeare (produced 1613).   1634; edited by G. R. Proudfoot, 1970.

The Captain, with Beaumont (produced 1613).   In *Comedies and Tragedies*, 1647; edited by L. A. Beaurline, in *Dramatic Works 1*, 1966.

The Honest Man's Fortune, with Nathan Field (produced 1613).   In *Comedies and Tragedies*, 1647; edited by J. Gerritsen, 1952.

The Scornful Lady, with Beaumont (produced 1613–17?).   1616; edited by Cyrus Hoy, in *Dramatic Works 2*, 1970.

Wit Without Money (produced 1614?).   1639; edited by R. B. McKerrow, in *Variorum Edition 2*, 1905.

The Nice Valour; or, The Passionate Madman, with Middleton (produced before 1616).   In *Comedies and Tragedies*, 1647.

Love's Pilgrimage, with Beaumont (produced 1616?).   In *Comedies and Tragedies*, 1647; edited by L. A. Beaurline, in *Dramatic Works 2*, 1970.

The Mad Lover (produced 1616?).   In *Comedies and Tragedies*, 1647.

The Queen of Corinth, with Nathan Field and Massinger (produced 1616–17?).   In *Comedies and Tragedies*, 1647.

The Knight of Malta, with Nathan Field and Massinger (produced 1616–19?).   In *Comedies and Tragedies*, 1647.

The Chances (produced 1617?).   In *Comedies and Tragedies*, 1647.

The Loyal Subject; or, The Faithful General (produced 1618).   In *Comedies and Tragedies*, 1647.

The Laws of Candy (produced 1619?).   In *Comedies and Tragedies*, 1647.

The Humorous Lieutenant; or, Generous Enemies (produced 1619?).   In *Comedies and Tragedies*, 1647; edited by M. Cook and F. P. Wilson, 1951.

Sir John Van Olden Barnevelt, with Massinger (produced 1619).   Edited by A. H. Bullen, in *A Collection of Old English Plays*, vol. 2, 1883; edited by W. P. Frijlinck, 1922.

The Custom of the Country, with Massinger (produced 1619–20?).   In *Comedies and Tragedies*, 1647.

The Island Princess (produced 1619–21?).   In *Comedies and Tragedies*, 1647.

Women Pleased (produced 1619–23?).   In *Comedies and Tragedies*, 1647.

The Little French Lawyer, with Massinger (produced 1619–23?).   In *Comedies and Tragedies*, 1647.

The False One, with Massinger (produced 1620?).   In *Comedies and Tragedies*, 1647.

Thierry, King of France, and His Brother Theodoret, with Massinger (produced ?).   1621; edited by Robert K. Turner, Jr., in *Dramatic Works 3*, 1976.

The Pilgrim (produced 1621?).   In *Comedies and Tragedies*, 1647.

The Wild Goose Chase, with Beaumont (produced 1621?).   1652.

The Double Marriage, with Massinger (produced 1621?). In *Comedies and Tragedies*, 1647.

The Spanish Curate, with Massinger (produced 1622?). In *Comedies and Tragedies*, 1647.

The Prophetess, with Massinger (produced 1622). In *Comedies and Tragedies* 1647.

The Sea Voyage, with Massinger (produced 1622). In *Comedies and Tragedies*, 1647.

The Beggars' Bush, with Massinger (produced 1622). In *Comedies and Tragedies*, 1647; edited by Fredson Bowers, in *Dramatic Works 3*, 1976.

The Lovers' Progress (produced 1623). Revised version by Massinger published in *Comedies and Tragedies*, 1647.

The Maid in the Mill, with Rowley (produced 1623). In *Comedies and Tragedies*, 1647.

Rule a Wife and Have a Wife (produced 1624). 1640.

A Wife for a Month (produced 1624). In *Comedies and Tragedies*, 1647.

The Elder Brother, with Massinger (produced 1625?). 1637; edited by W. H. Draper, 1916.

The Fair Maid of the Inn, with Massinger (produced 1625–26?). In *Comedies and Tragedies*, 1647.

The Noble Gentleman, with Beaumont (produced 1625–26?). In *Comedies and Tragedies*, 1647; edited by L. A. Beaurline, in *Dramatic Works 3*, 1976.

A Very Woman, with Massinger (produced 1634). In *Three New Plays*, by Massinger, 1655.

The Night Walker; or, The Little Thief (produced ?). 1640.

Love's Cure; or, The Martial Maid, with Massinger (produced ?). In *Comedies and Tragedies*, 1647; edited by George Walton Williams, in *Dramatic Works 3*, 1976.

Wit at Several Weapons, with Middleton and Rowley (produced ?). In *Comedies and Tragedies*, 1647.

Bibliography: *Beaumont and Fletcher: A Concise Bibliography* by S. A. Tannenbaum, 1938; supplement, 1946; supplement in *Elizabethan Bibliographies Supplements 8*, by C. A. Pennell and W. P. Williams, 1968.

Reading List: *Beaumont, Fletcher, and Company: Entertainers to the Jacobean Gentry* by L. B. Wallis, 1947; *The Pattern of Tragicomedy in Beaumont and Fletcher* by E. M. Smith, 1952; *Beaumont and Fletcher: A Critical Study* by W. W. Appleton, 1956; *Beaumont and Fletcher* by Ian Fletcher, 1967.

* * *

After Jonson and Shakespeare, John Fletcher was the most gifted and influential of the Elizabethan and Stuart dramatists. His mastery is most notable in two dramatic types, tragicomedy and comedy of manners, both of which exerted a pervasive influence on dramatists in the reign of Charles I and during the Restoration.

A characteristically heroic tragi-comedy is *The Island Princess*, based on a recent Spanish history, Bartomé Leonardo de Argensola's *La Conquist de las Isles Maluces* (1609). The setting is exotic and remote (the Moluccan island of Tidore); the plot tangled and swift-moving; the theme love and honor; the language both coarse and lyrical; the characters aristocratic and refined, and given over to sudden, inexplicable changes of moods and motives. As usual, Fletcher begins with a contrived, melodramatic situation: the beautiful pagan princess Quisara's father has been imprisoned by a ruthless tyrant, and, although she is in love with the Portuguese commander Ruy Dias, she offers to marry the suitor who frees her father. When this is accomplished by another young Portuguese, Armusia, she plots with Ruy Dias to murder him rather than fulfill her promise. Armusia conducts himself so nobly, however, that Ruy Dias repents of his treachery and magnanimously rescues Armusia from execution, whereupon Quisara, equally inspired by Armusia's resplendent virtues, is converted to Christianity and marries him. In the end, of course, her father is restored to his throne and the tyrant is exiled. Thus the characters simply alter their behavior to avert the many disasters ingeniously prepared for them by the author. The heroes are paradigms of cavalier virtues with almost perverse obsessions for making excruciatingly fine distinctions between love and honor; the heroine is a garrulous *précieuse* straight out of the French and Spanish heroic romances. The setting is not the bustling world of Jonson and Shakespeare, but the artificial landscape of Sidney's *Arcadia*, where action and dialogue serve to express certain aristocratic ideas about love and honor.

Fletcher had written a similar type of tragi-comedy in 1608 with his *Faithful Shepherdess*, an imitation of Guarini's pastoral drama *Il Pastor Fido*, but this effort to adapt the conventions of the formal pastoral love debate to the popular stage failed utterly. A year earlier Francis Beaumont's satiric comedy *The Knight of the Burning Pestle* had met with a similar fate, perhaps for similar reasons, and the two dramatists decided to combine their talents. In retrospect, the famous collaboration of Beaumont and Fletcher would appear almost inevitable. They were ardent disciples of Jonson, shared quarters on the Bankside, had written a number of plays for the boys' company at St. Paul's, and were shifting over to the King's Men, who, in turn, were contracting for plays more suitable to the genteel taste of the private theatres. No doubt the King's Men, in catering to the refined audience at the Blackfriars, felt they could trust the social instincts of Beaumont, scion of a distinguished Leicestershire family, and Fletcher, a bishop's son. In any event, their collaboration, extending from 1608 until Beaumont's retirement from the stage around 1613, produced a string of successes: *Cupid's Revenge, The Coxcomb, The Scornful Lady, Philaster, The Maid's Tragedy*, and *A King and No King*. The 1647 folio of their plays included thirty-four; the second edition of 1679 fifty-two. Most of these are now believed to have been by Fletcher, many in collaboration with dramatists other than Beaumont.

Beaumont and Fletcher's first notable success on behalf of Shakespeare's company came around 1610 with *Philaster; or, Love Lies A-Bleeding*, a flamboyant tragi-comedy that became the prototype of the cavalier dramas of the 1630's and the heroic plays of Dryden and Orrery in the Restoration. The similarities of *Philaster* and Shakespeare's *Cymbeline*, both written about the same time, have often been noted; but most resemblances derive from common appropriation of fairly conventional romantic situations, such as a virtuous heroine disguised as a page and falsely accused of treachery. Shakespeare's romance, set in ancient Britain, lacks the courtly rhetoric and idealized characterizations of Beaumont and Fletcher's tragi-comedy, which owes less to robust folklore or legend than to delicate sentiments and ritualistic deportment portrayed in French heroic pastorals and Sidney's *Arcadia*. In *Cymbeline* Shakespeare tells a wondrous, adventurous tale; in *Philaster* Beaumont and Fletcher depict niceties of courtly conduct and sentiments. Philaster's tortuous sensitivity and brooding melancholy, which prohibit any forthright action, are not maladies but aristocratic traits setting him apart from ordinary mortals. Hence, although apotheosized in testimony as "god-like" and "divine," he is ineffectual and "lily-livered," a kind of ranting Cambises more concerned with his lady-love's unaccountable petulances than with the rigors of war. As in many of Fletcher's tragi-comedies, beginning with his *Faithful Shepherdess*, the characters in *Philaster* are created to suggest various concepts of love in a manner resembling that of the French pastorals, the *Arcadia*, and *The Faerie Queene*, Book III. The noble Philaster and his virtuous Arethusa, appropriately long-suffering, are contrasted to the base, sensual Pharamond and his lascivious courtesan Megra, whereas "Bellario" (ethereal Euphrasia disguised as a page in the hero's service) represents Fletcher's flirtation with the idea of Platonic love, a theme seized upon and developed even less intellectually by Fletcher's imitators in the Caroline period.

In a play like *Philaster*, it is difficult to distinguish Beaumont's contributions from Fletcher's. Beaumont is credited with having been a more confident master of total plot construction, of deeper characterizations, of a firm, regular verse with frequent run-on lines. Fletcher was a skillful contriver of sensational, heart-rending individual scenes, a superb rhetorician in dialogue with a loose-flowing style of verse that melts into rhythmic prose with numerous feminine endings and end-stopped lines. Judging from those plays written by Fletcher alone, a critic surmises that he, rather than Beaumont, had a keen perception of the changing tastes of the times. This last quality is most apparent in Fletcher's comedy of manners *The Wild-Goose Chase* (revised in 1702 by George Farquhar as *The Inconstant*), which anticipates the urbane, cynical Restoration comedies of Wycherley, Etherege, and Congreve. In *The Wild-Goose Chase*, as in many of Fletcher's comedies of manners, he adopts his master Ben Jonson's technique of presenting a fixed comic situation with a variety of "humorous" characters. A prodigal young rake and his sportive companions, much to the chagrin of their wealthy, indulgent parents, seek to outmaneuver a covey of vivacious girls bent on matrimony. Thus Fletcher combines the themes of the battle of the sexes and the alienation of generations, but, unlike Jonson, he deals with these in a relaxed, amoral way totally pleasing to his sophisticated audience. The characters are drawn from the familiar background of Jonson's and Middleton's London comedies – madcap rakes, stodgy bourgeois fathers, confused matrons, nubile lasses and dotty "fantastics" – all given renewed vitality by Fletcher's single-minded concern with pure entertainment rather than moral exploration or didacticism.

Fletcher collaborated with a dozen dramatists (including Shakespeare in *Two Noble Kinsmen* and *Henry VIII*) in addition to Beaumont, and he succeeded Shakespeare as master dramatist of the King's Men, providing that company with three or four plays a year. In spite of his limitations of loose plot construction, careless versification, and indifference to any high seriousness, Fletcher's achievements and influence were immense. After Shakespeare and Jonson, he alone provided the stage with a large number of variegated plays unparalleled for their ingenuity and vitality.

—James E. Ruoff

FORD, John. English. Born in Islington, Devon, baptized 17 April 1586. Educated at Exeter College, Oxford, 1601–02; Middle Temple, London, 1602–05, 1608–17, but probably never practised law. Very little is known about his life: probably retired from London to Devon c. 1638. *Died c. 1640.*

PUBLICATIONS

Collections

Works, edited by William Gifford, revised by A. Dyce. 3 vols., 1869.
Dramatic Works, edited by W. Bang and Henry de Vocht. 2 vols., 1908–27.

Plays

The Witch of Edmonton, with Rowley and Dekker (produced 1621). 1658; edited by Fredson Bowers, in *Dramatic Works of Dekker,* 1953–61.

Perkin Warbeck: A Strange Truth (produced 1622–32?).   1634; edited by Peter Ure, 1968.
The Welsh Ambassador, with Dekker (produced 1623).   Edited by H. Littledale and W. W. Greg, 1920.
The Sun's Darling: A Moral Masque, with Dekker (produced 1624).   1656.
The Broken Heart (produced 1627–31?).   1633; edited by Donald K. Anderson, Jr., 1968.
The Lover's Melancholy (produced 1628).   1629.
'Tis Pity She's a Whore (produced 1629–33?).   1633; edited by Brian Morris, 1969.
Love's Sacrifice (produced 1632?).   1633.
The Fancies, Chaste and Noble (produced 1635–36?).   1638.
The Lady's Trial (produced 1638).   1639.
The Queen; or, The Excellency of Her Sex (produced ?).   1653.

Verse

Fame's Memorial; or, The Earl of Devonshire Deceased.   1606; edited by S. E. Brydges, 1810.
Christ's Bloody Sweat.   1613.

Other

Honour Triumphant; or, The Peers' Challenge.   1606.
The Golden Mean.   1613; revised edition, 1614, 1638.
A Line of Life, Pointing at the Immortality of a Virtuous Name.   1620.

Bibliography: *Ford: A Concise Bibliography* by S. A. Tannenbaum, 1941; supplement in *Elizabethan Bibliographies Supplements 8* by C. A. Pennell and W. P. Williams, 1968.

Reading List: *Ford* by M. J. Sargeaunt, 1935; *Burtonian Melancholy in the Plays of Ford* by S. Blaine Ewing, 1940; *The Tragic Muse of Ford* by George F. Sensabaugh, 1944; *The Problem of Ford* by H. J. Oliver, 1955; *Ford and the Drama of His Time* by Clifford Leech, 1957; *Ford and the Traditional Moral Order* by Mark Stavig, 1968; *Ford* by Donald K. Anderson, Jr., 1972; *The Tragic Vision of Ford* by Tucker Orbison, 1974.

*   *   *

John Ford's dramatic career begins in 1621 with *The Witch of Edmonton*, a tragedy based on a contemporary event involving accusations of witchcraft. The main plot is the work of Thomas Dekker and William Rowley; Ford's contribution consists of the sub-plot which deals with a star-crossed youth and his progress towards murder.

Fifteen years earlier Ford had produced two non-dramatic works which, in their different ways, are characteristic of the temperament we sense behind the plays. *Fame's Memorial* is an elegy on the death of Charles Blount, Earl of Devonshire and second husband of Sidney's Stella. Typically, Ford chose to eulogise a courtier who was, at the time of his death, out of favour at court. In *Honour Triumphant; or, The Peers' Challenge*, four young gallants conduct a highly mannered debate on certain vaguely paradoxical topics, such as that beautiful women are necessarily virtuous. This penchant for ethical paradox is also a feature of Ford's plays.

The first play written entirely by Ford was probably *The Lover's Melancholy*, performed in 1628. The hothouse atmosphere of self-generated emotion characteristic of all Ford's work is evident in this story of a father driven mad and a lover on the edge of despair because of the death of a daughter and mistress respectively. Ford's almost obsessive interest in abnormal psychology is very much a feature of his first independent play, and is a direct result of the influence on him of that compendious psychological treatise, Robert Burton's *The Anatomy of Melancholy*.

It was four years later that Ford's next play *Love's Sacrifice* was performed. Here too there is a good deal of emotion which seems to exist for its own sake, as in the scene where the Duchess, who had earlier spurned the advances of her husband's friend Fernando, presents herself to him in his chambers, swearing the while to kill herself after she has lost her honor. For all its emotional self-indulgence, this play is notable for the character of the villainous D'Avolos; Shakespeare's Iago influences but does not overwhelm Ford in his creation of this character.

Ford's interest in the psychology of individuals in emotional extremity and his fondness for ethical paradox find their most striking dramatic embodiment in his next two plays, *'Tis Pity She's a Whore* and *The Broken Heart*. The first of these is undoubtedly his finest play, in which the theme of incest is treated with an honesty and a sensitiveness which are in marked contrast to the evasiveness with which the same theme is handled by Beaumont and Fletcher in *A King and No King*. The superficial impression we gain that Giovanni, the incestuous brother, is the only honourable character in the play is, however, only apparently paradoxical. By contrast with his sister Annabella, he is finally revealed as totally lacking in self-discipline and therefore morally defective. It is doubtful, however, whether Ford is seriously interested in the moral predicament of his chief characters; their psychological states and the predictable reactions of the pillars of church and state around them are probably more important to him.

In *The Broken Heart* the tragic situation is more diffuse than it is in *'Tis Pity*, and, because the dramatist seems not to be fully in control of it, the general effect is orgiastic rather than tragic, a welter of torture and death rather than a truly tragic climax. A beautiful young girl who deliberately starves herself to death rather than endure marriage with an ancient and possessive husband, and the murder of her brother by her erstwhile lover – these events have all the trappings of melodrama. But Ford's gift for subtle psychological analysis redeems the play, and the final act, where Calantha continues dancing while she hears of the successive deaths of those near and dear to her until she falls down dead, is more than a mere theatrical coup.

Ford's other important play is rather different in style and scope from those already mentioned. Taking Bacon's history of Henry VII and Thomas Gainsford's *True and Wonderful History of Perkin Warbeck* as his sources, Ford produced his own highly individual version of that moribund genre, the chronicle play, *Perkin Warbeck*. The characterization of the hero is especially effective, and the whole play has an energy which recalls, if not Shakespeare, at least the Marlowe of *Edward II*.

Two inconsiderable romantic comedies, *The Fancies Chaste and Noble* and *The Lady's Trial*, bring Ford's dramatic career to its close. But it is on *'Tis Pity*, *The Broken Heart*, and *Perkin Warbeck* that his claim to be the finest dramatist of the years immediately preceding the closing of the theatres depends.

—Gāmini Salgādo

GLAPTHORNE, Henry. English.   Born in Whittlesey, Cambridgeshire, 28 July 1610.
Very little is known about his life: educated at Corpus Christi College, Cambridge; probably
enjoyed the patronage of a lord; presumed to be a Royalist and probably died in the Civil
War. *Died in 1644.*

PUBLICATIONS

Collections

   Plays and Poems, edited by R. H. Shepherd.   2 vols., 1874.

Plays

   Argalus and Parthenia (produced 1632–38?).   1639.
   The Lady's Privilege (produced 1632–40?).   1640.
   Albertus Wallenstein (produced 1634–39?).   1639.
   The Lady Mother (produced 1635).   Edited by A. H. Bullen, in *A Collection of Old
      English Plays,* 1883; edited by Arthur Brown, 1959.
   The Hollander (produced 1636).   1640.
   Wit in a Constable (produced ?).   1640.
   Revenge for Honour (produced 1640?).   1654.

Verse

   Poems.   1639.
   Whitehall, with Elegies and An Anniversary.   1643.

Other

   *His Majesty's Gracious Answer to the Message Sent from the Honourable City of London
      Concerning Peace.*   1643.

   Editor, *Poems, Divine and Humane,* by Thomas Beedome.   1641.

Reading List: *Glapthorne* by M. Zwickert, 1881; *The Sons of Ben: Jonsonian Comedy in
Caroline England* by J. L. Davis, 1967.

*   *   *

Henry Glapthorne is an obscure English dramatist who wrote for the popular theatre
during the last half of the reign of Charles I. He is perhaps best known for a play which in
fact he may not have written, *Revenge for Honour.* For although the Stationers' Register for
1653 lists Glapthorne as author, Chapman's name appears on the title page. Certainly he
wrote no other play in the Eastern heroic vein. During a short theatrical career of less than
ten years, Glapthorne set his hand to pastoral, tragedy, comedy, and tragi-comedy, producing
no play totally in a single theatrical mode. This is a generic eclecticism common to much
Caroline drama. For example, the Fletcherian pastoral, *Argalus and Parthenia,* is based on an

incident from Sidney's revision of his *Arcadia*. Although in Glapthorne's play Argalus still dies for honour and Parthenia for love, thus preserving the high heroics of Sidney's romantic epic, the suitor Demagorgas is reduced to a *miles gloriosus*, and the tragic main plot is filled out with a comic sub-plot of some proportion and with the masque-like pleasantries of pastoral song and dance. The tragedy *Albertus Wallenstein* concerns both the politics of the rebellion of Wallenstein from the German Emperor Ferdinand the Second and the romance of Albertus, Wallenstein's son, with Isabella, one of his mother's ladies-in-waiting. And *The Hollander* can't decide whether it is romantic comedy, the subject of the main plot, satire against the affectations of the "Galland naturaliz'd Dutchman" Sconce, the subject of its title, or simply farce.

Glapthorne's plays are interesting primarily for historical rather than for artistic reasons. Glapthorne seems to grasp at successful theatrical ideas from many earlier English Renaissance dramatists. Most noticeably, he looks back to Jonson for his comedies, especially for the ubiquitous humour characters, and back to Shirley, Fletcher, or Lyly for the florid surface and decorated pathos of his style. Yet the comedies adumbrate weakly the glittering intelligence of Restoration drama. Such a play is *Wit in a Constable*, a comedy of some vitality set in London and in fact revived, although perhaps unsuccessfully, in 1662. Two sets of suitors vie for the hands of the young cousins, Grace and Clare. The would-be's, Sir Timothy Shallowit and Jeremy Holdfast, have come to London, the one from the country and the other from Cambridge. Both pretend to the true wit needed to win the ladies, but Jeremy's flights into pedantry are matched by Sir Timothy's lapses into boorishness. The successful suitors are Thorowgood and Valentine, young gentlemen as well as friends. However, the lovers' difficulties are resolved not by their gentle intelligence but by Constable Busie and his common-sense wit. As the title suggests *Wit in a Constable* has a "citizen" bias, despite the more elevated status of the main characters.

The language of Glapthorne's plays is their major fault. The style is too often poetic, not dramatic. Glapthorne's plots have much theatrical possibility, his sense of the scene division is intelligent, and the threads of his sub-plots are interwoven ingeniously enough to provide variety and interest. But his characters do not talk; they recite. Too often Glapthorne clothes his simple thoughts in stiff and ill-fitting conceits, especially in those drawn from nature experienced through books.

The same stultifying inventiveness mars his poems. The subjects and forms of the poems – love poems to an imaginary mistress Lucinda, elegies or epistles to his friends – suggest an interest in the matter and manner of Latin literature common to many cavalier poets, including Glapthorne's "noble Friend and Gossip, Captaine Richard Lovelace." The Royalist sympathies which this dedication implies are also indicated by the curious poem "White-Hall," which employs the palace itself as narrator of the royal history of Tudor and Stuart England. The building itself is personified as the abandoned wife of Charles I, then in battle against his subjects, soon to be beheaded.

—Daniel DeMatteis

GREENE, Robert.   English.   Born in Norwich, Norfolk, baptized 11 July 1558. Educated at St. John's College, Cambridge, 1575–78, B.A. 1578; Clare Hall, Cambridge, M.A. 1583; incorporated at Oxford, 1588. Married in 1585, but later deserted his wife; one illegitimate son. Travelled in Italy and Spain, 1579–80; writer from 1580; settled in London, 1586, and quickly became known as a pamphleteer and romancer; associated with the University Wits; known for his profligate life. *Died 2 or 3 September 1592.*

PUBLICATIONS

Collections

Life and Complete Works in Prose and Verse, edited by A. B. Grosart.   15 vols., 1881–86.
Plays and Poems, edited by J. C. Collins.   2 vols., 1905.
Complete Plays, edited by T. H. Dickinson.   1909.

Plays

Alphonsus, King of Aragon (produced 1587?).   1599; edited by W. W. Greg, 1926.
Friar Bacon and Friar Bungay (produced 1589?).   1594; edited by J. A. Lavin, 1969.
A Looking Glass for London and England, with Thomas Lodge (produced 1590?).   1594; edited by T. Hayashi, 1970.
Orlando Furioso, One of the Twelve Peers of France (produced 1591?).   1594; edited by W. W. Greg, in *Two Elizabethan Stage Abridgements,* 1923.
The Scottish History of James the Fourth (produced 1591?).   1598; edited by Norman Sanders, 1970.
A Knack to Know a Knave (produced 1592).   1594.
George à Greene, The Pinner of Wakefield (produced before 1593).   1599; edited by E. A. Horsman, 1956.

Fiction

Mamillia: A Mirror or Looking Glass for the Ladies of England.   1583; augmented edition, 1583(?).
Arbasto: The Anatomy of Fortune.   1584.
Gwydonius: The Card of Fancy.   1584; edited by George Saintsbury, in *Shorter Novels 1,* 1929.
Morando the Tritameron of Love.   1584; augmented edition, 1587.
The Mirror of Modesty.   1584.
Planetomachia.   1585.
Euphues His Censure to Philautus.   1587.
Penelope's Web.   1587.
Pandosto: The Triumph of Time.   1588; as *Dorastus and Fawnia,* 1636; edited by James Winny, in *The Descent of Euphues,* 1957.
Perimedes the Blacksmith.   1588.
Ciceronis Amor: Tullie's Love.   1589; edited by Charles Howard Larson, 1974.
The Spanish Masquerado.   1589.
Menaphon: Camilla's Alarum to Slumbering Euphues.   1589; as *Greene's Arcadia,* 1610; edited by G. B. Harrison, with *A Margarite of America* by Thomas Lodge, 1927.
Greene's Never Too Late.   1590.
Greene's Mourning Garment.   1590.

Greene's Farewell to Folly. 1591.

The Black Book's Messenger: The Life and Death of Ned Browne. 1592; edited by A. V. Judges, in *The Elizabethan Underworld,* 1930.

Philomela: The Lady Fitzwater's Nightingale. 1592.

Greene's Groatsworth of Wit, Bought with a Million of Repentance. 1592; edited by A. C. Ward, 1927.

Greene's Orpharion, Wherein Is Discovered a Musical Concord of Pleasant Histories. 1599 (first extant edition).

Alcida: Greene's Metamorphosis. 1617 (first extant edition).

Verse

A Maiden's Dream: Upon the Death of Sir Christopher Hatton. 1591.

Other

A Notable Discovery of Cozenage. 1591; *The Second Part of Cony-Catching,* 1591; *Third and Last Part,* 1592; edited by A. V. Judges, in *The Elizabethan Underworld,* 1930.

A Disputation Between a He Cony-Catcher and a She Cony-Catcher. 1592; as *Thieves Falling Out, True Men Come by Their Goods,* 1615; edited by A. V. Judges, in *The Elizabethan Underworld,* 1930.

A Quip for an Upstart Courtier. 1592.

The Repentance of Robert Greene, Master of Arts. 1592; edited by G. B. Harrison, with *Greene's Groatsworth of Wit,* 1923.

Translator, *An Oration at the Burial of Gregory the 13th,* from the French. 1585.

Translator, *The Royal Exchange,* by Orazio Rinaldi. 1590.

Bibliography: *Greene Criticism: A Comprehensive Bibliography* by T. Hayashi, 1971; *Greene* by A. F. Allison, 1975.

Reading List: *Greene* by J. C. Jordan, 1915; *The Professional Writer in Elizabethan England* by E. H. Miller, 1959; *L'Opera Narrativa di Greene* by F. Ferrara, 1960; *The Aphorisms of Orazio Rinaldi, Greene, and Lucas Gracian Dantisco* by C. Speroni, 1968.

*   *   *

Robert Greene, in the few years between his graduation with an M.A. from Cambridge in 1583 and his early death in 1592, was a restless and indefatigable free-lance writer with a massive output. He turned his hand to several currently popular genres in succession. Beginning with prose romances (of which he wrote some dozen), he was then briefly involved in the Marprelate controversy, an angry exchange of theological pamphlets written for popular appeal deliberately in colloquial style. This led him to experiment with a series of prose pamphlets on "conny catching," for which he drew on his considerable knowledge of the seamy (and criminal) side of London life. These pamphlets, ostensibly designed to expose the "cosenages and villainies" of the Elizabethan underworld, met with great popular success as lively pieces of crime fiction.

Greene was associated with Lodge, Nashe, and other of the "university wits" and was inescapably drawn into working for the theatre. The full extent of his involvement (considering the collaborative writing common at the time) is not exactly determinable, but he is the certain author of five plays, four of them comedies produced by Queen Elizabeth's Men between 1589 and 1591.

Greene began by writing for a leisured and cultured audience – his romance, *Menaphon*, is, typically, dedicated to a noble lady and its preface is addressed "To the Gentlemen Readers." For these he wrote his prose romances (the best-known are *Menaphon* and *Pandosto*, the source of Shakespeare's *The Winter's Tale*), Arcadian love-tales marked by lively plotting, pastoral settings, interspersed lyrics, and a highly mannered prose style. His involvement with public controversy led to a great change in his attitude to writing. The later conny-catching and other pamphlets exploit the resources of a colloquial prose based on the speech of ordinary Londoners. With his friend Nashe, Greene expanded "downwards" the whole range of vocabulary and prose structures that could be admitted into literary English, and so paved the way for Defoe and the establishment of the English novel.

His skill in plotting, acquired in his prose fiction, is evident in all his work for the theatre. His best-known comedy, *Friar Bacon and Friar Bungay*, owes something to the magic scenes in Marlowe's *Faustus*, but Greene shows an independent mastery of the resources of the Elizabethan stage (the inset "glass perspective" scene, where he presents simultaneously scenes in two different places, both actions integrated into the forward movement of the plot). His portraits, in prose and drama, of lively and independent-minded young women (Margaret in *Friar Bacon*, Fawnia in *Pandosto*) foreshadow, and perhaps helped towards creating, the Rosalinds and Beatrices of Shakespeare; in one of his early works he announced himself as a "Homer of women."

Like many Elizabethan writers of any genre, in an age when poetry and music went hand-in-hand, he had an instinctive facility for lyric poetry. Twenty of his lyrics (from his plays and his prose romances) are included in the *Oxford Book of Sixteenth Century Verse*.

—Ian A. Gordon

HEYWOOD, Thomas. English. Born in Lincolnshire in 1573. Possibly educated at Cambridge University. Lived in London; wrote plays for Philip Henslowe from 1596; actor and possibly a shareholder in Henslowe's company, the Lord Admiral's Men, from 1598; later a member of other companies, including the Earl of Worcester's players; succeeded Dekker as writer of mayoral pageants for the City of London; claimed to have been involved in the writing of 220 plays, of which some 35 survive. *Died* (buried) *16 August 1641.*

PUBLICATIONS

Collections

Dramatic Works, edited by R. H. Shepherd.   6 vols., 1874.

Plays

The Four Prentices of London (produced 1592?).   1615.

King Edward the Fourth, 2 parts (produced before 1599).   1599; edited by S. de Ricci, 1922.

How a Man May Choose a Good Wife from a Bad (produced 1602?).   1602; edited by A. E. H. Swaen, 1912.

The Royal King and the Loyal Subject (produced 1602?).   1637; edited by K. W. Tibbals, 1906.

Sir Thomas Wyatt, with Dekker and Webster (produced 1602–07?).   1607; edited by Fredson Bowers, in *Dramatic Works* by Dekker, 1953–61.

A Woman Killed with Kindness (produced 1603).   1607; edited by R. Van Fossen, 1961.

The Rape of Lucrece (produced 1603–08?).   1608; edited by A. Holaday, 1950.

The Wise Woman of Hogsdon (produced 1604?).   1638.

If You Know Not Me, You Know Nobody; or, The Troubles of Queen Elizabeth (produced 1605).   1605; edited by Madeleine Doran, 1935.

The Second Part of If You Know Not Me, You Know Nobody (produced 1605).   1606; as *The Second Part of Queen Elizabeth's Troubles,* 1609; edited by Madeleine Doran, 1935.

Fortune by Land and Sea, with William Rowley (produced 1607?).   1655; edited by J. E. Walker, 1899.

The Miseries of Enforced Marriage, with George Wilkins (produced 1607).   1607; edited by G. H. Blayney, 1964.

Appius and Virginia, with Webster (produced 1608?).   1654; edited by F. L. Lucas, in *Works* by Webster, 1927.

The Fair Maid of the West; or, A Girl Worth Gold, part 1 (produced before 1610).   1631; edited by Brownell Salomon, 1975; *The Fair Maid of the West,* part 2 (produced 1630?), 1631; edited by R. K. Turner, with part 1, 1967.

The Golden Age (produced 1611?).   1611.

The Silver Age (produced 1612?).   1613.

The Brazen Age (produced 1613?).   1613.

The Iron Age, 2 parts (produced 1613).   1632.

The Martyred Soldier, with Henry Shirley (produced before 1619).   1638; edited by A. H. Bullen, in *A Collection of Old English Plays 1,* 1882.

The Captives; or, The Lost Recovered (produced 1624).   Edited by A. H. Bullen, in *A Collection of Old English Plays,* 1885; edited by A. Brown, 1953.

A Maidenhead Well Lost (produced 1625–34?).   1634.

The English Traveller (produced 1627?).   1633.

Pleasant Dialogues and Dramas, from Lucian, Erasmus, Ovid (produced 1630–36?).   1637.

London's Jus Honorarium, Expressed in Sundry Triumphs, Pageants, and Shows (produced 1631).   1631.

Londini Artium et Scientiarum Scaturigo; or, London's Fountain of Arts and Sciences (produced 1632).   1632; edited by Arthur M. Clark, in *Theatre Miscellany,* 1953.

Londini Emporia; or, London's Mercatura (produced 1633).   1633; edited by Arthur M. Clark, in *Theatre Miscellany,* 1953.

The Late Lancashire Witches, with Richard Brome (produced 1634).   1634.

Love's Mistress; or, The Queen's Masque (produced 1634).   1636; edited by H. M. Blake, 1910.

A Challenge for Beauty (produced 1634–35?).   1636.

Londini Sinus Salutis; or, London's Harbour of Health and Happiness (produced 1635).   1635.

Londini Speculum; or, London's Mirror (produced 1637).   1637.

Porta Pietatis; or, The Port or Harbour of Piety (produced 1638). 1638.
Londini Status Pacatus; or, London's Peaceable Estate (produced 1639). 1639.

Verse

Oenone and Paris. 1594; edited by Elizabeth Story Donno, in *Elizabethan Minor Epics,*
 1963.
Troia Britannica; or, Great Britain's Troy. 1609.
A Marriage Triumph. 1613; edited by E. M. Goldsmid, 1884.
A Funeral Elegy upon King James. 1625.
The Hierarchy of the Blessed Angels. 1635.
The Life and Death of Queen Elizabeth, in Heroical Verse. 1639.
*Reader, Here You'll Plainly See Judgement Perverted by These Three: A Priest, A Judge,
 A Patentee.* 1641.

Other

An Apology for Actors. 1612; as *The Actors' Vindication,* 1658; shortened version,
 edited by E. K. Chamber, in *The Elizabethan Stage,* 1923.
Nine Books of Various History Concerning Women. 1624; as *The General History of
 Women,* 1657.
England's Elizabeth: Her Life and Troubles During Her Minority. 1631.
Philocothonist; or, The Drunkard Opened, Dissected, and Anatomized. 1635.
The Wonder of This Age. 1635.
The New Year's Gift. 1636.
The Three Wonders of This Age. 1636.
*A True Discourse of the Two Prophets, Richard Farnham, Weaver, and John Bull,
 Weaver.* 1636.
A Curtain Lecture, As It Is Read by a Country Farmer's Wife to Her Good Man. 1637.
The Phoenix of These Times; or, The Life of Mr. Henry Welby. 1637.
*A True Description of His Majesty's Royal Ship Built This Year 1637 at Woolwich in
 Kent.* 1637; revised edition, 1638.
*A True Relation of the Lives and Deaths of the Two Most Famous English Pirates, Purser
 and Clinton.* 1639.
*The Exemplary Lives and Memorable Acts of Nine of the Most Worthy Women of the
 World.* 1640.
The Black Box of Rome Opened. 1641.
Brightman's Predictions and Prophecies. 1641.
A Dialogue Betwixt Mr. Alderman Abell and Richard Kilvert. 1641.
*The Life of Merlin, Surnamed Ambrosius, His Prophecies and Predictions
 Interpreted.* 1641.
Machiavel's Ghost. 1641; as *Machiavel, as He Lately Appeared,* 1641.
A New Plot Discovered. 1641.
The Rat Trap; or, The Jesuits Taken in Their Own Net. 1641.
A Revelation of Mr. Brightman's Revelation. 1641.
Sir Richard Whittington. 1656.

Translator, *De Arte Amandi; or, The Art of Love,* by Ovid. 1600(?).
Translator, *The Two Most Worthy and Notable Histories of Catiline and Jugurtha,* by
 Sallust. 1608.

Bibliography: *Heywood: A Concise Bibliography* by S. A. Tannenbaum, 1939, supplement in *Elizabethan Bibliographies Supplements 2* by Dennis Donovan,1967.

Reading List: *The Bourgeois Elements in the Dramas of Heywood* by F. M. Velte, 1922, revised edition, 1966; *Heywood: A Study in the Elizabethan Drama of Everyday Life* by Otelia Cromwell, 1928; *Heywood, Playwright and Miscellanist* by Arthur M. Clark, 1931; *Heywood* by F. S. Boas, 1950; *An Index to the Figurative Language in Heywood's Tragedies* by Louis Charles Stagg, 1967; *Images of Women in the Work of Heywood* by Marilyn L. Johnson, 1974.

*   *   *

Thomas Heywood of Lincolnshire, Tucker Brooke's "drama bridge" between Marlowe and Jonson, eminent actor, non-dramatic poet, translator, critic, composer of Lord Mayor pageants and masques (notably *Love's Mistress*, in the Platonic love tradition), wrote his 220 plays (10% surviving) in the classical, English history, romance, and bourgeois realism traditions.

Heywood's classical plays include *The Rape of Lucrece*, a Roman tragedy from Livy, its tragic impact partly blunted by songs worthy of *The Beggar's Opera*, and a five-part study of Greek myth ranging from *The Golden Age*, dealing with the earliest legends of Greek gods, through the two-part *Iron Age*, dealing with the fates of warriors who fought at Troy, the vigor and variety sometimes suggesting Marlowe and Shakespeare.

"Bourgeois" "untrammeled Elizabethan" zest for life during Elizabeth's reign comes through well in Heywood's two-part English history, *If You Know Not Me, You Know Nobody*, especially part two, but nearly drowns in *King Edward the Fourth* because of the songs and the sentimentality of the Jane Shore plot. For example, Jane, the mistress of Edward, submits in a flood of tears and kisses to Edward's queen for chastisement, a scene in which Edward is present; such sentimentality is topped only by the finally reconciled Shores' death agonies, as they join hands across a grave and sing till they expire.

Heywood's masterpiece of romance, the two-part *Fair Maid of the West*, features true, simple, frank, chaste, loyal, English Bess's exotic adventures to rescue her lover, ranging from the Raleigh-Essex Island Voyage to the court of Mulisheg, Morocco, successful because of her honesty, courage, and beauty. Part two gets the two chief couples safely married and home. Heywood's absurd but entertaining chivalric romance set during the crusades, *The Four Prentices of London* (satirized in *The Knight of the Burning Pestle*), has the apprentices become kings and their sister marry an Italian prince.

A Woman Killed with Kindness, Heywood's masterpiece of bourgeois realism and domestic tragedy, abandons the romantic tradition in *Othello* so dominant in Spanish and English theatre, demanding the adulterous wife's death. Frankford "heaps coals of fire" upon the heads of the conscience-stricken lovers by offering Anne forgiveness, becoming as eloquent for forgiveness as Wendoll was for sin. Keeping his dignity as betrayed husband, Frankford creates a mood of pathetic sorrow, anguish, and consternation, mixed with some righteous indignation; he weeps with, not hates, the evil doers, persuading the audience to do likewise, experiencing only one outburst of rage during which he would have killed them had not an accident intervened. The plot unfolds against a very realistic background, but the imagery presents Frankford as God and Adam in Eden, then Christ (betrayed), St. Paul, and God (in judgment), while Wendoll is Satan, Cain, and Judas.

—Louis Charles Stagg

JONSON, Ben(jamin).   English.   Born in Westminster, London, probably 11 June 1572. Educated at Westminster School, London, under William Camden. Fought for the Dutch against the Spanish in the Low Countries. Married Anne Lewis c. 1593; had several children. Actor, then playwright, from 1595; acted for Philip Henslowe, 1597; killed a fellow actor in a duel, 1598, but escaped the gallows by pleading benefit of clergy; enjoyed the patronage of Lord Albany and Aurelian Townshend; appointed Poet Laureate, and given royal pension, 1616, and wrote and presented masques at court, 1616–25; gained a reputation as the "literary dictator" of London and in later life attracted a circle of young writers who styled themselves the "Sons of Ben"; visited Scotland, and William Drummond of Hawthornden, 1618–19: elected a Burgess of Edinburgh, 1619; appointed City Chronologer of London, 1628. M.A.: Oxford University, 1619. *Died 6 August 1637.*

PUBLICATION

Collections

> *Works,* edited by C. H. Herford and P. and E. M. Simpson.   11 vols., 1925–52.
> *Complete Masques,* edited by S. Orgel.   1969.
> *Complete Poems,* edited by Ian Donaldson.   1975.

Plays

> *The Case Is Altered* (produced 1597–98?).   1609.
> *Every Man in His Humour* (produced 1598).   1601; edited by G. B. Jackson, 1969.
> *Every Man Out of His Humour* (produced 1599).   1600.
> *The Fountain of Self-Love; or, Cynthia's Revels* (produced 1600).   1601.
> *Poetaster; or, The Arraignment* (produced 1601).   1602.
> *Sejanus His Fall* (produced 1603).   1605; edited by W. Bolton, 1966.
> *Entertainment of the Queen and Prince at Althorp* (produced 1603).   1604.
> *King James His Royal and Magnificent Entertainment,* with Dekker (produced 1604). With *Entertainment of the Queen and Prince at Althorp.*   1604.
> *A Private Entertainment of the King and Queen at Highgate* (produced 1604).   In *Works,* 1616.
> *Eastward Ho,* with Chapman and Marston (produced 1605).   1605; edited by C. G. Petter, 1973.
> *Volpone; or, The Fox* (produced 1605).   1607; edited by J. Creaser, 1978.
> *The Masque of Blackness* (produced 1605).   In *The Characters of Two Royal Masques,* 1608.
> *Hymenaei* (produced 1606).   1606.
> *The Entertainment of the Two Kings of Great Britain and Denmark at Theobalds* (produced 1606).   In *Works,* 1616.
> *An Entertainment of King James and Queen Anne at Theobalds* (produced 1607).   In *Works,* 1616.
> *The Masque of Beauty* (produced 1608).   In *The Characters of Two Royal Masques,* 1608.
> *The Hue and Cry after Cupid* (produced 1608).   In *Works,* 1616.
> *The Description of the Masque Celebrating the Marriage of John, Lord Ramsey, Viscount Haddington* (produced 1608).   In *Works,* 1616.
> *The Masque of Queens* (produced 1609).   1609.

Epicoene; or, The Silent Woman (produced 1609).   In *Works*, 1616; edited by L. A. Beaurline, 1966.

The Speeches at Prince Henry's Barriers (produced 1610).   In *Works*, 1616.

The Alchemist (produced 1610).   1612; edited by Alvin B. Kernan, 1974.

Oberon, The Faery Prince (produced 1611).   In *Works*, 1616.

Love Freed from Ignorance and Folly (produced 1611).   In *Works*, 1616.

Catiline His Conspiracy (produced 1611).   1611; edited by W. Bolton and J. F. Gardner, 1972.

Love Restored (produced 1612).   In *Works*, 1616.

The Irish Masque (produced 1613).   In *Works*, 1616.

A Challenge at Tilt (produced 1614).   In *Works*, 1616.

Bartholomew Fair (produced 1614).   1631; edited by Edward B. Partridge, 1964.

The Golden Age Restored (produced 1616).   In *Works*, 1616.

Mercury Vindicated from the Alchemists (produced 1616).   In *Works*, 1616.

The Devil Is an Ass (produced 1616).   1631; edited by M. Hussey, 1967.

Christmas His Masque (produced 1616).   In *Works*, 1640.

The Vision of Delight (produced 1617).   In *Works*, 1640.

Lovers Made Men (produced 1617).   1617.

Pleasure Reconciled to Virtue (produced 1618).   In *Works*, 1640; revised version, as *For the Honour of Wales* (produced 1618), in *Works*, 1640.

News from the New World Discovered in the Moon (produced 1620).   In *Works*, 1640.

An Entertainment at the Blackfriars (produced 1620).   In *The Monthly Magazine; or, British Register*, 1816.

Pan's Anniversary; or, The Shepherd's Holiday (produced 1620).   In *Works*, 1640.

The Gypsies Metamorphosed (propoduced 1621).   In *Works*, 1640; edited by W. W. Greg, 1952.

The Masque of Augurs (produced 1622).   1622.

Time Vindicated to Himself and to His Honours (produced 1623).   1623.

Neptune's Triumph for the Return of Albion.   1624; revised version, as *The Fortunate Isles and Their Union* (produced 1625), 1625.

The Masque of Owls (produced 1624).   In *Works*, 1640.

The Staple of News (produced 1625).   1631; edited by Devra Rowland Kifer, 1976.

The New Inn; or, The Light Heart (produced 1629).   1631.

Love's Triumph Through Callipolis (produced 1631).   1631.

Chloridia (produced 1631).   1631.

The Magnetic Lady; or, Humours Reconciled (produced 1632).   In *Works*, 1640.

A Tale of a Tub (produced 1633).   In *Works*, 1640.

The King's Entertainment at Welbeck (produced 1633).   In *Works*, 1640.

Love's Welcome at Bolsover (produced 1634).   In *Works*, 1640.

The Sad Shepherd; or, A Tale of Robin Hood (incomplete), in *Works*.   1640; edited and completed by Alan Porter, 1944.

Other

Works (plays and verse).   1616; revised edition, 2 vols., 1640.

Timber; or, Discoveries Made upon Men and Matter, in *Works*.   1640; edited by R. S. Walker, 1953.

The English Grammar, in *Works*.   1640; edited by S. Gibson, 1928.

Leges Convivales.   1692.

Literary Criticism, edited by J. D. Redwine.   1970.

Translator, *Horace His Art of Poetry*, in *Works*.   1640; edited by E. H. Blakeney, 1928.

Bibliography: *Jonson: A Concise Bibliography* by S. A. Tannenbaum, 1938; supplement 1947; supplement in *Elizabethan Bibliographies Supplements 3* by G. R. Guffey, 1968.

Reading List: *Jonson, Poet* by George B. Johnston, 1945; *The Satiric and Didactic in Jonson's Comedies* by Helena W. Baum, 1947; *Apologie for Bartholomew Fayre: The Art of Jonson's Comedies* by Freda L. Townsend, 1947; *Jonson of Westminster* (biography) by Marchette Chute, 1953; *The Accidence of Jonson's Plays, Masques, and Entertainments* by Astley C. Partridge, 1953; *Jonson and the Comic Truth* by John J. Enck, 1957; *The Broken Compass: A Study of the Major Comedies of Jonson* by Edward B. Partridge, 1958; *Jonson and the Language of Prose Comedy* by Jonas A. Barish, 1960; *Jonson: Studies in the Plays* by Calvin G. Thayer, 1963; *Jonson's Plays: An Introduction* by Robert E. Knoll, 1965; *Jonson's Dotages: A Reconsideration of the Late Plays* by L. S. Champion, 1967; *Jonson's Romish Plot: A Study of Catiline and Its Historical Context* by B. N. De Luna, 1967; *Vision and Judgment in Jonson's Drama* by Gabriele B. Jackson, 1968; *The Aristophanic Comedies of Jonson* by Coburn Gum, 1969; *Jonson* by John B. Bamborough, 1970; *Jonson's Moral Comedy* by A. C. Dessen, 1971; *Jonson, Public Poet and Private Man* by George Parfitt, 1976.

*　　*　　*

The opening lines of T. S. Eliot's famous essay on Ben Jonson are now nearly sixty years old, yet they are almost as applicable today as when they were first written: "The reputation of Jonson," Eliot wrote, "has been of the most deadly kind that can be compelled upon the memory of a great poet. To be universally accepted; to be damned by the praise that quenches all desire to read the book; to be afflicted by the imputation of the virtues which excite the least pleasure; and to be read only by historians and antiquaries – this is the most perfect conspiracy of approval." Substitute "academics and students" for "antiquaries" and you have a fair summary of Jonson's current reputation. That this state of affairs is partly of Jonson's own making is certainly true but hardly sufficient justification. In his own day Jonson saw himself as the self-appointed arbiter of true critical taste, the upholder of classical standards of decorum, construction, and moral didacticism against the undiscriminating popular appetite for sensation and extravagant spectacle, and the champion of high erudition against barbarous ignorance. So successful was he in imposing this version of himself on his own age and those that followed that it was not long before the contrast was drawn by which Jonson's reputation is still largely defined – the contrast between the warm, spontaneous, generous-hearted inclusiveness of the "romantic" Shakespeare and the chilly learning and cold perfection of the "classical" Jonson. Like all such sweeping contrasts, this one has enough plausibility to survive as the received truth, though it is as misleading about Shakespeare as it is about Jonson.

By way of building up a fairer picture of the nature of Jonson's achievement we may begin by recalling one of Drummond's remarks about him: "He hath consumed a whole night in lying looking to his great toe, about which he hath seen Tartars and Turks, Romans and Cartheginians, fight in his imagination." Such a detail serves to draw attention to an element in Jonson's work which meets us at every turn and which is at least as important as his undoubted learning and his emphasis on classical precept and precedent. It is a facet of his imagination at once childlike, romantic, and grotesque, and one which clearly contributed to some of his finest comic creations as well as to his tenderest lyrics and his most savage satirical epigrams.

The exuberance of Jonson's imagination is already apparent in his first great stage success, *Every Man in His Humour*, first performed in 1598 by the Lord Chamberlain's Men, the most famous theatrical company of the time. (The tradition that Shakespeare himself arranged for his company to present the play is attractive, though it cannot be traced beyond the eighteenth century.) In terms of plot and setting there is nothing to distinguish Jonson's play from many others deriving from classical Roman Comedy, with its conflict of generations and the convoluted manoeuvrings of wily servants. Jonson's distinctive contribution appears in his conception of the "humorous man," a dramatic character whose personality is shaped by some leading trait (or "humour") in his temperament which was itself, according to prevailing medical notions, based on the predominance of one of the four bodily fluids, blood, choler, melancholy, and phlegm. Jonson's contemporary George Chapman had been the first to put "humorous" characters on the stage (in *A Humorous Day's Mirth* performed a year before Jonson's comedy), but the vigour and extravagance of Jonson's presentation set it apart. The sharp distinction he draws between true "humour" as an element of character and mere affectation is typical of the energy and inventiveness of Jonson's imagination:

> As when some one peculiar quality
> Doth so possess a man, that it doth draw
> All his affects, his spirits, and his powers,
> In their confluctions, all to run one way,
> This may be truly said to be a Humour.
> But that a rook, in wearing a pied feather,
> The cable hat-band, or the three-piled ruff,
> A yard of shoe-tie, or the Switzer's knot
> On his French garters, should affect a Humour!
> Oh, 'tis more than most ridiculous.

Like most sequels, Jonson's attempt to capitalize on the success of this play with *Every Man Out of His Humour* was a comprehensive failure and appears to have led to the Chamberlain's Men dispensing with his services. The Children of the Queen's Chapel, one of the companies of boy actors which sprouted up towards the end of the century, were his new theatrical patrons and for them he wrote the satiric comedies which involved him in the "war of the theatres" with his contemporaries John Marston and Thomas Dekker. In spite of occasional passages of great satirical energy and some beautiful lyrics such as "Queen and huntress, chaste and fair," Jonson's contributions to this "war" are not by any means among his best plays. *Cynthia's Revels* deserves to be remembered for its portrait of Jonson himself as Crites, the impartial and well-informed judge of society and the arts; and in *Poetaster* Jonson as Horace feeds Marston (Crispianus) an emetic that makes the latter spew great quantities of words in his typically turgid style. But Jonson's greatest achievements in drama were yet to come.

This achievement is certainly not to be found in Jonson's two classical tragedies *Sejanus His Fall* and *Catiline His Conspiracy*; though the latter especially has some magnificent speeches as well as dramatic moments of great intensity, both suffer by comparison with Shakespeare's excursions into Roman history, especially *Julius Caesar*. Jonson's enduring reputation as a dramatist rests squarely on three great comedies, *Volpone; or, The Fox*, *The Alchemist*, and *Bartholomew Fair*. Each of them exemplifies Jonson's enormous capacity to dramatize the grotesque aberrations of human appetite, his zest for the variety of life, and his unfailing delight in the villain as artist. *Volpone* is scrupulously classical in its didactic import, yet what delights us is chiefly the artistry of Volpone and his henchman Mosca. *The Alchemist* is a model of the observance of the Aristotelian unities, but its dramatic appeal lies in the breakneck momentum of its plot and the almost unbearable comic tension created by it. And in *Bartholomew Fair* Jonson abandoned even the pretence of being the classical moralist in favour of the unbuttoned enjoyment of Jacobean London in all its colour and richness.

The opening years of the seventeenth century witnessed Jonson's finest dramatic productions, not only for the public stage, but in the sphere of royal entertainment, when Jonson's collaboration with the scene designer and architect Inigo Jones led to a splendid flowering of that most ephemeral of theatrical forms, the court masque. Rooted as it was in time, place, and occasion, the masque can give us little sense of its splendour through the text alone, though Jonson's scripts for such works as *Pleasure Reconciled to Virtue* and *The Gypsies Metamorphosed* are eloquent enough even in the reading. It was precisely the disagreement between Jonson and Jones as to the relative importance of words versus spectacle in masque which led to the dissolution of this brilliant partnership in 1631.

Jonson's last years present a sad picture of commercial failure, declining creative powers, and increasing bodily decrepitude. Apart from the comedies already mentioned, *The Silent Woman*, *The Devil Is an Ass*, and *The Staple of News* deserve to be remembered for their occasional inventiveness and keen-eyed observation of London life and manners. But if Jonson's principal claim to fame lies in his three great comedies, his achievements as lyric and epigrammatic poet are not inconsiderable. Contemporary practitioners of verse esteemed him so highly that a group of them, which included Herrick, Suckling, and Carew styled themselves the Sons of Ben and produced a commemorative volume *Jonsonus Virbius* after his death in 1637. As a critic, too, Jonson was of the first rank, forthright, well-informed, and catholic in taste by the standards of the time. All these qualities are well illustrated in the splendid commendatory verses which he contributed to the Folio edition of Shakespeare's works published in 1623.

That Jonson was a classicist and an erudite one need not be disputed, though he was by no means the most learned classical scholar of his day (his mentor Camden and his contemporary John Selden were far better versed in the classics). But the emphasis should finally fall on the originality of his imagination, his roots in the popular idiom he affected to despise, and his enormous sense of theatre which is illustrated by the continued success on the stage of his great comedies.

—Gāmini Salgādo

KILLIGREW, Thomas.   English.   Born in Lothbury, London, 7 February 1612. Married 1) Cecilia Crotts in 1636, one son; 2) Charlotte de Hesse in 1655, four sons and two daughters. Page to Charles I, 1633; imprisoned on taking up arms for the king, 1642–43; followed Prince Charles into exile in Paris, 1647; appointed by Charles Resident in Vienna, 1651–52; after the Restoration appointed groom of the bedchamber to Charles II, and, later, Chamberlain to the queen; also received a patent to erect a playhouse: manager of the King's Servants players; built the Theatre Royal in Drury Lane, 1663; Master of the Revels from 1673. *Died 19 March 1683.*

PUBLICATIONS

Plays

The Prisoners (produced 1632–35?).   With *Claracilla*, 1641.
Claracilla (produced 1636).   1641.
The Princess; or, Love at First Sight (produced 1661).   In *Comedies and Tragedies*, 1664.
The Parson's Wedding (produced 1664).   In *Comedies and Tragedies*, 1664.

Cicilia and Clorinda; or, Love in Arms, from a novel by Mme. Scudéry, *Thomaso; or,
The Wanderer, Bellamira Her Dream; or, The Love of Shadows,* and *The Pilgrim,* in
Comedies and Tragedies. 1664.

Reading List: *Killigrew, Cavalier Dramatist* by Alfred Harbage, 1930.

*   *   *

Thomas Killigrew was a courtier and man of the world who wrote plays only intermittently. He was willing to jest at his possible insufficiency as an author; a character in his comedy *The Parson's Wedding* speaks of "the illiterate Courtier that made this Play." But though not a university man he must have read a great deal, he possessed a quick and rather whimsical mind, and from an early age he was in a position to learn whatever the court of Charles and Henrietta Maria could teach, including the arts by which a gentleman without private means might hope to thrive.

His first three plays, tragi-comedies based on popular French romances, present a breathless sequence of surprising events, interspersed with lofty sentiments and occasional moments of comic relief. *The Parson's Wedding,* written some years later, abandons romance for realistic comedy in its portrayal of a company of wits in the contemporary London of 1639–40. Real persons may have provided models – if not exactly as they were, at least perhaps as they would have liked to appear. Pepys was to declare it "a bawdy loose play," and so it is. But it moves with compelling gusto.

As an exile on the Continent with other Royalists, Killigrew wrote a tragedy, *The Pilgrim,* which he conceivably intended for production by Prince Charles's short-lived company at Paris. Heavily influenced by Shirley, and with distant echoes of *Hamlet,* the five acts press to a harrowing outcome in which the princely hero, disguised as a pilgrim, unwittingly kills his evil father and is himself killed unwittingly by his evil mother. Killigrew's three remaining plays, also from this period, are closet dramas, each in two parts so as to extend to ten acts. Two of these long works attest his continuing love of the romances; the third, a comedy called *Thomaso; or, The Wanderer,* seems meant as romanticised autobiography. In Madrid with other English exiles ("remnants of the broken regiments; royal and loyal fugitives"), the supremely valiant Thomaso ("being bred with the wolf he grew wise enough to thrive in the forest") immediately proves himself by winning the passionate love of a beautiful and elegant courtesan – so elegant, indeed, that her portrait which hangs outside her house is by Van Dyck. Further exploits, mingled with fantastic scrapes involving the other characters, multiply through the seventy-two scenes, and by Act V of Part II the hero has married a beautiful Spanish heiress. At this romantic height Killigrew's career as an author ends. After the Restoration he was more closely concerned with the stage than ever before, thanks to the theatrical monopoly which he shared with Davenant, and he seems to have done some revising, but he attempted nothing new.

He wrote his plays in a mixture of prose and what looks like verse, though many of the lines are not at all metrical. The collection which he published in 1664 prints everything as prose.

—Rhodes Dunlap

KYD, Thomas. English. Born in London, baptized 6 November 1558. Educated at Merchant Taylors' School, London, from 1565. Little is known about his life: perhaps worked in early life as a scrivener; in the service of an unknown lord, 1587–93; arrested for heresy, because of his association with Christopher Marlowe, 1593, but subsequently released. *Died in December 1594.*

PUBLICATIONS

Collections

    Works, edited by F. S. Boas. 1901.

Plays

    The Spanish Tragedy (produced 1589?). 1592; revised edition, 1602; edited by J. R. Mulryne, 1970; edited by Andrew S. Cairncross, with *The First Part of Hieronimo,* 1967.
    Cornelia, from a play by Robert Garnier. 1594; as *Pompey the Great His Fair Cornelia's Tragedy,* 1595.

Other

    The Truth of the Most Wicked and Secret Murdering of John Brewen. 1592.

    Translator, *The Householder's Philosophy,* by Tasso. 1588.

Bibliography: *Kyd: A Concise Bibliography* by S. A. Tannenbaum, 1941; *Kyd: 1940–66* by R. C. Johnson, 1968.

Reading List: *"The Spanish Tragedy"* by William Empson, in *Nimbus,* 1956; *"Kyd's Spanish Tragedy*: The play Explains Itself" by E. Jenson, in *Journal of English and Germanic Philology,* 1965; *Kyd and Early Elizabethan Tragedy* by Philip W. Edwards, 1966; *Kyd: Facts and Problems* by Arthur Freeman, 1967; *Kyd* by P. B. Murray, 1970.

*   *   *

No single play is more important in the development of English Renaissance drama than *The Spanish Tragedy,* yet it is not two hundred years since its authorship was generally recognized. In 1773, Thomas Hawkins in his *The Origin of the English Drama* mentioned a reference to Thomas Kyd as the author of *The Spanish Tragedy* made by Thomas Heywood in *Apology for Actors* (1612). Although ten editions of the play were published between 1592 and 1633 none of them bore the author's name, a fact which tells us something of the relative unimportance of the author's name as a "selling point" in late 16th- and early 17th-century publishing.

Most of the plays now commonly attributed to Kyd were printed anonymously; as a result we know very little for certain about his dealings with the professional theatre of his day, though the continuing popularity of *The Spanish Tragedy* in performance is attested not only by its printing history but the many contemporary allusions to lines, scenes, and characters from the play. Is is also noteworthy that fifteen years after the play was written that shrewd theatre manager Philip Henslowe found it worth his while to employ no less a man than Ben Jonson to revise the play for a revival at the Rose Theatre by the Lord Admiral's Company. The only publication to bear Kyd's name in his own lifetime is *Pompey the Great His Fair Cornelia's Tragedy*, a translation of the French Senecan tragedy *Cornélie* by Robert Garnier, which may have been inspired by the translation in the previous year of another of Garnier's tragedies, *Marc Antoine*, by the Countess of Pembroke. Also attributed to Kyd with varying degrees of confidence are *Soliman and Perseda* (1589), which forms the play within the play in the last act of *The Spanish Tragedy*, *The Rare Triumphs of Love and Fortune* (1589), and all or part of *Arden of Feversham* (1592), a play based on a contemporary murder which began the vogue for "documentary" domestic tragedy. A prose pamphlet, *The Householder's Philosophy*, based on an Italian story by Torquato Tasso, is more confidently attributed to Kyd. He is also widely believed to have been the author of an earlier version of *Hamlet* (sometimes referred to as the *Ur-Hamlet*) on which Shakespeare drew when he came to write his celebrated tragedy.

It is truer of Kyd than of most dramatists that his achievement resides in a single play. As far as is known, the plot of *The Spanish Tragedy* is Kyd's own invention. In adapting the Senecan form of tragedy to the conventions of the Elizabethan theatre, Kyd showed the born playwright's instinct for what to use, what to discard, and what to add. He abandoned Seneca's mythological plot and characters in favour of a contemporary setting. He also rejected the Senecan device of the *nuntius* or messenger who reports crucial phases of the action. The theatrical tradition of the miracle plays, with their emphasis on violence and spectacle, had equipped the Elizabethan inheritors of that tradition to show rather than tell, and, in leaving out the messenger, Kyd offered them ample scope for their resources and expertise. With these exceptions Kyd took over virtually all the paraphernalia of Senecan tragedy. These included the theme of revenge (soon to spawn a long line of descendants among which *Hamlet* is the most famous), the ghost, the dumb-show and the play within the play, the soliloquy, and the interest in madness and violent action. Though Kyd's debt to Seneca is thus fairly obvious, it is perhaps worth noting that some of the features mentioned are to be found in the popular miracle plays.

To this Senecan stock, Kyd grafted a character, Lorenzo, who embodied the contemporary interest in Machiavelli (as the Elizabethans understood him) and the amoralism associated with his ideas. Lorenzo is thus the ancestor of the unscrupulous figure whose only goal is success and whose only criterion is expediency, though he wears the mask of moral virtue. It is a tribe to which belong some of the most dazzling dramatic creations of the period – Flamineo, De Flores, Edmund, and Iago among a host of others.

If Kyd had merely adapted Senecan conventions for the popular English stage, he would still have a place in any history of the drama, but it would be grossly unjust to imply that *The Spanish Tragedy* is a play whose importance is solely or mainly historical. It is one of the most powerful plays of its time, and modern revivals have shown that it is still full of life. It draws this life from two sources, Kyd's masterly dramatic construction and the richness of his dramatic style. In terms of sheer stagecraft, *The Spanish Tragedy* is one of the most successful English plays of any period. The entire action is presided over by the ghost seeking vengeance and the spirit of Revenge itself, giving effects of resonant irony, while such scenes as the discovery by Hieronimo of his murdered son's body and the climactic moment where the pretended killings of the play within the play erupt into "real life" are unforgettable. Kyd's linguistic virtuosity is fully equal to his constructional skill. He uses all the elaborate rhetorical devices of Elizabethan English –stichomythia, sententiae, and the rest – with confident zest, and the more mannered his verse the more powerful it sounds on the stage:

> Oh eyes, no eyes, but fountains fraught with tears;
> Oh life, no life, but lively form of death;
> Oh world, no world, but mass of public wrongs,
> Confused and filled with murder and misdeeds.

The most convincing evidence of the impact of Kyd's play is the fact that it was parodied and imitated for decades afterwards, but independent of all influence it remains a great tragedy in its own right.

—Gāmini Salgādo

LYLY, John.   English.   Born in the Weald of Kent c. 1553. Educated at King's School, Canterbury, Kent; Magdalen College, Oxford, B.A. 1573, M.A. 1575; also studied at Cambridge University, M.A. 1579. Married Beatrice Browne in 1583; two sons and one daughter. In the service of Lord Delawarr, 1575–80, and the Earl of Oxford, from 1580; leased Blackfriars Theatre, London, 1584, but subsequently gaoled for debt in the same year; wrote for the children's acting companies of the Chapel Royal and St. Paul's, London, until 1591; Member of Parliament for Hindon, Aylesbury, and Appleby, 1589–1601. *Died* (buried) *30 November 1606.*

PUBLICATIONS

Collections

> *Dramatic Works,* edited by F. W. Fairholt.   2 vols., 1858–92.
> *Complete Works,* edited by R. W. Bond.   1902.

Plays

> *Alexander, Campaspe, and Diogenes* (produced 1584).   1584; as *Campaspe,* 1584; edited by W. W. Greg, 1933.
> *Sappho and Phao* (produced 1584).   1584.
> *Galathea* (produced 1584–88?).   1592; edited by A. B. Lancashire, with *Midas,* 1969.
> *Mother Bombie* (produced 1587–90?).   1594; edited by A. Harriette Andreadis, 1975.
> *Endymion, The Man in the Moon* (produced 1588).   1591; edited by W. H. Neilson, 1911.
> *Love's Metamorphosis* (produced 1589–90?).   1601.
> *Midas* (produced 1590?).   1592; edited by A. B. Lancashire, with *Galathea,* 1969.
> *The Woman in the Moon* (produced 1590–95?).   1597.

Fiction

> *Euphues: The Anatomy of Wit.*   1578; augmented edition, 1579; edited by J. Winny, 1957.

Euphues and His England.   1580.
Euphues (both parts).   1617; edited by M. W. Croll and H. Clemons, 1916.

Other

Pap with a Hatchet, Alias a Fig for my Godson; or, Crack Me This Nut; or, A Country Cuff, That Is, A Sound Box of the Ear, for the Idiot Martin.   1589.
A Whip for an Ape; or, Martin Displayed.   1589; as *Rhythms Against Martin Marprelate*, 1589 (possibly by Lyly).

Bibliography: *Lyly: A Concise Bibliography* by S. A. Tannenbaum, 1940; *Lyly 1935–65* by R. C. Johnson, 1968.

Reading List: *Lyly and the Italian Renaissance* by V. M. Jeffery, 1928; *Lyly: The Humanist and Courtier*, 1962, and *Lyly and Peele*, 1968, both by George K. Hunter; *The Court Comedies of Lyly: A Study in Allegorical Dramaturgy* by Peter Saccio, 1969.

*   *   *

John Lyly graduated as Master of Arts from Oxford, where he had enjoyed the patronage of Lord Burleigh, Queen Elizabeth's Lord High Treasurer. He gained a position as secretary to the Earl of Oxford, Burleigh's son-in-law and a supporter of a company of boy actors. Lyly's humanistic education, and his entry as a young man to court circles, determined both his audience and his entire literary output. He first appeared in print with a pastoral prose romance, *Euphues: The Anatomy of Wit*, and followed it up with an even more successful sequel, *Euphues and his England*, both parts continuing during his lifetime to be regularly reprinted.

He was appointed vice-master of Paul's Boys (the cathedral choristers who also acted as boy actors) and later to a position in the Revels Office, which was responsible for mounting the Queen's entertainments. He was (with Nashe) drawn in for a time on the side of the bishops in the theological Marprelate controversy to which he contributed one pamphlet, *Pappe with an Hatchet* in colloquial prose. But unlike Nashe, who found in the pamphlet a new and effective prose style, Lyly preferred the prose style of which he was a master and the audience with which he was familiar. His later work, all theatrical, was written to be acted (and sung) by Paul's Boys for performance before Elizabeth and her court.

Euphues, a love-romance, was directed particularly towards an audience of leisured ladies. "Euphues had rather lie shut in a lady's casket then open in a scholar's study," claims its preface. Lyly drew on the stylistic devices of medieval and renaissance rhetoric to produce a skilled, highly mannered, prose (which has always since Lyly's time been termed Euphuism, the sentence quoted above being a relatively simple example). Euphuism was characterised by (a) a balance of similar parts of speech in successive clauses, the matching words generally reinforced by alliteration or by "like endings," (b) equal-length phrases or clauses used in a parallel series, (c) the repetition of words derived from the same stem, (d) the use of antithesis, and (e) frequent far-fetched similes many of them drawn from the natural world and derived from Pliny's *Natural History*. The style was much admired and was fashionable for a few years. It was brilliantly parodied by Shakespeare in a speech by Falstaff, and echoes of it can be found in mannered prose as late as that of Dr. Johnson.

When Lyly came to write for the theatre, he generally used some variation of his Euphuistic prose style, though he could vary it with a more colloquial (but never vulgar) idiom if the situation demanded. Apart from *Campaspe* (derived from Classical history) and *Mother Bombie* (a Terence-type comedy on an English folk-theme), his plays are fantasies based on themes and characters from Classical mythology. The format encouraged lavish spectacle, allegorical references to current affairs in court (in *Endymion*, Cynthia and Endymion could be readily interpreted as Elizabeth and Leicester), aristocratic comedy to evoke what the preface to *Sapho and Phao* called "soft smiling, not loud laughing"; and it could very easily (as in the close of *Endymion*) be diverted to open praise of the monarch who was present at the performance. All was presented with a high degree of wit and dazzling verbal displays.

With a cast of boy actors and choristers, and an audience who demanded glitter, Lyly made no attempt to present real human feelings. His comedy was pantomimic and non-realistic, and (given the terms in which it was written) extremely effective. He made full use of the resources at his disposal. *Endymion*, for instance, contains several lyrics for his choristers, a dumb-show representing a dream, a dance of fairies for his troop of boy actors, and indications in the stage directions for spectacular costumes, changing scenic effects, and a final transformation in full view ("Bagoa recovers human shape").

The drama of the Elizabethan and Jacobean period ranges over a spectrum. At one end is the "drumming decasyllabon" of Marlowe's *Doctor Faustus* and *Tamburlaine* and the poetry and human insights of Shakespeare. Lyly's plays are at the other end of the spectrum. They are scripts for a kind of extended *commedia dell' arte*, and their real affinities are with the later Court Masque of Inigo Jones and Ben Jonson.

—Ian A. Gordon

MARLOWE, Christopher. English. Born in Canterbury, Kent, 6 February 1564. Educated at King's School, Canterbury, 1579; Benet College, now Corpus Christi College, Cambridge, matriculated 1581, B.A. 1584, M.A. 1587. Settled in London c. 1587: wrote plays for the Lord Admiral's Company and Lord Strange's Company; charged with heresy, 1593: stabbed to death in a tavern brawl before the case was considered. *Died 30 May 1593.*

PUBLICATIONS

Collections

> *Works*, edited by R. H. Case and others.   6 vols., 1930–33.
> *Poems*, edited by Millar Maclure.   1968.
> *Plays*, edited by Roma Gill.   1971.
> *Complete Works*, edited by Fredson Bowers.   2 vols., 1973.
> *Complete Plays and Poems*, edited by E. D. Pendry.   1976.

Plays

> *Tamburlaine the Great, Divided into Two Tragical Discourses* (produced 1587).   1590; edited by Irving Ribner, 1974.

Doctor Faustus (produced 1588? or 1592?).   1604; alternative text, 1616; both texts
   edited by W. W. Greg, 1950; edited by Keith Walker, 1973.
The Rich Jew of Malta (produced 1589?).   1633; edited by N. W. Bawcutt, 1977.
Edward the Second (produced 1592?).   1594; edited by Irving Ribner, 1970.
Dido, Queen of Carthage (produced 1593?).   1594.
The Massacre at Paris (produced 1593?).   1594(?).

Verse

Epigrams and Elegies of Ovid, with John Davies.   1595(?); as *All Ovid's Elegies: 3
   Books, with Epigrams by John Davies,* 1598(?).
Hero and Leander, Begun by Marlowe, Completed by Chapman.   1598; edited by Louis
   L. Martz, 1972.
Lucan's First Book Translated Line for Line.   1600.

Bibilography: *Marlowe: A Concise Bibliography* by S. A. Tannenbaum, 1937; supplement,
1947; supplement by R. C. Johnson, 1967.

Reading List: *Marlowe* by M. Poirier, 1951; *The Overreacher: A Study of Marlowe* by Harry
Levin, 1952; *Marlowe and the Early Shakespeare* by F. P. Wilson, 1953; *Suffering and Evil
in the Plays of Marlowe* by D. Cole, 1962; *Marlowe: A Collection of Critical Essays* edited by
Clifford Leech, 1964; *Marlowe: A Critical Study* by J. B. Steane, 1964; *In Search of Marlowe:
A Pictorial Biography* by A. D. Wraight and V. F. Stern, 1965; *Marlowe* by R. E. Knoll,
1968; *Critics on Marlowe* edited by J. O'Neill, 1969; *Marlowe's Agonists* by C. C. Fanta,
1970; *Marlowe, Merlin's Prophet* by Judith Weil, 1977.

*   *   *

A "Coblers eldest son" (as Robert Greene jealously scorned him) Christopher Marlowe
earned for himself the education of a gentleman at the University of Cambridge, and almost
immediately after graduating as Master of Arts startled London with *Tamburlaine.* The play's
"high astounding terms" (Prologue to Part 1) conquered the new world of the theatre with
the same *éclat* as its eponymous hero overcame the Turks and Persians; for many years after
its presumed first production, no dramatist could shake himself free of its cadences.
   The echoes of *Tamburlaine* in other sixteenth-century plays whose dates are more certain
is almost the only objective means of establishing a date for the play; the same is true of all
Marlowe's works. Subjective evidence, from its style, suggests that *Dido, Queen of Carthage*
was his earliest dramatic production, and that it belongs with the translations of Lucan and
Ovid, perhaps accomplished while he was still at Cambridge. Translating the Latin taught
him to handle his native language, and a steady progression can be observed in the facility
with which he treats the classical authors. Book 1 of his version of Lucan's *Pharsalia* is a line-
for-line·rendering of the original; the *Elegies* convert Ovid's verse form (hexameter followed
by pentameter) into racy, sometimes witty, English heroic couplets. *Dido* takes the whole of
the first part of Virgil's *Aeneid* as its provenance; the plot centres on Book 4, but details of
character and episode are snatched up with easy deliberation from Books 1 to 6.
   The titlepage presents *Dido* as having been performed by the Children of the Chapel Royal,
and it ought to be judged by the criteria obtaining for children's plays written by such authors
a Lyly and Marston. Its distinction is unmistakable. Marlowe exploits the delight in costume
and effect, making his characters draw attention to what they are wearing or to the efforts of
the stage technicians. Children's plays aspired to verisimilitude only in the accidentals of a
performance; by no stretch of the imagination could boys with unbroken voices imitate to the
life the great heroes of classical mythology who were the protagonists of these plays. But if

they could not act, they could recite; they had been chosen for their voices, and they were highly trained in all the Renaissance arts of elocution. In Aeneas's account of the fall of Troy Marlowe writes a stirring "aria" which augurs well for his subsequent career as a dramatist writing for the public theatres.

The Prologue to the first part of *Tamburlaine*, written perhaps in 1585, disdains the "jigging veins of rhyming mother-wits," preferring language more appropriate to its tale of the Scythian shepherd whose personal magnetism and force of arms raised him to imperial status and won the love of his captive Egyptian princess, Zenocrate. The success of Part 1 "made our poet pen his second part" (Prologue to Part 2), and the two parts together show the complete revolution of Fortune's Wheel. Tamburlaine is not vanquished by any human power; mortality itself brings about his overthrow: he falls sick, and dies, lamenting that he must "die, and this unconquered." The play is a tragedy only in the Elizabethan sense; the hero suffers no Aristotelian flaw, and the dramatist does not presume to criticize any of his callous slaughters as errors. The pride with which Tamburlaine identifies himself as "the scourge of God" is no *hubris* but a factual description of the English drama's first superman, larger than life in every sense. In comparison with Tamburlaine, the rest of the *dramatis personae* are two-dimensional, of interest merely as they enhance their conqueror's achievement in Part 1, and show in their deaths the waning of his power in Part 2.

In *Tamburlaine* the famous "mighty line" praised by Ben Jonson (in a poem prefixed to the First Folio of Shakespeare's works), is appropriate to the "aspiring mind" of its great hero. In Marlowe's next play, *The Jew of Malta*, rhetoric is inflated for comic purposes. In this story of a Jew's battle against Christians, neither of the opposing factions is worthy of respect; admiration is compelled only for the skill of unscrupulous dealings, and sentiment is dismissed by cruel laughter. The Jew's daughter is murdered by her father, but calls upon two friars to witness that she dies a Christian; any pathos arising from this situation is dispelled by the friar's response: "Ay, and a virgin too; that grieves me most." The audience's sympathy is with the Jew, Barabas – not because he is virtuous but because he makes no secret of his double-dealings, confiding in elaborate asides his schemes to outwit the no-less villainous, but hypocritical, Christians. Barabas of course overreaches himself and meets an appropriate end in the boiling cauldron that he had prepared for his chief enemy – but not until he has engineered the deaths of his daughter and her two suitors, an entire convent of nuns, the two friars, the army of Turkish soldiers, a prostitute, her pimp, and one of her clients (who happens to be Barabas's blackmailing slave). Like Tamburlaine, Barabas is larger than life; the rest of the characters, in this play too, are insignificant in comparison with the protagonist, and chiefly remarkable as objects or agents of his malevolence.

Marlowe probably wrote *The Massacre at Paris*, which survives only in a mangled, reported text, at much the same time as he wrote *The Jew of Malta*. Both have the same black comedy, in which murder is committed with a jest – and the laugh is the murderer's. *The Massacre at Paris* is a political play, dealing with recent events in the struggle between Catholics and Protestants in France in the late 1580's. The central figure is the Duke of Guise, a professed villain like Barabas but more menacing than him because the crimes are not imagined but historical. In a reported text, which relies on the memory of actors, poetry suffers more damage than plot, but one can still detect in the Guise the note of true Marlovian aspiration:

> What glory is there in a common good,
> That hangs for every peasant to achieve?
> That like I best that flies beyond my reach.

In *The Jew of Malta* and *The Massacre at Paris* Marlowe makes great play with the popular concept of the machiavellian "politician" who parodied the Florentine statesman by putting self before state. In *Edward II* he treats Machiavelli's ideas more seriously, showing in the character of Young Mortimer a hot-headed patriot who, for the first half of the play, is genuinely distressed by the king's weakness and profligacy. But as the play progresses, covering twenty-three years of chronicled history, Mortimer loses principle as he gains power until, when Edward is imprisoned in the dungeon sewers of Kenilworth Castle and he himself is, as he believes, secure as Protector over the prince and lover of the queen, he manifests all the characteristics of the Italianate villain who so appealed to the Elizabethan imagination: "Fear'd am I more than lov'd; let me be fear'd,/And when I frown, make all the court look pale." Mortimer contrasts with Edward, passively homosexual and ambitious for nothing more than "some nook or corner" in which to "frolic with [his] dearest Gaveston."

Marlowe manipulates the sympathies of the audience, turning them away from Edward and his recklessness to support Mortimer and the barons in their care for the realm. But this care is not flawless: pride and ambition vitiate it from the start. Mortimer's regime is hateful, and the treatment meted out to Edward is brutal and obscene. There is no "mighty line" in this play, but the quick cut and thrust of conversations between conspirators and enemies. Isabella, Edward's queen, is allowed a languid romanticism as the despised wife, but when she comes under Mortimer's domination her speeches are at first hollow and hypocritical, and later subdued by fear. In some ways *Edward II* is Marlowe's best play: its structure is shapely, with Mortimer's fortunes rising as Edward's decline; its characterisation is diversified, and for the first time the protagonist has a worthy antagonist and a supporting cast who are characters and not merely names; its verse, though businesslike to the point of drabness, is nevertheless suited to the unheroic action. *Dr. Faustus*, the play that followed *Edward II* and which was Marlowe's last play, has none of these qualities, but while *Edward II* is a good play, *Dr. Faustus* is a great one.

Two texts of *Dr. Faustus* survive, but neither represents the play as Marlowe intended it. The earlier was published in 1604 and seems to be the work of actors who repeated their lines inaccurately, were sometimes vague about meaning, and often confused about which speech came next. The 1616 text is longer and more coherent, being based probably upon some theatrical document such as a prompt-book. But this too is unreliable. An "editor" has been at work, simplifying, censoring, and adding the extra material for which Henslowe, the actor-manager, paid Bird and Rowley four pounds in 1602. A twentieth-century text can only be eclectic in its attempts to approach the play that Marlowe wrote.

The plot of *Dr. Faustus* is simple: a brilliant scholar, frustrated by the limitations imposed on human learning, sells his soul to the devil for four and twenty years of knowledge, power, and voluptuousness. At the end of the play only one hour is left, after which "The devil will come, and Faustus must be damn'd." The play is remarkable for its first two and last acts. In the first, Faustus reviews the whole scope of learning available to Renaissance man in a speech where the names of Aristotle, Galen, and Justinian glitter for a while until they are extinguished by the logic which sees death as the inevitable climax of all human endeavour, and by the perverse will that presents necromancy as the only means of escaping human bondage. An interview with Mephostophilis, one of the "Unhappy spirits that fell with Lucifer," does nothing to shake Faustus's resolution even though the troubled spirit begs him to "leave these frivolous demands/Which strikes a terror to my fainting soul." The play disintegrates in the middle acts, where clownage distracts Faustus's mind from contemplation of his deed. The 1616 text's comic scenes are fully developed, but the rudiments are present in the 1604 text, forcing the conclusion that although Marlowe may not have written them himself, he nevertheless acquiesced to their presence in his play. Parts of 1616's Act V, however, are not to be found anywhere in 1604; among them is the interchange between Faustus and Mephostophilis where Faustus blames the devil for his damnation and Mephostophilis proudly claims responsibility. Eleven lines (V, ii, 80–91) are crucial to an interpretation of the play. If they are included as part of Marlowe's design, then Dr. Faustus is no more than a puppet, manipulated by external forces of good and evil, and in no way responsible for his fate; the play is in that case a Morality Play which lacks the traditional happy ending in which God's mercy prevails over His justice. But if the lines are discarded (as I think they should be), Faustus appears as an independent being who, of his own free will, although with imperfect knowledge, chooses damnation; and the play is a true tragedy.

Plague raged in London during the last year of Marlowe's life. The theatres were closed, to avoid the spread of infection; and there was consequently no demand for new plays. Like Shakespeare, Marlowe spent some of the time writing a long narrative poem. His subject, the love between Hero and Leander, is a tragic one, but the poem stops with the consummation of the love; it is not clear whether Marlowe intended to proceed to the catastrophe. The eight hundred lines that he wrote reveal a marvellously rich invention that combines tenderness with sardonic wit in a form that is, in the best sense, artificial. Describing his two protagonists, Marlowe counterpoises the elaborateness of Hero's garments with the sensuous simplicity of Leander's naked body. Of "Venus' nun" he tells us:

> Buskins of shells all silver'd used she
> And branch'd with blushing coral to the knee,
> Where sparrows perch'd, of hollow pearl and gold,
> Such as the world would wonder to behold.

Sight and sound predominate in the description of Hero, but Marlowe refers to touch and taste when he speaks of Leander:

> Even as delicious meat is to the taste,
> So was his neck in touching, and surpass'd
> The white of Pelops' shoulder. I could tell ye
> How smooth his breast was, and how white his belly.

The ease with which he moves through the polished couplets is assurance enough that Marlowe, when he died in the spring of 1593, had by no means exhausted his genius.

—Roma Gill

MARMION, Shakerley. English. Born at Aynho, near Brackley, Northamptonshire, in January 1603. Educated at the free school at Thame; Wadham College, Oxford, 1620–25, B.A. 1622, M.A. 1624. Served as a soldier in the Netherlands. Settled in London; enjoyed the patronage of Ben Jonson; indicted for murder, 1629, but apparently was not convicted; gained some reputation as a playwright, especially with the court of Charles I; joined Sir John Suckling's expedition to Scotland in 1638 but became ill en route and was removed back to London. *Died in January 1639.*

PUBLICATIONS

Collections

Dramatic Works, edited by James Maidment and W. H. Logan.   1875.

Plays

Holland's Leaguer (produced 1631).   1632.

A Fine Companion (produced 1632–33?).   1633.
The Antiquary (produced 1634–36?).   1641.

Verse

A Moral Poem Entitled the Legend of Cupid and Psyche.   1637; as Cupid's Courtship,
1666; edited by A. J. Nearing, 1944.

Reading List: The Sons of Ben: Jonsonian Comedy in Caroline England by J. L. Davis, 1967.

*   *   *

During his short career as a dramatist Shakerley Marmion produced three plays, Hollands
Leaguer, A Fine Companion, and The Antiquary, a few occasional poems, and a long verse
narrative, Cupid and Psyche.

Hollands Leaguer was performed at the Salisbury Court Theatre by the newly constituted
Prince Charles' Men in December 1631, and it appeared in print in an untidy censored quarto
early in 1632. Marmion evidently prepared his text for the press, and the quarto is divided
into acts and scenes according to classical criteria, containing a list of actors in the new
company. This was one of the first plays to introduce the technique of "place realism" to the
Caroline Stage, although the scenes depicting Elizabeth Holland and her notorious
Southwark brothel serve primarily as a thematic contrast to the loosely chivalric temper of
the main plot. This is an apprenticeship piece rigid in its structure, crude in irony and moral
design, and clumsy in its attempts to assimilate material from a variety of dramatic and
classical sources. But Marmion's handling of blank verse dialogue demonstrates his
undoubted ability to evoke moods of lyrical intensity, and he makes a genuine effort to vary
the pace of the dramatic action.

A Fine Companion was performed by the same company, and appeared in quarto in 1633.
The play takes its name from a fashionable dance, and is often cited as evidence that Marmion
was one of the "Sons of Ben" who frequented the Apollo Room of the Devil Tavern. The
influence of Jonson's The New Inn (1629) is recognizable, and its apologetic Induction recalls
the critical debate following the earlier play's stage failure. A Fine Companion, like Hollands
Leaguer, is a Jonsonian "humours" comedy, although Marmion learned quickly to work
within the confines of this form and managed to produced memorable social types like the
braggadocio Captain Whibble. Generally, type-characterization is handled more decorously
in the later play, the irony is more refined, and the dramatic design more confident. Although
these plays lack the satiric venom of Marston or the earlier Jonson, or the exuberant raciness
of Middleton, they demonstrate a developing awareness on Marmion's part of the technical
requirements of stage comedy.

The Antiquary, acted probably in 1635 by Queen Henrietta's Men at the Phoenix Theatre,
but not published in quarto until a year after Marmion's death, is clearly his best play. It
shares with the two earlier plays a boldness of scenic design, and manages to exploit parallel
dramatic situations for their ironic as well as their comic potentiality. The play deals with the
follies of old age, and shows Marmion's eclecticism at its most fertile and inventive, as he
assimilates material and plot devices from Petronius, Shakespeare, Middleton, and Jonson.
Despite minor technical flaws, which are present in all his plays, The Antiquary demonstrates
a competent awareness of comic form, and even within the constricting framework of
"humours" comedy, manages to move easily and naturally from vigorous prose dialogue to
substantial blank verse. Marmion returned to the problems of writing verse in Cupid and
Psyche, skilfully dramatising his source, Apuleius's The Golden Ass, and successfully
circumventing the limitations of the rhyming couplet form. In his three plays and in Cupid
and Psyche, Marmion looks back to the poetry and drama of the Elizabethan period, but his

growing confidence in the handling of theme and dialogue point forward to the more refined world of Restoration comedy.

—John Drakakis

MARSTON, John.   English.   Born in Wardington, Oxfordshire, baptized 7 October 1576. Educated at Brasenose College, Oxford, 1592–94, B.A. 1594; Middle Temple, London, 1595–1606. Married Mary Wilkes c. 1605; one son. Wrote for Paul's boys company after 1599, and shareholder in the Queen's Revels company after 1604; imprisoned (for unknown reasons), 1608; ordained deacon, then priest, 1609, and ceased writing for the theatre after taking orders; Rector of Christchurch, Hampshire, 1616 until his resignation, 1631. *Died 25 June 1634.*

PUBLICATIONS

Collections

  Works, edited by A. H. Bullen.   3 vols., 1887.
  Plays, edited by H. H. Wood.   3 vols., 1934–39.
  Poems, edited by Arnold Davenport.   1961.

Plays

  Antonio and Mellida, part 1 (produced 1599).   1602; edited by G. K. Hunter, 1965.
  Antonio's Revenge (part 2 of *Antonio and Mellida*) (produced 1599).   1602; edited by Reavley Gair, 1977.
  Histriomastix; or, The Player Whipped, from an anonymous play (produced 1599).   1610.
  Jack Drum's Entertainment; or, The Comedy of Pasquill and Katherine (produced 1600).   1601.
  What You Will (produced 1601?).   1607.
  The Dutch Courtesan (produced 1603–04?).   1605; edited by Peter Davison, 1968.
  The Malcontent (produced 1604).   1604; edited by Bernard Harris, 1967.
  Parasitaster; or, The Fawn (produced 1604–05?).   1606; edited by David A. Blostein, 1978.
  Eastward Ho, with Chapman and Jonson (produced 1605).   1605; edited by C. G. Petter, 1973.
  The Wonder of Women; or, The Tragedy of Sophonisba (produced 1606).   1606.
  The Honorable Lord and Lady of Huntingdon's Entertainment at Ashby (produced 1607).   In *Works,* 1887, in *Poems,* 1961.
  The Insatiate Countess, completed by William Barksted (produced 1610?).   1613.
  Works (tragedies and comedies).   1633.

Verse

> The Metamorphosis of Pygmalion's Image, and Certain Satires.   1598; edited by
> Elizabeth Story Donno, in Elizabethan Minor Epics, 1968.
> The Scourge of Villainy: Three Books of Satires.   1598; revised edition, 1599.

Bibliography: Marston: A Concise Bibliography by S. A. Tannenbaum, 1940; supplement in Elizabethan Bibliographies Supplements 4 by C. A. Pennel and W. P. Williams, 1968.

Reading List: Marston: Satirist by A. Caputi, 1961; The Satire of Marston by M. S. Allen, 1965; Jacobean City Comedy: A Study of Satiric Plays by Jonson, Marston, and Middleton by B. Gibbons, 1968; Marston of the Middle Temple: An Elizabethan Dramatist in His Social Setting by P. J. Finkelpearl, 1969.

*   *   *

John Marston's crabbed and bitter satire quickly established his literary reputation. In the "Parnassus Plays" of 1598–1601 at Cambridge University, Marston's satiric style was parodied in the character of "W. Kinsayder": "What, Monsieur Kinsayder, lifting up your leg and pissing against the world? Put up, man, put up for shame. Methinks he is a ruffian in his style." His literary quarrels with Ben Jonson and Joseph Hall created a furor at the time; Drummond of Hawthornden notes that Jonson "had many quarrels with Marston, beat him and took his pistol from him, wrote his Poetaster on him." Jonson also attacked him in Every Man Out of His Humour and Cynthia's Revels, since Marston had "represented him on stage." This so-called Poetomachia was not enduring, though, and the two eventually became friends.

Marston's tendency to stumble in and out of quarrels, jails and royal favour has marked him for centuries of literary criticism as a railing and often incoherently self-defeating malcontent. This is not entirely justified, however, as in all his works, from the most violent to the most flippant, there is an underlying moral concern. Many details of Marston's life are anomalous, but it is not altogether surprising that at the age of thirty-two he set aside his writing and, like his fellow satirists John Donne and Joseph Hall, took Holy Orders.

Marston's literary career begins with two collections of verse satires: the semi-erotic Metamorphosis of Pygmalion's Image and the snarling and snapping Scourge of Villainy, in which Marston ridicules the poses and pretenses of the young gallants of the Inns of Court and London. In both volumes, the satire shifts uneasily from a range of effete social pastimes to vulgar depravities; both were considered immoral, and burned in 1599. The harsh and contentious style of the verse satires is carried over to Marston's first play, Histriomastix, a pageant-like allegory performed at the Inns of Court, which deals with the function of law in a crumbling society. Jack Drum's Entertainment and What You Will reflect the lighter side of the verse satires, again attacking the foppish young gallants, though love themes and Shakespearean echoes complement the satire in these romantic comedies.

Antonio and Mellida and Antonio's Revenge introduce the dark qualities of Marston's satiric vision. In spite of its tentative comic reconciliation, the first play is largely influenced by evil and unjust characters, and the moral climate of the Venetian court is oppressive and sordid. The second play, however, lurches into perhaps the most violent and painful revenge tragedy in Elizabethan drama. As the protagonist degenerates both psychologically and morally, his "barbarism and blood lust" confirm the play's assertion that men are "vermin bred of putrifacted slime."

The Malcontent is generally considered Marston's greatest play. His tragi-comic satire of the court and of a morally degenerating world is successfully accomplished, while at the same time the play is well-structured and temperate in plot, character, and language. Through the character of Malevole, Marston probes the moral complexities of the human condition by dramatically juxtaposing neo-stoicism with worldy epicureanism. The play's Induction reveals that the King's Men stole it from the Children of Blackfriars in response to their theft of *The First Part of Jeronimo*. While *The Malcontent* was clearly influenced by Shakespeare's *Measure for Measure*, and particularly by *Hamlet*, it was also performed at the Globe, and the title role of Malevole was played by Shakespeare's Hamlet, Richard Burbage.

After *The Malcontent*, *The Dutch Courtesan* is perhaps Marston's next best work. It is a very entertaining comedy dealing again with complex moral values, in particular the relationship of love and lust, set against a colourful city background of prostitutes, rakes, and mountebanks. The satire in *Parasitaster; or, The Fawn* is to a large degree directed against James I and his Court: flattering and deluded courtiers, corrupting and corrupted governors. The Fawn's speeches expose the moral vacuum in this society, but the play ends on a reconciliatory note with a masque that acknowledges both the "Ship of Fools" and the "Parliament of Cupid." These two comedies are more epicurean than Marston's earlier works.

Marston's part in the collaborative *Eastward Ho* with Ben Jonson and George Chapman is generally accepted as the entirety of the first act, as well as various parts throughout the play, though it is difficult to determine his specific authorship beyond this point. The play is a delightful parody of the "citizen comedy" tradition that was so popular on the London stage in the first decade of the seventeenth century. Several references to the Scots proved objectionable enough to James to result in the imprisonment of Chapman and Jonson, though Marston apparently escaped.

In his preface to *The Fawn*, Marston observes that comedies are "writ to be spoken, not read" because they consist solely in action. He wrote *The Wonder of Women; or, The Tragedy of Sophonisba*, however, as a tragedy that "shall boldly abide the most curious perusal." While sensation and spectacle abound, the highminded rhetoric in such an austere Roman tragedy demands our close reading, or "curious perusal." The play is often quite moving, and the moral dichotomy in this classical world is presented in great earnest, though there is little memorable action. Contrasted with the Stoic integrity of Sophonisba is the pathological lust of the heroine in Marston's unfinished play, *The Insatiate Countess*. Marston presumably left the various plots and characters in the play unresolved when he was sent to prison in 1608, though his hand is traceable in the 1613 edition completed by William Barksted.

Recent criticism has begun to acknowledge the considerable range and variety of Marston's dramatic works. His bold experimentation and unique characterization, particularly in the *Antonio* plays and *The Malcontent*, were completely new to Elizabethan audiences. Studies of the individual plays reveal a dramatic craftsmanship and originality that liberate him from his contemporary reputation as Kinsayder, "pissing against the world." There are many aspects of Marston's life and writings that deserve further critical analysis. His greater defects are very apparent, but T. S. Eliot's observation is still true: "for both scholars and critics he remains a territory of unexplored riches and risks."

—Raymond C. Shady

MASSINGER, Philip. English. Born in Salisbury, Wiltshire, baptized 24 November 1583. Educated at St. Alban Hall, Oxford, 1602–06, left without taking a degree. Married; possibly had children. Settled in London, 1606, and quickly gained a reputation as a playwright; collaborated with Field, Daborne, Tourneur, and Dekker, and regularly with Fletcher, 1613–25; wrote for the King's Men, 1613–23, and the Cockpit Company, 1623–25;

after Fletcher's death in 1625 rejoined the King's Men as their chief writer and continued to write for them until his death. *Died* (buried) *18 March 1640.*

PUBLICATIONS

Collections

Plays and Poems (excludes those plays written with Beaumont and Fletcher), edited by Philip Edwards and Colin Gibson. 5 vols., 1976; *Selected Plays* (includes *A New Way to Pay Old Debts, The City Madam, The Duke of Milan, The Roman Actor*), edited by Gibson, 1978.

Plays

The Queen of Corinth, with Fletcher and Nathan Field (produced 1616–17?). In *Comedies and Tragedies* by Beaumont and Fletcher, 1647.

The Knight of Malta, with Fletcher and Nathan Field (produced 1616–19?). In *Comedies and Tragedies* by Beaumont and Fletcher, 1647.

The Fatal Dowry, with Nathan Field (produced 1616–19?). 1632.

Sir John Van Olden Barnavelt, with Fletcher (produced 1619). Edited by A. H. Bullen, in *A Collection of Old English Plays 2,* 1883; edited by W. P. Frijlinck, 1922.

The Custom of the Country, with Fletcher (produced 1619–20?). In *Comedies and Tragedies* by Beaumont and Fletcher, 1647.

The Little French Lawyer, with Fletcher (produced 1619–23?). In *Comedies and Tragedies,* by Beaumont and Fletcher, 1647.

The Virgin Martyr, with Dekker (produced 1620?). 1622; edited by Fredson Bowers, in *Dramatic Works of Dekker,* 1958.

The False One, with Fletcher (produced 1620?). In *Comedies and Tragedies* by Beaumont and Fletcher, 1647.

Thierry, King of France, and His Brother Theodoret, with Fletcher (produced ?). 1621; edited by Robert K. Turner, Jr., in *Dramatic Works in the Beaumont and Fletcher Canon 3,* 1976.

The Maid of Honour (produced 1621?). 1632.

The Double Marriage, with Fletcher (produced 1621?). In *Comedies and Tragedies* by Beaumont and Fletcher, 1647.

The Duke of Milan (produced 1621–22?). 1623.

A New Way to Pay Old Debts (produced 1621–22?). 1633.

The Unnatural Combat (produced 1621–25?). 1639.

The Spanish Curate, with Fletcher (produced 1622?). In *Comedies and Tragedies* by Beaumont and Fletcher, 1647.

The Beggars' Bush, with Fletcher (produced 1622). In *Comedies and Tragedies* by Beaumont and Fletcher, 1647; edited by Fredson Bowers, in *Dramatic Works in the Beaumont and Fletcher Canon 3,* 1976.

The Sea Voyage, with Fletcher (produced 1622). In *Comedies and Tragedies* by Beaumont and Fletcher, 1647.

The Prophetess, with Fletcher (produced 1622). In *Comedies and Tragedies* by Beaumont and Fletcher, 1647.

The Bondman: An Ancient Story (produced 1623). 1624.

The Parliament of Love (produced 1624). Edited by William Gifford, 1805.

The Renegado (produced 1624). 1630.

The Elder Brother, with Fletcher (produced 1625?). 1637.
Fair Maid of the Inn, with Fletcher (produced 1625–26?).   In *Comedies and Tragedies* by Beaumont and Fletcher, 1647.
The Roman Actor (produced 1626). 1629.
The Great Duke of Florence (produced 1627?). 1636.
The Picture (produced 1629). 1630.
The Emperor of the East (produced 1631). 1632.
Believe As You List (produced 1631). Edited by T. C. Croaker, 1849.
The City Madam (produced 1632?). 1658.
The Guardian (produced 1633). In *Three New Plays,* 1655.
The Bashful Lover (produced 1633–37?). In *Three New Plays,* 1655.
A Very Woman; or, The Prince of Tarent, with Fletcher (produced 1634). In *Three New Plays,* 1655.
Love's Cure; or, The Martial Maid, with Fletcher (produced ?). In *Comedies and Tragedies* by Beaumont and Fletcher, 1647; edited by George Walton Williams, in *Dramatic Works in the Beaumont and Fletcher Canon 3,* 1976.

Bibliography: *Massinger: A Concise Bibliography* by S. A. Tannenbaum, 1938; supplement in *Elizabethan Bibliographies Supplements 8* by C. A. Pennel and W. P. Williams, 1968.

Reading List: *Massinger* by Alfred H. Cruickshank, 1920; *Massinger and Fletcher: A Comparison* by Henri J. Makkink, 1927; *Massinger, The Man and the Playwright* by Thomas A. Dunn, 1957; *Massinger and His Associates* by Donald S. Lawless. 1967.

*   *   *

Together with his older contemporary Thomas Middleton, Philip Massinger shares the distinction of being the boldest Jacobean dramatist in his dealings with controversial religious and political questions of the day, at a time when such boldness incurred official displeasure which was often expressed in terms more severe than mere censorship. He began his dramatic career as part of a group of playwrights working for Philip Henslowe, and his earliest plays were written in collaboration with John Fletcher and Nathan Field. The first play to carry his name on the title page was *The Virgin Martyr* (1622), of which he was joint author with Thomas Dekker. Already Massinger's unorthodox religious and political attitudes can be seen in his sympathetic portrayal of Catholicism at a time when the general temper was fiercely anti-Catholic. Later, in *The Renegado* he makes a Jesuit priest the most admirable character in the play. In 1630 the censor refused to allow the performance of *Believe As You List* because of its strongly anti-Spanish bias, whereupon Massinger changed the setting from modern Spain and Portugal to ancient Asia and classical Rome, an alteration which fooled the censor but not apparently the audience. In *The Maid of Honour* Charles I's brother-in-law, Frederick V, Elector Palatine, was the object of attack, while *The Bondman* satirized the powerful George Villiers, Duke of Buckingham, an enemy of Massinger's patron Philip Herbert, Earl of Montgomery.

The first play known to be entirely Massinger's work is *The Duke of Milan,* a work which has many resemblances to *Othello.* Massinger's debt to Shakespeare is visible throughout his work, and it has even been suggested that it was Massinger and not John Fletcher who collaborated with Shakespeare in *Henry VIII* and *The Two Noble Kinsmen.*

Massinger himself regarded his tragedy *The Roman Actor* as his finest dramatic work: "I ever held it the most perfit birth of my Minerva." Posterity has not agreed with him. The only two plays by Massinger which have survived into the modern repertory are *A New Way to Pay Old Debts* and *The City Madam.* Both are comedies and the first is undoubtedly a masterpiece. Its plot is based on Middleton's *A Trick to Catch the Old One* written twenty years earlier, but there is nothing in Middleton's play to match the central character Sir Giles

Overreach, a usurer, extortioner, and rack-renter of monstrous proportions based on an actual historical figure, Sir Giles Mompesson. The sheer demonic energy of Overreach threatens to swamp the conventional romantic plot through which he blusters his way. It is not surprising that the celebrated nineteenth-century actor Edmund Kean had one of his greatest successes in this role, as did Donald Wolfit in the twentieth century.

The City Madam is also based on an earlier play, Eastward Ho by Chapman, Jonson and Marston. Here again Massinger has created a monster of capacity in the character of Luke Frugal. Both plays are savage satires against the pretensions of the new city rich whom Massinger depicted as destroying the traditional virtues which he saw in the hereditary landed aristocracy and which, in his view, kept society ordered and stable.

In addition to the plays already mentioned, Massinger also wrote several romantic tragi-comedies, the best of them The Beggars' Bush (1622) in collaboration with Fletcher. His was the finest satirical dramatic talent in the years immediately before the curtain came down on the theatres in 1642.

—Gāmini Salgādo

MAY, Thomas.   English.   Born in Mayfield, Sussex, in 1595. Educated at Sidney Sussex College, Cambridge (fellow-commoner), 1609–12, B.A. 1612; entered Gray's Inn, London, 1615. Settled in London; gave up the law because of a speech defect, and turned to literature; enjoyed patronage of Charles I, but was disappointed in his hopes for preferment and later supported the parliamentary cause during the civil war: served as Secretary of the Parliament, 1646 until his death. *Died 13 November 1650.*

PUBLICATIONS

Plays

The Heir (produced before 1620).   1622; edited by W. C. Hazlitt, in Dodsley's Old Plays, 1875.
Cleopatra Queen of Egypt (produced 1626).   1639.
Antigone, The Theban Princess (produced 1627–31?).   1631.
Julia Agrippina, Empress of Rome (produced 1628).   1639; edited by F. Ernst Schmid, in Bang's Materialen, 1914.
The Old Couple (produced 1636).   1658; edited by M. Simplicia Fitzgibbons, 1943.

Verse

Lucan's Pharsalia.   1626; with A Continuation till the Death of Julius Caesar, by May, 1630.

The Reign of King Henry the Second.   1633.
The Victorious Reign of King Edward the Third.   1635.

Other

A Discourse Concerning the Success of Former Parliaments.   1642.
The Character of a Right Malignant.   1644.
The Lord George Digby's Cabinet and Dr. Goff's Negotiations.   1646.
The History of the Parliament [of] 1640.   1647; edited by F. Maseres, 1812.
The Changeable Covenant.   1650.
A Breviary of the History of the Parliament of England (in Latin and English).   1650.

Translator, Virgil's Georgics.   1628.
Translator, Selected Epigrams of Martial.   1629.
Translator, Barclay His Argenis (verse sections only).   1629.
Translator, The Mirror of Minds; or, Icon Animorum, by Barclay.   1631.

Reading List: May, Man of Letters by Allan Griffith Chester, 1932.

*   *   *

A solid classicist, and at his best as a translator, Thomas May wrote poetry both English and Latin, comedies, tragedies, and prose history. His most substantial achievement is his translation of Lucan's Pharsalia in heroic couplets; Ben Jonson, in verses "To my chosen Friend, the learned Translator," praises Lucan and May as exhibiting "the self-same genius." Subsequently May himself continued Lucan's unfinished poem with seven additional books in both English and Latin versions – an ambitious project carried out with a competence that gained him something of a reputation on the Continent. The successful Lucan, which was admired by Charles I, led directly ("by His Majesty's Command") to two original "historical poems" in English heroic couplets, The Reign of King Henry the Second and The Victorious Reign of King Edward the Third, in seven books each. Both poems have epic pretensions, with formal invocations and supernatural machinery; there is even a vision of the future which extends to the renowned Charles, "A King in virtue as in Royalty." For all the heroic trappings, May does not succeed in making the action in either poem amount to much more than versified chronicle. In a prose note he suggests that Henry II's life may be looked at as a five-act tragedy, but the suggestion seems stillborn.

May's two comedies take Jonson as their main model, but The Heir pays tribute to Shakespeare as well with a comic Watch and a Constable who might as well be named Dogberry – "For your better destruction, I will deride my speech into two parts" – and a pair of lovers whose marriage will reconcile their two warring houses. The Old Couple, with less complex a plot but more skilful dramatic writing, draws on a long tradition of usury comedy. Much of the action involves the "old miserly niggard" Earthworm, but the title-roles are those of Sir Argent Scrape and Lady Covet, each eager for marriage in hope of inheriting the other's wealth. Thus touched by Cupid's golden-headed arrow, they court each other from invalid chairs; both are deaf; she is eighty years old, and he ninety-five. A happy ending shows avarice foiled and Earthworm reformed.

May's three tragedies, Antigone, Cleopatra, and Julia Agrippina, are respectable learned drama which echo both Seneca and the Jonson of the Roman plays. He shows some originality in his manipulation of the three actions, and for the Cleopatra draws upon Plutarch quite independently of Shakespeare.

The King had called May "my poet," but during the conflicts of the 1640's it was as "Secretary for the Parliament" that he published his History of that body. He professes to offer a "plain and naked discourse" with truth as its sole object, but in spite of occasional refusal to pass judgment he is hardly even-handed in his reporting of events, in which he incorporates a glowing personal tribute to Oliver Cromwell. The classical bent of his earlier writings is recognisable in the way that he explains his own times by analogy with ancient history: London had no walls "but such as old Sparta used for their guard, the hearts of courageous citizens," and Lucan and Claudian are made to comment on the Earl of Strafford.

—Rhodes Dunlap

MAYNE, Jasper. English. Born in Hatherleigh, Devon, baptized 23 November 1604. Educated at Westminster School, London; Christ Church, Oxford, matriculated 1623, student 1627, B.A. 1628, M.A. 1631, B.D. 1642, D.D. 1646. Ordained: given college living of Cassington, near Woodstock, 1639; because of his Royalist views, deprived of his studentship and living at Cassington, 1648; Rector of Pyrton, Oxfordshire, 1648 until he was ejected, 1656; maintained by the Earl of Devonshire in late 1650's; after the Restoration returned to his benefices, and appointed canon of Christ Church, archdeacon of Chichester, and chaplain-in-ordinary to the king. *Died 6 December 1672.*

PUBLICATIONS

Plays

　　The City Match (produced 1637–38?).　1639; edited by W. C. Halitt, in *Dodsley's Old Plays,* 1875.
　　The Amorous War (produced 1628–48?).　1648.

Verse

　　To the Duke of York on Our Late Sea-Fight.　1665.

Other

　　Certain Sermons and Letters.　1653.

　　Translator, *Part of Lucian Made English.*　1664.

Reading List: *The Sons of Ben: Jonsonian Comedy in Caroline England* by J. L. Davis, 1967.

*　　*　　*

Jasper Mayne's extant works consist of two plays, a handful of poems, and several sermons. The sermons, which reveal him as a reasonable, charitable man, have no literary merit; their only interest for the purposes of this essay lies in the awareness Mayne shows of Puritan linguistic habits and of the part that language was playing in exacerbating the conflicts of the age.

The poems also are mainly of value for the light they throw on contemporary attitudes, in this case cultural ones. Mayne's elegy in Donne's *Poems* (1633), has received attention for its comment on Donne's poetry, "We are thought wits, when 'tis understood"; but its description of Donne in the pulpit is also worth reading. An encomium on Jonson in *Parnassus Biceps* (1656), praises his dramatic art in some detail. A poem lauding Denham (in Bodleian MS. Engl.poet.e.4) also shows Mayne capable of neat couplets very much in Denham's manner. Elsewhere he expresses views on art and gardening. His longest poem, a fulsome address to the Duke of York, is devoid of interest.

Mayne's comedy *The City Match* uses ingredients from Jonson and his successors; the plot is derived from *Epicoene*. The action is unsatisfactory, however, partly because of excessive reliance on the convention that a change of attire makes one's nearest relations instantly unrecognisable, partly because of the inconsistency and uncertainty of the author's moral attitudes. Like Jonson, Middleton, and Massinger, Mayne deals with the duping of a rich uncle by a scheming nephew; unlike his predecessors, he omits to ensure that our sympathies lie with the nephew, and in the unexplained reconciliations of the dénouement moral problems are shelved, not solved. *The Amorous War*, a romantic tragi-comedy, repeats and magnifies the faults of the earlier play; the plot is silly and unconvincing, and Mayne's ethical insensitivity is a serious flaw in a play purporting to deal with the themes of love and faithfulness.

Yet comedy is undoubtedly the genre to which Mayne is best suited. Scenes such as that in which the drunken Timothy, suitably attired, is exhibited as a monstrous fish, or one in which three dandified courtiers are forced to change clothes with their ragged flea-bitten captors, have genuine dramatic potentiality. Mayne possessed a sense of theatre as well as a sense of humour, and in his loosely structured blank verse has achieved much easy, humorous dialogue, particularly in the London setting of *The City Match*. The later play also contains two songs with complex stanza-forms which reveal a lyric gift which one may wish that Mayne had cultivated further. One of these, "Time is a feathered thing," treats with some poignancy the theme of "Gather ye rosebuds," and deserves to be better known.

—Margaret Forey

———————

MIDDLETON, Thomas. English. Born in London, baptized 18 April 1580. Educated at Queen's College, Oxford, and possibly at Gray's Inn, London. Married Mary (or Magdalen) Morbeck in 1602; one son. Playwright for Philip Henslowe by 1602, and wrote for Paul's boys company, 1602 to 1606–07; City Chronologer of London, 1620–27. *Died* (buried) *4 July 1627.*

PUBLICATIONS

Collections

Works, edited by A. H. Bullen.   8 vols., 1885–86.

Selected Plays (includes *The Changeling, Women Beware Women, A Chaste Maid in Cheapside, A Mad World, My Masters*), edited by David L. Frost. 1978.

Plays

The Phoenix (produced 1603–04?). 1607.

The Honest Whore, with Dekker (produced 1604). 1604; as *The Converted Courtesan*, 1604; edited by Fredson Bowers, in *Dramatic Works of Dekker*, 1953–62.

A Mad World, My Masters (produced 1604–06?). 1608; in *Selected Plays*, 1978.

A Trick to Catch the Old One (produced 1604–06?). 1608; edited by G. J. Watson, 1968.

The Family of Love (produced 1604–07?). 1608.

Michaelmas Term (produced 1606?). 1607; edited by Richard Levin, 1967.

Your Five Gallants (produced 1607). 1608(?).

Sir Robert Shelley, His Royal Entertainment (produced 1609 ?). 1609.

The Roaring Girl; or, Moll Cut-Purse, with Dekker (produced 1610?). 1611; edited by Andor Gomme, 1976.

The Witch (produced 1610–16?). 1778; edited by W. W. Greg and F. P. Wilson, 1950.

A Chaste Maid in Cheapside (produced 1611). 1630; in *Selected Plays*, 1978.

No Wit, No Help Like a Woman's (produced 1613?). Revised version published 1657; edited by Lowell E. Johnson, 1976.

The Manner of His Lordship's Entertainment on Michaelmas Day Last (produced 1613). 1613; edited by J. Nichols, in *Progresses of James I*, 1828.

The Triumphs of Truth: A Solemnity (produced 1613). 1613; edited by J. Nichols, in *Progresses of James I*, 1828.

More Dissemblers Besides Women (produced 1615?). In *Two New Plays*, 1657.

A Fair Quarrel, with William Rowley (produced 1615–17?). 1617; edited by George R. Price, 1976.

The Nice Valour; or, The Passionate Woman, with Fletcher (produced before 1616). In *Comedies and Tragedies* by Beaumont and Fletcher, 1647.

The Widow (produced 1616?). 1652; edited by Robert Trager Levine, 1975.

Civitatis Amor, The City's Love: An Entertainment by Water (produced 1616) 1616; edited by J. Nichols, in *Progresses of James I*, 1828.

The Mayor of Quimborough (produced 1616–20?). 1661; edited by R. C. Bald, as *Hengist, King of Kent*, 1938.

The Triumphs of Honour and Industry: A Solemnity (produced 1617). 1617.

The Peace-Maker; or, Great Britain's Blessing (produced 1618?). 1618.

The Old Law; or, A New Way to Please You, with William Rowley (produced 1618?). 1656.

The Inner Temple Masque; or, Masque of Heroes (produced 1619). 1619; edited by R. C. Bald, in *A Book of Masques in Honour of Allardyce Nicoll*, 1967.

The Triumphs of Love and Antiquity: An Honourable Solemnity (produced 1619). 1619; edited by J. Nichols, in *Progresses of James I*, 1828.

The World Tossed at Tennis, with William Rowley (produced 1619–20?). 1620.

The Marriage of the Old and New Testament (produced 1620?). 1620; as *God's Parliament House*, 1627.

Honourable Entertainments, Composed for the Service of This Noble City. 1621; edited by R. C. Bald and F. P. Wilson, 1953.

The Sun in Aries: A Noble Solemnity (produced 1621). 1621.

Any Thing for a Quiet Life, with Webster (produced 1621?). 1662; edited by F. L. Lucas, in *Complete Works of Webster*, 1927.

An Invention Performed for the Service of Edward Barkham, Lord Mayor of London (produced 1622). In *Works*, 1885–86.

The Triumphs of Honour and Virtue: A Noble Solemnity (produced 1622).   1622.
The Changeling, with William Rowley (produced 1622).   1653; in *Selected Plays*, 1978.
The Triumphs of Integrity: A Noble Solemnity (produced 1623).   1623.
The Spanish Gipsy, with William Rowley (produced 1623).   1653; edited by C. M. Hayley, in *Representative English Comedies*, 1914.
A Game at Chess (produced 1624).   1625; edited by J. W. Harper, 1966.
Women Beware Women (produced 1625–27?).   In *Two New Plays*, 1657; in *Selected Plays*, 1978.
The Triumphs of Health and Prosperity: A Noble Solemnity (produced 1626).   1626.
Wit at Several Weapons, with Fletcher and William Rowley (produced ?).   In *Comedies and Tragedies*, by Beaumont and Fletcher, 1647.

Verse

The Wisdom of Solomon Paraphrased.   1597.
Microcynicon: Six Snarling Satires.   1599.
The Ghost of Lucrece.   1600; edited by Joseph Quincy Adams, 1937.

Other

The Ant and the Nightingale; or, Father Hubbard's Tales.   1604; revised edition, as *Father Hubbard's Tales*, 1604.
The Black Book.   1604.

Bibliography: *Middleton: A Concise Bibliography* by S. A. Tannenbaum, 1940; supplement in *Elizabethan Bibliographies Supplements 1*, by D. G. Donovan, 1967.

Reading List: *Non-Dramatic Sources for the Rogues in Middleton's Plays* by M. G. Christian, 1936; *Middleton's Tragedies* by Samuel Schoenbaum, 1955; *Middleton* by Richard H. Barker, 1958; *The Art of Middleton: A Critical Study* by David M. Holmes, 1970; *Parody and Burlesque in the Tragicomedies of Middleton* by John F. MacElroy, 1972; *Middleton and the Drama of Realism* by Dorothy M. Farr, 1973; *The Lust Motif in the Plays of Middleton* by Barbara J. Baines, 1973; *The Most Unvaluedst Purchase: Women in the Plays of Middleton* by Caroline L. Cherry, 1973; *A Study of Middleton's Tragicomedies* by Carolyn Asp, 1974; *The Canon of Middleton's Plays* by David J. Lake, 1975.

*   *   *

An attempt to narrate the plot of any one of Thomas Middleton's plays could only end in disastrous confusion. Comedies and tragedies alike are composed of multiple actions which, when the dramatist is at his best, intertwine, sharing characters and themes, so that each is enriched by the conjunction. In the comedy *A Chaste Maid in Cheapside* a single character, Sir Walter Whorehound, is common to all the actions, and makes unity out of diversity. He provides Master Allwit with comfort and children, and he schemes to rid himself of a former mistress by presenting her as an heiress, a desirable daughter-in-law for the avaricious Master and Mistress Yellowhammer. They in turn intend Sir Walter as a husband for their daughter, Moll, who is in love with Touchwood Junior. By marrying Moll, Sir Walter could breed legitimate heirs to inherit the wealth of the childless Sir Oliver and Lady Kix. Preoccupations with sex and procreation, wealth and gentility, are shared by all the characters, usually to the total exclusion of any other quality; and yet they are more than personifications, having a vitality which re-creates seventeenth-century Cheapside. They live in a world where everything has its price, and where double-dealing is the normal practice of young and old alike – of Touchwood Junior as much as Master Yellowhammer. Sir Walter is the villain, and at the end of Act V he has been defeated in a duel by Touchwood; disappointed of his hopes because Lady Kix has been made pregnant; and disowned by Mistress Allwit. But the duel is not an assertion of the triumph of good over evil, or innocent youth over unprincipled age. Touchwood wins his Moll, and romance ends the play, but the hero of *A Chaste Maid in Cheapside* is the least romantic and idealistic of the characters, Master Allwit. He has stood by, as door-keeper and bawd to his wife, and thanked Sir Walter for making him a comfortable cuckold:

> I thank him, h'as maintained my house this ten years,
> Not only keeps my wife, but a keeps me,
> And all my family; I am at his table,
> He gets me all my children, and pays the nurse,
> Monthly, or weekly, puts me to nothing,
> Rent, nor church duties, not so much as the scavenger:
> The happiest state that ever man was born to.

But when the ruined knight turns to him for support, Allwit's rejection of him is as unequivocal as Henry V's "I know thee not, old man" to Falstaff. Allwit and his wife have a future to plan together: to set up a bawdy-house in the Strand.

Middleton sees that luxury, in its Elizabethan double sense (both "extravagance" and "lechery"), will continue to thrive. His comedies are moral, but realistic. He examines the vices of contemporary middle-class society, and displays them for laughter; but for the most part he eschews poetic justice in his endings. As a moralist, he is no visionary.

In the tragedy *Women Beware Women* Livia occupies a similar pivotal position to Sir Walter, having a part in both plots as a manipulator, drawing Bianca and Isabella into sin and corruption. Eventually she becomes entangled in her own snares. In the tragic catastrophe the injured revenge themselves on the guilty – but so widespread is the guilt that only two characters, the foolish ones, are left alive at the end of the play, together with the Cardinal whose well-intentioned sermon triggered off the first murder. In this play, and in another late tragedy, *The Changeling*, Middleton is still the moralist, although his emphasis has shifted a little and lust, as a theme, is largely independent of avarice. In the sub-plot of *Women Beware Women* Isabella is a mere commodity, to be sold by her father to the highest bidder. Isabella has been, he tells the Duke, a "dear child" to him: "dear to my purse, I mean,/Beside my person; I nev'r reckoned that." Beatrice-Joanna, however, the heroine of *The Changeling*, is accustomed to having her every want supplied, and she has no hesitation in demanding the removal of one suitor to make place for a new one when her fancy has changed. Both tragedies are set in the exotic "abroad," and Spanish passions are hot in *The Changeling*. But although Middleton is careful to make occasional references to location in *Women Beware Women* these are not strong enough to counter the strong impression that Jacobean England and its mercantile middle classes are once more the object of the moralist's concern.

At the very beginning of his career as a writer, Middleton seized on the extravagances of his affluent society; in *Microcynicon* he sets himself firmly in the tradition of the satirists who regarded sartorial excess as the emblem of prodigality, likely to bring about the ruin both of the individual and of the nation:

> Suit upon suit, satin too, too base;
> Velvet laid on with gold or silver lace
> A mean man doth become; but he must ride
> In cloth of fined gold, and by his side
> Two footmen at the least, with choice of steeds,
> Attired, when he rides, in gorgeous weeds.

He always has criticism, varying in its degree of severity, for the wastrel who has sacrificed property, the legacy of generations, for the transitory splendour of an appearance at Court, or the "poor benefit of a bewitching minute." But he is still more scornful of those who, having (in the words of Henry Peacham) "by Mechanicke and base meanes ... raked up a masse of wealth," seek to acquire gentility. The Yellowhammers in *A Chaste Maid in Cheapside* presume to send their son to Cambridge, and we are encouraged to agree that they get their just deserts when the boy is married to Sir Walter's discarded whore in the mistaken belief that she is a Welsh heiress. Ephestian Quomodo in *Michaelmas Term* is a London woollen-draper who dreams of the respectability which will be his when he has bought an estate from the impecunious gentleman, Easy: "Oh, that sweet, neat, comely, proper, delicate parcel of land, like a fine gentlewoman i'th'waist, not so great as pretty, pretty; the trees in summer whistling, the silver waters by the banks harmoniously gliding...." His vocabulary registers his inability to lay claim to the status of a gentleman: he is very much the draper when he compares the land to a gentlewoman's waist, although he has certainly learned some of the appropriate literary pastoral language. Similarly, Leantio in *Women Beware Women* cannot attain the status to which he has aspired in marrying Bianca, and here again his language betrays his deficiency: employed as a "factor" in buying and selling, he can only appreciate Bianca as a "most unvalued'st purchase."

Middleton's verse never glitters, but it is always taut and smooth, firm in its rhythms, which approximate to speech but never permit slackness. As a dramatic craftsman he is almost impeccable. His early experience was in writing as one of a hard-pressed team of collaborators for Henslowe's two dramatic companies. In this work he so successfully subdued any idiosyncrasies that his voice is not audible in the few surviving collaborated plays. He went on to write for the two children's companies (as did such writers as Jonson and Marston), and then joined the many playwrights who, with Fletcher at their head, supplied the London stage with escapist fiction in tragi-comedies. His play *A Game at Chess* defies categorization. A political play, it describes the struggles between Spain and England, Catholicism and Protestantism, in terms of a chess game. The Black Knight was immediately recognized by the audiences as the Spanish Ambassador, Count Gondomar, who earned English hatred for his attempts to secure an Anglo-Spanish alliance through the marriage of Prince Charles. The play was an instant success, and it was (as the titlepage says) "Acted *nine days to gether at the Globe on the banks side*" – after which the play was banned, the King's Men forbidden to act, and a warrant issued for the arrest of the dramatist. Once the topicality was gone, of course, the play lost its impact, and today the text is swamped with footnotes. Yet although the meaning is obscure and the characters unrecognizable, the strength of the plot is clear; the action is conducted with the firm sense of direction that marks all Middleton's plays, from the beginning to the end of his career.

Some scholars have also credited Middleton with the authorship of *The Revenger's Tragedy*, which was published anonymously. In the absence of overwhelming evidence to prove Middleton's claim, this play has been discussed together with the work of Cyril Tourneur, to whom it was attributed in 1656.

—Roma Gill

MUNDAY, Anthony. English. Born in London in 1560. May have travelled, and may have been an actor, prior to being apprenticed to the stationer John Allde, 1576–78. Married; four daughters and one son. Visited Rome, to gather material on the English seminary there, 1578–79; actor with the Earl of Oxford's Company, London, 1579–84; involved in the writing of some 18 plays, 1584–92, and also known for his ballads and songs; served as Messenger to Her Majesty's Chamber, 1584–93; wrote most of the City of London pageants, and was keeper of the pageant properties, 1592–1623; travelled as "pageanter" with the Earl of Pembroke's Men to Holland, 1598–99; may have followed his father's trade of draper in the latter years of his life. *Died* (buried) *10 August 1633.*

PUBLICATIONS

Plays

Fedele and Fortunio: The Deceits in Love, with Chapman and Stephen Gosson, from a play by L. Pasqualigo (produced 1584?). 1585; edited by P. Simpson, 1909.
John a Kent and John a Cumber (produced 1594). Edited by J. P. Collier, 1851; edited by M. St. C. Byrne, 1923.
Sir Thomas More, with Shakespeare (produced 1596?). Edited by A. Dyce, 1844; edition of W. W. Greg revised by H. Jenkins, 1961.
The Downfall of Robert, Earl of Huntingdon, with Henry Chettle (produced 1598). 1601; edited by J. C. Meagher, 1965.
The Death of Robert, Earl of Huntingdon, with Henry Chettle (produced 1598). 1601; edited by J. C. Meagher, 1967.
Sir John Oldcastle, part 1, with others (produced 1599). 1600; edited by P. Simpson, 1908.
The Triumphs of Re-United Britannia, Performed in Honor of Sir Leonard Holliday, Lord Mayor (produced 1605). 1605.
Campbell; or, The Ironmonger's Fair Field (produced 1609). 1609.
London's Love to the Royal Prince Henry, Meeting Him on the River of Thames (produced 1610). 1610.
Chruso-Thriambos: The Triumphs of Gold, at the Inauguration of Sir James Pemberton in the Dignity of Lord Mayor (produced 1611). 1611; edited by J. H. P. Pafford, 1962.
Himatia-Poleoa: The Triumphs of Old Drapery at the Entertainment of Sir Thomas Hayes, Lord Major (produced 1614). 1614.
Metropolis Coronata: The Triumphs of Ancient Drapery in a Second Year's Entertainment in Honour of Sir John Jolles, Lord Mayor (produced 1615). 1615.
Chrysanaleia: The Golden Fishing, Applauding the Advancement of Mr. John Leman to the Dignity of Lord Mayor (produced 1616). 1616; edited by J. G. Nichols, as *The Fishmongers' Pageant,* 1884.
Sidero-Thriambos; or, Steel and Iron Triumphing, Applauding the Advancement of Sir Sebastian Harvey to the Dignity of Lord Mayor (produced 1618). 1618.
The Triumphs of the Golden Fleece, Performed at the Installment of Sir Martin Lumley in the Mayoralty (produced 1623). 1623.

Fiction

Zelauto: The Fountain of Fame. 1580; edited by Jack Stillinger, 1963.
A True and Admirable History of a Maiden of Consolens in Poitiers. 1603.

Verse

The Mirror of Mutability; or, Principal Part of the Mirror of Magistrates, Selected Out of the Sacred Scriptures. 1579.
The Pain of Pleasure. 1580.
A Banquet of Dainty Conceits. 1588.

Other

A Second and Third Blast of Retreat from Plays and Theatres, with Salvianus. 1580.
A View of Sundry Examples, Reporting Many Strange Murders. 1580(?).
An Advertisement and Defense for Truth Against Her Backbiters. 1581.
The True Report of the Prosperous Success Which God Gave unto Our English Soldiers in Ireland. 1581.
A Brief Discourse of the Taking of Edmund Campion. 1581.
A Courtly Controversy Between Love and Learning Between a Lady and a Gentleman of Siena. 1581.
A Discovery of Edmund Campion and His Confederates. 1582.
A Brief Answer Made unto Two Seditious Pamphlets. 1582.
A Brief and True Report of the Execution of Certain Traitors at Tyburn. 1582.
The English Roman Life, Discovering the Lives of the Englishmen at Rome. 1582; edited by G. B. Harrison, 1925.
A Watch-Word to England, to Beware of Traitors. 1584.
The Admirable Deliverance of 166 Christians by J. Reynard, Englishman, from the Turks. 1608.
A Brief Chronicle of the Success of Times from the Creation of the World to This Instant. 1611.
A Survey of London, by John Stow, revised by Munday. 1618; revised edition, with D. Dyson and others, 1633; edited by H. B. Wheatley, 1960.

Translator, *Palmerin D'Oliva.* 2 vols., 1588–97.
Translator, *The Famous, Pleasant, and Variable History of Palladine of England,* by Claude Colet. 1588.
Translator, *The Declaration of the Lord de la Noue, upon His Taking Arms.* 1589.
Translator, *The Honorable, Pleasant, and Rare Conceited History of Palmendos,* by Francisco de Moraes. 1589.
Translator, *Amadis of Gaul.* 3 vols., 1590–1618.
Translator, *The Copy of the Anti-Spaniard.* 1590.
Translator, *The Masque of the League and the Spaniard Discovered.* 1592; as *Falsehood in Friendship,* 1605.
Translator, *Archaioplutos; or, The Riches of Elder Ages,* by Guillaume Thelin. 1592.
Translator, *Gerileon of England,* part 2, by Estienne de Maisonneufve. 1592.
Translator, *The Defense of Contraries: Paradoxes Against Common Opinion,* by Charles Estienne. 1593.
Translator, *Primaleon of Greece.* 3 vols., 1595–1619.
Translator, *Palmerin of England,* by Francisco de Moraes. 3 vols., 1596–1602; edited by Robert Southey, 1807.
Translator, *A Brief Treatise of the Virtue of the Cross.* 1599.
Translator, *The True Knowledge of a Man's Own Life,* by Philippe de Mornay. 1602.
Translator, *The Dumb Divine Speaker,* by Fra. Giacomo Affinati d'Acuto Romano. 1605.
Translator, *The Conversion of a Most Noble Lady of France.* 1608.

Bibliography: *Munday: A Concise Bibliography* by S. A. Tannenbaum, 1942; *Munday 1941–66* by R. C. Johnson, 1968.

Reading List: *Munday, An Elizabethan Man of Letters* by Celeste Turner, 1928; *The Palmerin Romances in Elizabethan Prose Fiction* by Mary Patchell, 1947; *Amadis de Gaul and Its Influence on Elizabethan Literature* by J. J. O'Connor, 1970; *English Civic Pageantry 1558–1642* by D. M. Bergeron, 1971.

*   *   *

Anthony Munday is the most fascinating of all the minor dramatists of his time, and very unusually it was a very long time: he was born in 1560 (not 1553 as used to be thought) and died when the Jacobean period had largely run its course (1633). He was a stationer's apprentice, a failed comedian of the Tarlton and Kemp type, a spy, a translator, a writer of pamphlets, ballads, and city pageants, and – *Histriomastix* calls him Posthaste – an industrious original and collaborative dramatist for Henslowe. Turner's *Life* and Tannenbaum's bibliography have many interesting details of his active career.

He plays an important part in the history of the prose romances that were so popular in the late Elizabethan period, and, though Southey thought them inaccurate, produced influential translations of Palmerin romances: three parts of *Palmerin of England, Palmerin D'Oliva, History of Palmendos, Gerileon of England, Primaleon of Greece*, and *Amadis of Gaul*. This makes him of interest to scholars of the semi-Arthurian romance (of whom there are many) and of the origins of the English novel (of whom there have not been enough).

Like Marlowe, he was a spy against the Jesuit plotters; if ever the whole story of Sir Thomas Walsingham's Elizabethan "CIA" is told (which is unlikely), it could reveal exciting secrets.

Munday was the author of numerous pamphlets about sensational crimes and executions in the days of Deloney, Nashe, and Lodge, and was involved in the much-studied "War of the Theatres" when he followed up Stephen Gosson's *Schoole of Abuse*, which asked the public to "shut up our ears to poets, pipers, and players" in the Puritan tradition, in *A Second and Third Blast of Retrait from Plays and Theatres*, a reformed-Bohemian effort in the style of Robert Greene which earned a resounding riposte from Lodge.

Yet while he on that occasion seemed even more sincere than the Puritans and the parsons in regarding the theatre as the sink of sin, Munday wrote (in addition to a number of adequate civic pageants in the 1600's) many plays himself. Most of the Elizabethan drama is lost, so it should be no surprise that among Munday's probable works now missing are *The Rare Triumphs of Love and Fortune, The Funeral of Richard Coeur de Lion, Chance Medley, Mother Redcap, Valentine and Orson*, the first part of *Fair Constance of Rome, Owen Tudor, The Rising of Cardinal Wolsey, Caesar's Fall (Two Shapes), Jephthah, The Set at Tennis*, and *The Widow's Charm*. It should be remembered, however, that Henslowe was keeping a diary for his own use, not for posterity, and also that The Stationer's Register noted plays it was intended to print and not simply those that were actually published.

Extant works indicate the range and quality of this dramatist whom Francis Meres in *Palladis Tamia* (1598) called "the best for comedy" and "our best plotter" (George Saintsbury sensed a gibe in that). These are a court play of 1584 (or earlier) called *Fedele and Fortunio* derived from Pasquaglio's *Il Fedele*, with the interesting *miles glorioso* Captain Crackstone and connections with Shakespeare's intrigue comedies; *John a Kent and John a Cumber*; a hand in *Sir Thomas More*, a fascinating MS representing collaborative revision of a play of c.1590–1593, itself dating anywhere from about 1593 to 1601 and involving Shakespeare; two Robin Hood plays, *The Downfall of Robert, Earl of Huntingdon* and *The Death of Robert, Earl of Huntingdon*, both with Chettle; a hand in the first part of *Sir John Oldcastle*; and several entertainments and pageants.

Munday's work has still not been fully studied, though his collaborations bring him importantly into examinations of a number of much-discussed playwrights. His work with mythological subjects connects him with Lyly and others, biblical subjects with Peele and others, history and folklore sources with Greene and his followers, while his period inevitably involves him in abstruse discussions of anonymous and lost plays and the apocryphal and actual plays of Shakespeare. Shakespeare is said to have quoted only Marlowe (the "dead shepherd") among his contemporaries, but *Macbeth* in a famous line echoes *The Downfall of Robert, Earl of Huntingdon*'s "made the green sea red" and "the multitudes of seas dyed red with blood" from *The Death of Robert, Earl of Huntingdon.*

Jonson's mention of his pageants in *The Case is Altered* ("Antonio Balladino" is hired, he says, "when a worse cannot be had") is prejudiced and not wholly fair, and I strongly agree with George Sampson (*Cambridge History of English Literature*) that "Munday is one of the minor Elizabethans eminently worthy of sympathetic study."

—Leonard R. N. Ashley

NABBES, Thomas.   English.   Born in Worcestershire in 1605. Educated at Exeter College, Oxford, matriculated 1621, left without taking a degree. Subsequently employed in the household of a nobleman near Worcester; settled in London, 1630; nothing is recorded about him after 1639.

PUBLICATIONS

Collections

  Works, edited by A. H. Bullen.   1887.

Plays

  Covent Garden (produced 1632–33?).   1638.
  Tottenham Court (produced 1633).   1638.
  Hannibal and Scipio (produced 1635).   1637.
  Microcosmus: A Moral Masque (produced 1637).   1637.
  The Spring's Glory, in a Masque, in *The Spring's Glory, with Other Poems.*   1638;
      edited by J. R. Brown, in *A Book of Masques in Honour of Allardyce Nicoll,* 1967.
  A Presentation Intended for the Prince on His Birthday.   1638.
  The Bride (produced 1638).   In *Plays ...,* 1639.
  The Unfortunate Mother, in *Plays. ...*   1639.

Other

  The Spring's Glory, with Other Poems, Epigrams, Elegies, and Epithalamiums.   1638.
  Plays, Masques, Epigrams, Elegies, and Epithalamiums.   1639.

Reading List: *Nabbes: A Critical Monograph* by A. C. Swinburne, 1914; *The Dramatic Works of Nabbes* by Charlotte Moore, 1918.

*   *   *

In the last half of the 1630's, two generations of playwrights and two monarchs removed from the vigour of the English theatre under Elizabeth, Thomas Nabbes produced his half dozen or so comedies, tragedies, and masques. His dramatic activity may have been cut short by the climate of anxiety preceding the close of the theatres in 1642. Perhaps he found his competence written out in the works he left us and, lacking genius, retired rather than repeat himself. All that we know is that Nabbes's surviving works were published from 1637–39, and then Nabbes disappears from literary history.

His two comedies, *Covent Garden* and *Tottenham Court*, seem to have been written first. Their titles indicate their strength, a palpable realism of locale, as well as their dependence on the London or citizen comedies and the theatre of humours of Ben Jonson. *Covent Garden* is especially lively, filled as it is with the clumsy pretensions of the would-be country gentleman, Dungworth, and the hectic antics of Dasher, the "complementing Vintner" whom Swinburne found a "really humorous and original figure." The plots of both comedies involve the amorous wooing of gentlewomen by gallants or libertines, who ultimately reform their ways, and by "deserving" gentlemen, whose common-sense virtue wins the day.

Nabbes's last comedy, *The Bride*, attempts a religious or moral allegory symbolized in the names of its principals: Goodlove, his son Theophilus, the "villane" Raven, and the object of their interest, a maiden called simply The Bride. Of the three comedies this is the most crammed with humorous characters – the antiquarian Horten, the French cook Kickshaw, Justice and Mrs. Ferret, and the Vintner Squirrel, among others. Its serious moral vision may be shaken out of focus at times by the vitality of the humours, but the earnestness of the author is evident here, as throughout his comedies. The satire is always gentle and accepting in these three "easy" Caroline sentimental comedies.

His two tragedies are less appealing. *Hannibal and Scipio*, modelled on Marston's *Sophonisba*, is at times inflated, at times inane. *The Unfortunate Mother*, a tragedy of intrigue, was never performed: the actors refused to go through with the performance.

His poems are likewise negligible, although the few poems that concern Worcester, its steeple and its beer, have some, if only biographical, interest.

Nabbes wrote three masques, *Microcosmus*, *The Spring's Glory*, and *A Presentation Intended for the Prince on His Birthday*. The first, a fairly substantial production, combines the visual splendour of the masque with the seriousness of an allegorical moral interlude. Physander (the Body) betrothed to Bellanima (the Soul) is tempted by Malus Genius (evil spirit) to jilt his beloved for Sensuality. He ruins his health courting her, but is ultimately cured, tried, acquitted, and reunited with Bellanima. This combination of masque and theatre is important because it represents an attempt to curb the empty extravagance of the Caroline masque; it domesticates the masque from court to private house (*Microcosmus* was the first masque performed on the public stage in England); and it leads toward the redefinition of the masque form that culminates in Milton's *Comus*. Both *The Spring's Glory* and *A Presentation* also have charm. That they were not presented in Nabbes's lifetime may be a consequence of their old-fashioned moral seriousness, out of favour with those who relished the elaborate spectacle of the Caroline court masque.

These masques, as well as the three comedies, are attractive in their gentleness and their lack of pretension. Perhaps the finest compliment, and the most perceptive, payable to Nabbes is Swinburne's: a "modest and good-humoured author."

—Daniel DeMatteis

NORTON, Thomas. English. Born in London in 1532. Nothing is known about his academic career except that he was created M.A. by Cambridge University in 1570; admitted to the Inner Temple, London, 1555, and subsequently practised law in London. Married 1) Margery Cranmer, the daughter of Archbishop Cranmer, in 1555 (died); 2) her cousin Alice Cranmer c. 1568; three sons and two daughters. Secretary to the Protector, the Duke of Somerset, in the early 1550's; elected Member of Parliament for Gatton, 1558, Berwick, 1562, and for the City of London, 1571, 1572, and 1580, and sponsored or strongly supported all measures against Roman Catholics; Standing Counsel to the Stationers' Company, 1562; Remembrancer of the City of London, 1571; Solicitor to the Merchant Taylors' Company, 1581; Official Censor of the Queen's Catholic Subjects from 1581, and conducted examinations of numerous Roman Catholic prisoners under torture: accused of treason because of his extreme Protestant views, imprisoned in the Tower of London, then released, 1584. *Died 10 March 1584.*

PUBLICATIONS

Play

> *The Tragedy of Gorboduc,* with Thomas Sackville (produced 1561). 1565; as *The Tragedy of Ferrex and Porrex,* 1570(?); edited by Irby B. Cauthen, 1970.

Verse

> *25 Psalms,* in *The Whole Book of Psalms Collected into English by Sternhold and Hopkins.* 1562.

Other

> *Orations.* 1560(?).
> *To the Queen's Deceived Subjects of the North Country.* 1569.
> *A Warning Against the Dangerous Practices of Papists.* 1570(?).
>
> Translator, *The Institution of Christian Religion,* by John Calvin. 1561.
> Translator, *A Catechism,* by Alexander Nowell. 1570.

*   *   *

See the essay on Thomas Sackville.

PEELE, George. English. Born in London in 1558. Educated at Christ's Hospital School, London, 1565; Broadgates Hall, later Pembroke College, Oxford, 1571–74, and Christ

Church, Oxford, matriculated 1574, B.A. 1577, M.A. 1579. Married in 1583. Very little is known about his life: settled in London, 1581, and began to write for the stage; recognized as one of the "university wits"; wrote several of the lord mayor's pageants for the City of London; his later life was spent in poverty and sickness. *Died* (buried) *9 November 1596.*

PUBLICATIONS

Collections

Life and Works, edited by C. T. Prouty.   3 vols., 1952–70.

Plays

The Arraignment of Paris: A Pastoral (produced 1584?).   1584.
The Device of the Pageant Borne Before Wolstan Dixie, Lord Mayor of London (produced 1585).   1585.
The Battle of Alcazar (produced 1589?).   1594.
The Hunting of Cupid (produced before 1591).   Edited by W. W. Greg, 1911.
Descensus Astraeae: The Device of a Pageant Borne Before William Webb, Lord Mayor of London (produced 1591).   1591.
The Old Wives Tale (produced 1591–94?).   1595.
King Edward the First, Surnamed Edward Longshanks (produced 1593?).   1593.
The Love of King David and Fair Bethsabe (produced 1594?).   1599.

Verse

Pareus (in Latin).   1585.
An Eclogue Gratulatory to Robert, Earl of Essex for His Welcome into England from Portugal.   1589.
A Farewell to Sir John Norris and Sir Francis Drake; A Tale of Troy.   1589; revised edition of *A Tale of Troy,* 1604.
Polyhymnia, Describing the Honourable Triumph at Tilt Before Her Majesty.   1590.
The Honour of the Garter.   1593.
Anglorum Feriae: England's Holidays, edited by R. Fitch.   1830(?).

Other

Life and Minor Works of Peele, by D. H. Horne.   1952.

Bibliography: *Peele: A Concise Bibliography* by S. A. Tannenbaum, 1940; *Peele 1939–65* by R. C. Johnson, 1968.

Reading List: *Peele* by P. H. Cheffaud, 1913; *Authorship and Evidence: A Study of Attribution and the Renaissance Drama, Illustrated by the Case of Peele* by Leonard R. N. Ashley, 1968; *Lyly and Peele* by George K. Hunter, 1968.

*   *   *

George Peele was an Oxford graduate who returned to his native London to earn a living by writing occasional poems, occasional pageants, and plays. He was a representative "University Wit," a free-lance author whose range, while confined to poetry and drama, embraced the taste of the court and that of the city and included most of the dramatic types fashionable in his day.

Having at Oxford translated one of Euripides's *Iphigenia* plays and written a digest of the Trojan war in under 500 lines of heroic couplets, he pursued his classical and mythological themes in his first extant original play, *The Arraignment of Paris*, written for the Children of the Chapel Royal to act before Elizabeth I. Paris awards the golden apple to Venus, whose disappointed rivals indict him for partiality before a court of gods and goddesses (hence the title); after his spirited defence the prize is adjudged to be re-awarded by Diana, who delivers a panegyric on the nymph Eliza, "whom some Zabeta call," and actually delivers the apple into the hand of the spectator-Queen. Though Peele celebrated several courtly occasions this seems to have been his only court play. Its slight, complimentary structure is somewhat filled out by introducing Oenone and her desertion by Paris, and, to balance this male infidelity, the constant unrequited lover Colin (drawn from Spenser's recent *Shepherd's Calendar*): but neither of these episodes is developed, and the play's attraction lies chiefly in its lyricism (there is considerable metrical variety, and several songs) and its eloquence.

Peele's next play was *The Battle of Alcazar*, a drama of violent deeds (mostly, however, symbolized by dumbshows or described in speeches) centred upon a recent battle in Morocco where Sebastian of Portugal and the English expatriate adventurer Tom Stukeley were slain. Like all his later ones, this play was written for the public theatre – another of its principal characters, the revengeful Moor, was played by Alleyn – and in its technique it is related to Marlowe's *Tamburlaine* and also to Kyd's *Spanish Tragedy*.

The order of Peele's remaining plays is not certainly known. *Edward I* is a history play insofar as it introduces historical characters and something of their story (the king's wars with the Scots and the Welsh, with the birth of the English Prince of Wales at Caernarvon), but it is a romance insofar as many incidents are apocryphal: from time to time Queen Elinor is portrayed (with anti-Spanish feeling) as a proud and cruel woman; the Welsh prince Lluellen takes to a Robin-Hood life in the woods, where he is joined by the disguised Lord Mortimer (his rival in love) and by a robust Friar who provides most of the comedy in this thoroughly mingled play.

In *David and Bethsabe* Peele dramatizes biblical incidents (from 1 Samuel and 2 Kings) into a play far more unified in structure and in style. It is a moral treatment, unrelieved by comedy, of David's sin and repentance, introducing also the revenge theme in Absalon's slaying of his brother for ravishing their sister, and the military-heroic in the seige of the enemy city and in Absalon's rebellion and death. Peele has here cultivated decorum of style by drawing on biblical language and imagery, without suppressing his characteristic lyricism and eloquence. All Peele's plays discussed so far are notable for the lengthy speeches they contain. They are also all highly spectacular.

His *Old Wives* (i.e. Wife's) *Tale*, though it too has spectacle, eloquence, and lyricism, is unique, not only in Peele's work but in English literature. This romance of an adventurous knight who rescues a princess abducted by a magician suggests Ariosto (from whose *Orlando Furioso* the magician Sacrapant takes his name), but the grateful ghost who is his loyal servant comes from homelier folklore, as do the pair of unlike sisters who go to a magic well to find their allotted husbands, one of whom is a comic braggart who speaks in the "English hexameters" with which poets were then experimenting. All these threads of plot – and others – are supposed to be united in a rambling tale told by an old woman to entertain benighted travellers at her cottage. To regard the play as quite serious would be unjust to Peele's sophistication; to regard it as a burlesque of popular drama would be unjust to his delight (seen in *Edward I*, for example) in simple and abundant storytelling.

It is by this play that Peele is best known. His verses for civic pageants (*Descensus Astraeae*, and Sir Wolstan Dixie's Lord Mayor's Show) and for court ceremonies (*Polyhymnia*; *The Honour of the Garter*; *Anglorum Feriae*) have the stylistic qualities of the verse in his plays:

he developed a lucid expressiveness in his blank verse, while some of his lyrics (specially the gravely beautiful valedictory poem for the Royal Champion in *Polyhymnia*, "His golden locks Time hath to silver turned") have the literal memorability which is one of the marks of true poetry.

—T. W. Craik

RANDOLPH, Thomas. English. Bo000in Newnham-cum-Badby, near Daventry, Northamptonshire, baptized 15 June 1605. Educated at Westminster School, London (King's Scholar); Trinity College, Cambridge, matriculated 1624, B.A. 1628, minor fellow 1629, major fellow 1632, M.A. 1632; also incorporated M.A. at Oxford, 1632. Became famous at Cambridge as a writer of verse; visited London frequently from 1628, and became acquainted with the writers and patrons surrounding Ben Jonson; settled in London, 1632, and lived an increasingly dissipated life which undermined his health. *Died* (buried) *17 March 1635.*

PUBLICATIONS

Collections

> *Poetical and Dramatic Works*, edited by W. C. Hazlitt.   2 vols., 1875.
> *Poems and Amyntas*, edited by John Jay Parry.   1917.
> *Poems*, edited by G. Thorn-Drury.   1929.

Plays

> *Aristippus; or, The Jovial Philosopher* (produced 1625–26?).   1630.
> *The Drinking Academy* (produced 1626?).   Edited by Hyder Rollins, in *Publications of the Modern Language Association*, 1924; edited by Rollins and S. A. Tannenbaum, 1930.
> *The Conceited Pedlar* (produced 1627).   With *Aristippus*, 1630.
> *The Muses' Looking-Glass* (produced 1630).   In *Poems* ..., 1638.
> *Amyntas; or, The Impossible Dowry* (produced 1630).   In *Poems* ..., 1638.
> *Praeludium* (produced 1630?).   In *Poems and Amyntas*, 1917.
> *The Jealous Lovers* (produced 1632).   1632.
> *The Constant Lovers* (produced 1634).   Edited by B. H. Newdigate, in *Times Literary Supplement*, 18 and 25 April 1942.
> *Hey for Honesty, Down with Knavery*, from a play by Aristophanes.   1651.

Other

> *Poems, with The Muses' Looking-Glass and Amyntas.*   1638; revised edition, 1640.

Bibliography: *Randolph: A Concise Bibliography* by S. A. and D. R. Tannenbaum, 1946.

Reading List: *Randolph* (lecture) by G. C. Moore Smith, 1927; *Pastoral Poetry and Pastoral Drama* by W. W. Greg, 1959; *The Poetry of Randolph* by Ila Mullick, 1974.

*   *   *

For reasons which it is now hardly possible to discern, Thomas Randolph's contemporary popularity was very great. Adopted by Jonson as a "son of Ben," he impressed his acquaintance as his great mentor's most worthy successor, and his early death was seen as a disaster for English letters. Precocity and facility may account for the effect Randolph had on those who knew him, for nothing that survives in his poetry or his plays justifies this high estimate of his work.

"An Ode to Master Anthony Stafford" is Randolph's main poetic achievement. It is his own version of the classical encomium of country life, "where old simplicity,/Though hid in gray,/Doth look more gay/Than foppery in plush and scarlet clad," and abandons his usual easy couplets for a swinging 12-lined stanza, where alternating short and long lines allow the rush of impatience or exuberance into the verse ("More of my days/I will not spend to gain an idiot's praise"; "The thrush and blackbird lend their throats/Warbling melodious notes;/ We will all sports enjoy, which others but desire"). The ode is only faintly tinged with the stale pastoral vocabulary in which so many of Randolph's poems are phrased, and gives fresh and lively treatment to a theme which he also dealt with several times in neat and competent translations from classical authors. Of his other pastorals, the "Eclogue ... upon Predestination" achieves an unexpectedly powerful close, but the rest are undistinguished. The wit of such poems as those on "his well-timbered mistress" or "a very deformed gentlewoman" is now tedious, but rueful poems to his empty purse, his creditors, and his lost finger show something of the gaiety and charm that delighted his contemporaries.

Randolph's dramatic works give the impression that, had the age allowed it, he would have found his vocation as a writer of sketches for reviews. The lively monologue *The Conceited Pedlar* is in effect cabaret material; the opportunities it offered a performer in the Cambridge setting for which it was designed are still evident. *Aristippus*, a longer but equally topical sketch, burlesques university life by adding the philosophy of drinking to the syllabus; its wit was well calculated to appeal to an undergraduate audience. *The Drinking Academy*, a similar piece, is less academic and shows Jonson's influence. *The Muses' Looking-Glass* is likewise more a sketch than a play; its demonstration of comedy's power to purge excesses by ridicule is hardly amusing today, except for the presentation of the Puritans whose prejudices are overcome. Randolph's two full-length plays are written in nondescript verse and show little power of dramatic construction on a larger scale. His pastoral drama, *Amyntas*, though admired by W. W. Greg, comes to life only in the comic scenes which Randolph added to the genre; while *The Jealous Lovers*, in which an improbable plot is unconvincingly resolved by a *deus ex machina*, shows Randolph deficient in the ability to portray plausible serious action or genuine feeling.

—Margaret Forey

ROWLEY, William.   English.   Born in England c. 1585. Actor: with the Duke of York's Company, later Prince Charles's Company, 1609–17; with the King's Men from 1623; noted for his portrayals in comic parts; collaborated with several other dramatists in writing for the stage, and may have assisted with as many as 50 plays. *Died in February 1626.*

PUBLICATIONS

Plays

Fortune by Land and Sea, with Thomas Heywood (produced 1607?).   1655; edited by J. E. Walker, 1899.

The Travels of the Three English Brothers, Sir Thomas, Sir Anthony, Mr. Robert Shirley, with John Day and George Wilkins (produced 1607).   1607; edited by A. H. Bullen, in *Works* by Day, 1881.

A Shoemaker a Gentleman (produced 1608?).   1638; edited by Charles Wharton Stork, with *All's Lost by Lust*, 1910.

A Fair Quarrel, with Middleton (produced 1615–17?).   1617; edited by George R. Price, 1976.

The Old Law; or, A New Way to Please You, with Middleton (produced 1618?).   1656; edited by A. H. Bullen, in *Works* by Middleton, 1885–86.

The World Tossed at Tennis, with Middleton (produced 1619–20?).   1620.

All's Lost by Lust (produced 1619–20?).   1633; edited by Charles Wharton Stork, with *A Shoemaker a Gentleman*, 1910.

The Birth of Merlin; or, The Child Hath Found His Father (produced 1620?).   1662; edited by C. F. Tucker Brooke, in *Shakespeare Apocrypha*, 1908.

The Witch of Edmonton, with Dekker and Ford (produced 1621).   1658; edited by Fredson Bowers, in *Dramatic Works of Dekker*, 1953–61.

The Changeling, with Middleton (produced 1622).   1653; edited by Kenneth Muir, in *Three Plays* by Middleton, 1975.

The Maid in the Mill, with Fletcher (produced 1623).   In *Comedies and Tragedies* by Beaumont and Fletcher, 1647.

The Spanish Gipsy, with Middleton (produced 1623).   1653; edited by C. M. Hayley, in *Representative English Comedies*, 1914.

A Cure for a Cuckold, with Webster (produced 1624–25?).   1661; edited by F. L. Lucas, in *Works* by Webster, 1927.

A New Wonder: A Woman Never Vexed (produced ?).   1632; edited by W. C. Hazlitt, in *Dodsley's Old Plays*, 1875.

A Match at Midnight (produced ?).   1633; edited by W. C. Hazlitt, in *Dodsley's Old Plays*, 1875.

Wit at Several Weapons, with Fletcher and Middleton (produced ?).   In *Comedies and Tragedies* by Beaumont and Fletcher, 1647.

Fiction

A Search for Money; or, The Lamentable Complaint for the Loss of the Wandering Knight M. l'Argent; or, Come Along with Me, I Know Thou Lovest Money.   1609.

Reading List: *An Inquiry into the Authorship of the Middleton-Rowley Plays* by P. G. Wiggin, 1897; "The Canon of Rowley's Plays" by D. M. Robb, in *Modern Language Review 45*, 1950; *Middleton's Tragedies* by Samuel Schoenbaum, 1955.

*   *   *

William Rowley was at his best as a dramatist when writing in collaboration, especially with Thomas Middleton. In their finest work, *The Changeling*, Rowley's sub-plot moves quickly and satisfyingly on its own account and, by ironic connections with the main plot, it powerfully reinforces the play's themes of lust, deceit, and corruption. In his early work, Rowley's dialogue is stilted and choppy, but his verse style developed a strength and natural flexibility, seen at their finest in the opening and closing scenes of *The Changeling*. His command of characterization is weak as a whole, but from about 1616 onward his clowns are markedly individual, probably because he played these roles himself. Compass of *A Cure for a Cuckold* and the justly praised Cuddy Banks of *The Witch of Edmonton,* for example, are both credibly human in the Shakespearian mould. Of his unaided plays, *A Woman Never Vexed* and *A Match at Midnight* are citizen comedies which owe something of their tone and setting, if little of their artlessness, to Middleton's influence. His one tragedy, *All's Lost by Lust*, is complex in plot, and though the verse is generally rough it occasionally rises to a melodramatic eloquence; the characterization is unsubtle and the structure crude. It was, however, acted "divers times" and "with great applause," according to the title page of its only early edition. Rowley's prose pamphlet, *A Search for Money*, is a goodhumoured satire which incidentally throws light on the topography and society of contemporary London. He also wrote commendatory verses for Webster's *Duchess of Malfi* (1623) and John Taylor's *Nipping and Snipping of Abuses* (1614) and verses on the death of Prince Henry for Taylor's *Great Britain All in Black* (1612) and William Drummond's *Mausoleum* (1613). Although Rowley has been neglected by modern critics, according to the late seventeenth-century stage historian Gerard Langbaine he was "beloved by those Great Men, Shakespear, Fletcher and Johnson."

—Alan Brissenden

SACKVILLE, Thomas; 1st Earl of Dorset; Baron Buckhurst. English. Born in Buckhurst, Withyham, Sussex, in 1536. Educated at the grammar school in Sullington, Sussex; possibly at Hart Hall, Oxford, or St. John's College, Cambridge; entered the Middle Temple, London; called to the bar. Married Cecily Baker in 1554; four sons and three daughters. Elected Member of Parliament for Westmorland, 1558, for East Grinstead, Sussex, 1559, and for Aylesbury, Buckinghamshire, 1563; toured France and Italy, 1563–66; inherited family estates and returned to England, 1566; served in the House of Lords from 1567; on diplomatic missions for the crown to France, 1568, 1571; Privy Councillor, from 1571, and served as Commissioner at State Trials; sent to the Low Countries by the queen to survey political affairs after Leicester's return to England, incurred her displeasure, was recalled, confined to his house, then restored to favour, 1587–88; appointed Commissioner for Ecclesiastical Causes, 1588; again sent on an embassy to the Low Countries, 1589; commissioner to sign treaty with France on behalf of the queen, 1591; with Burghley unsuccessfully attempted to negotiate peace with France, 1598; appointed Lord Treasurer, 1599, and confirmed in the position for life by James I, 1603; Lord High Steward, presiding at the trial of the Earl of Essex, 1601; a commissioner in the successful negotiation of a new peace treaty with Spain, and pensioned for his services by the king, 1604. Grand Master of the Order of the Freemasons, 1561–67; Chancellor of Oxford University, 1591. M.A.:

Cambridge University, 1571; Oxford University, 1592. Knighted, and created Baron Buckhurst, 1567; Knight of the Garter, 1589; Earl of Dorset, 1604. *Died 19 April 1608.*

PUBLICATIONS

Collections

> *Works,* edited by R. W. Sackville-West.   1859.
> *Poems,* edited by M. Hearsey.   1936.

Play

> *The Tragedy of Gorboduc,* with Thomas Norton (produced 1561).   1565; as *The Tragedy of Ferrex and Porrex,* 1570(?); edited by Irby B. Cauthen, 1970.

Verse

> *Induction,* and *Complaint of Henry, Duke of Buckingham,* in *Mirror for Magistrates.*   1563; edited by L. B. Campbell, 1938.

Reading List: *Sackville* by Normand Berlin, 1974.

*   *   *

In the first edition of *Gorboduc,* the first three acts are attributed to Norton and the last two to Sackville, but some current opinion also ascribes the play's first scene to Sackville and its final one to Norton. *Gorboduc,* the first English tragedy properly so called, is based on a story from the British pseudo-history written by Geoffrey of Monmouth. The authors have altered this story (of brother-princes' rivalry, leading to the death of one of them in battle and their mother's murder of the survivor, after which the nobles fall to civil war) by making it begin with the king's abdication of rule in favour of both his sons, by causing the king and queen to be slain in a popular rebellion which is then put down by the nobles, and by introducing in the last act an ambitious nobleman who covets the vacant throne. Their play is therefore concerned both with tragic passions (which destroy a fated royal house) and with political lessons (particularly the dangers of civil war and the importance of a settled succession): it partakes both of the world of Senecan tragedy and of that of the *Mirror for Magistrates.* In form it resembles classical tragedy, though actually defective in all three unities of time, place, and (finally, when the chief characters are dead) action. It is divided into acts and scenes, with choruses between the acts; there are long speeches containing many *sententiae*; physical action, instead of being shown, is narrated by messengers. From non-classical tradition come the symbolic dumb-shows between the acts. The speeches are in blank verse, the choruses in quatrains (sometimes double) rounded off with couplets.

Sackville also contributed to the 1563 edition of the *Mirror for Magistrates,* supplying one of the tragic narratives (the "complaint" of the Duke of Buckingham, Richard III's right-hand-man) and a long 76-stanza "induction" to the whole work. In the induction, the poet, musing in a dreary winter landscape, encounters Sorrow personified, who escorts him to the underworld, where he sees various other appropriate personifications – Remorse of Conscience, Dread, Revenge, Misery, Care, Sleep, Age, Malady, Famine, Death, War, and

Debate – before crossing in Charon's boat to interview the great men whose falls are the subject of the *Mirror*. Written in rhyme-royal pentameter, this induction powerfully evokes the sombre mood of the collection of "tragedies" by drawing partly on Virgilian and partly on medieval artistic conventions; it looks forward towards Spenser in this mingling, as also in its deliberate use of archaic words for their emotional associations.

—T. W. Craik

SHAKESPEARE, William. English. Born in Stratford upon Avon, Warwickshire, baptized 26 April 1564. Probably educated at the King's New School, Stratford, 1571–77. Married Anne Hathaway in 1582; two daughters, one son. May have taught school in or near Stratford; settled in London c. 1588, and was well-known as an actor and had begun to write for the stage by 1592: Shareholder in the Lord Chamberlain's Company (after James I's accession, called the King's Men) by 1594, performing at the Globe Theatre from 1599, and, after 1609, at the Blackfriars Theatre; bought New Place in Stratford, 1597, and acquired land in Stratford; retired to Stratford in 1611. *Died 23 April 1616.*

PUBLICATIONS

Collections

    Comedies, Histories, and Tragedies (First Folio), edited by John Heming and Henry Condell. 1623.
    Works (New Variorum Edition), edited by H. H. Furness and H. H. Furness, Jr. 27 vols., 1871–
    Works (New Cambridge Edition), edited by J. Dover Wilson and A. H. Quiller-Couch. 1921–66.
    The New Arden Shakespeare, edited by Una Ellis-Fermor and others. 1951–
    The New Penguin Shakespeare. 1967–

Plays

    King John (produced 1589). In First Folio, 1623.
    1 Henry VI (produced 1591?). In First Folio, 1623.
    2 Henry VI (produced 1592?). 1594 (bad quarto).
    3 Henry VI (produced 1592?). 1595 (bad quarto).
    Richard III (produced 1592?). 1597.
    The Comedy of Errors (produced 1593?). In First Folio, 1623.
    Titus Andronicus (produced 1594). 1594.
    The Taming of the Shrew (produced 1594). In First Folio, 1623.
    Love's Labour's Lost (produced 1594?). 1598.
    Romeo and Juliet (produced 1594–95?). 1597 (bad quarto); 1599.
    Two Gentlemen of Verona (produced 1595?). In First Folio, 1623.
    A Midsummer Night's Dream (produced 1595). 1600.

Richard II (produced 1595–96?). 1597.
Sir Thomas More, with Munday (produced 1596?). Edited by A. Dyce, 1844; edition of W. W. Greg revised by H. Jenkins, 1961.
The Merchant of Venice (produced 1596?). 1600.
Henry IV, part 1 (produced 1596–97?). 1598.
Henry IV, part 2 (produced 1597–98?). 1600.
Much Ado about Nothing (produced 1598?). 1600.
Henry V (produced 1599). 1600 (bad quarto).
Julius Caesar (produced 1599). In First Folio, 1623.
The Merry Wives of Windsor (produced 1599–1600?). 1602 (bad quarto).
As You Like It (produced 1600?). In First Folio, 1623.
Hamlet (produced 1601?). 1603 (bad quarto); 1604.
Twelfth Night; or, What You Will (produced 1601–02?). In First Folio, 1623.
Troilus and Cressida (produced 1602?). 1609.
All's Well That Ends Well (produced 1602?). In First Folio, 1623.
Measure for Measure (produced 1604?). In First Folio, 1623.
Othello (produced 1604?). 1622.
King Lear (produced 1605). 1608 (bad quarto).
Macbeth (produced 1606). In First Folio, 1623.
Antony and Cleopatra (produced 1606?). In First Folio, 1623.
Coriolanus (produced 1606?). In First Folio, 1623.
Timon of Athens (produced 1607?). In First Folio, 1623.
Pericles, with George Wilkins (produced 1608?). 1609.
Cymbeline (produced 1609?). In First Folio, 1623.
The Winter's Tale (produced 1610?). In First Folio, 1623.
The Tempest (produced 1611). In First Folio, 1623.
Henry VIII, with Fletcher(?) (produced 1613). In First Folio, 1623.
The Two Noble Kinsmen, with Fletcher (produced 1613). 1634; edited by G. R. Proudfoot, 1970.

Verse

Venus and Adonis. 1593.
The Rape of Lucrece. 1594.
Sonnets. 1609.
Poems. 1640.

Bibliography: *A Shakespeare Bibliography* by Walther Ebisch and Levin L. Schücking, 1931, supplement, 1937; *A Classified Shakespeare Bibliography 1936–1958* by Gordon Ross Smith, 1963.

Reading List: *Shakespeare: A Study of the Facts and Problems* by E. K. Chambers, 2 vols., 1930; *Narrative and Dramatic Sources of Shakespeare* edited by Geoffrey Bullough, 8 vols., 1957–75; *The Printing and Proof-Reading of the First Folio of Shakespeare* by C. Hinman, 2 vols., 1963; *Four Centuries of Shakespeare Criticism* edited by Frank Kermode, 1965; *A Shakespeare Encyclopaedia* edited by O. J. Campbell and E. G. Quinn, 1966; *A New and Systematic Concordance to the Works of Shakespeare* by M. Spevack, 6 vols., 1968–70; *A New Companion of Shakespeare Studies* edited by Kenneth Muir and Samuel Schoenbaum, 1971; *Shakespeare: The Critical Heritage* edited by Brian Vickers, 6 vols., 1973–74; *Shakespeare: A Documentary Life* by Samuel Schoenbaum, 1975, compact edition, 1977.

*   *   *

Shakespeare, "of all modern, and perhaps ancient poets, had the largest and most comprehensive soul." Dryden's tribute, the more generous for coming from an age that prided itself on a superior standard of polish and "politeness," sums up what students of Shakespeare have at all times sought to express. No writer of comparable greatness is more elusive to final definition. None has exercised a more diverse appeal or shown a greater capacity for continual and fruitful renewal in the minds of succeeding generations.

This protean genius came only gradually to full expression. Shakespeare's earliest work is that of a man engaged in exploring, and in some measure creating, the possibilities of his art. The earliest work attributed to him, the three plays on *Henry VI*, show him engaged in shaping chronicle material to dramatic ends. They lead, in *Richard III*, to the creation of a character who stands out by his passionate dedication to the achievement of power against the world of short-sighted time-servers, ambitious politicians, and helpless moralists in which he moves.

Side by side with these early chronicle dramas we find Shakespeare, in a series of plays running from *The Comedy of Errors* through *The Taming of the Shrew* to *Love's Labour's Lost*, shaping the conventions of comedy into an instrument for expressing the finished statements about life – and more especially about love and marriage as central aspects of it – that he was already concerned to make.

In the 1590's Shakespeare also wrote two narrative poems, *Venus and Adonis* and *The Rape of Lucrece*, possibly stimulated by the success of Marlowe's *Hero and Leander* of 1593, and he was also at work on his sonnets, though the 1609 *Sonnets* is now generally thought to contain poems from virtually all the periods of his development. Many of the sonnets are exercises in the conventions of the period, addressed to a patron or to an imaginary mistress. But Shakespeare was able to use the thematic conventions in a fresh way, investigating – as he would do in his later plays – the relation of individual experience (in particular the heightened emotions of friendship and love) to time. At the same time Shakespeare developed a distinctively intense and immediate language to meet the strict formal limitations of the sonnet. The stress of feeling informing the language and the exploration of shifting attitudes to a particular emotion are essentially *dramatic*, and mark out linguistic and thematic areas that Shakespeare was to explore in his "problem" plays and later.

His early works led, approximately from 1595 to 1596, to a first remarkable explosion of creative energy. Within a brief period of time, Shakespeare produced his first great tragedy, *Romeo and Juliet*, a comedy of outstanding brilliance, *A Midsummer Night's Dream*, and a historical play, *Richard II*, which gives the chronicle type of drama an entirely new dimension. In *Romeo and Juliet* a pair of young lovers seek to affirm the truth of their mutual dedication in the face of an intolerably hostile world. Their attempt ends, inevitably, in separation and death; but because it is a true emotion, involving an intuition of *value*, of life and generosity, it achieves, even in the doom which overtakes it, a measure of triumph over external circumstance. *A Midsummer Night's Dream* could be regarded as a comic counterpoise to the "romantic" tragedy. Within the framework of a rational and social attitude to marriage, it transports two pairs of youthful lovers to the mysterious woods, where the irrational but potent impulses which men ignore at their peril are released and their capacity to master them tested. By the end of their misadventures, and when the central theme of the play has been presented in the infatuation of Titania, the queen of the fairies, for Bottom the weaver with his ass's head, there is a return to daylight reality and, with it, a resolution of the issues raised by the play in terms of creative paradox. Love is seen at once to be a folly and to contain within itself, absurd indeed but not the less real, a glimpse of the divine element by which human life is imaginatively transformed in terms of "wonder."

The third play of this period, *Richard II*, is the starting-point for a series, continued in *Henry IV*, Parts I and II and *Henry V*, which traces the downfall of a traditional conception of royalty and its replacement by a political force at once more competent, more truly self-aware, and more precariously built on the foundation of its own desire for power. The Lancastrian Bolingbroke, having achieved the crown by deposing and murdering his predecessor, is seen striving to impose unity upon his realm, but foiled in his efforts by the consequences of his original crime. The success which eludes him is finally attained, in *Henry V*, by his son, but in a way which underlines the cost as well as the necessity of his triumph. The presence of Shakespeare's greatest comic creation, Falstaff, and his final rejection, underline the human complexity involved in the new king's necessary choices. As King, he can hardly do otherwise than banish the companion of his youth, and it would surely be wrong to sentimentalize Falstaff in any way; but we are required, in a manner that is very essentially Shakespearean, to weigh the *cost* against the success, and perhaps to conclude that the human and the political orders – both necessary aspects of human life – are in the real world barely to be reconciled.

At about the time that he was writing this second series of history plays, Shakespeare was engaged in developing further his concept of comedy to cover other aspects of human behaviour. In *Much Ado about Nothing* he produced a highly formal comedy which works, through strict conventions and largely in prose, to illuminate facets of truth and illusion in the reality of love. In *As You Like It* the consideration of the basic realities of love and friendship is extended to cover a concept of sociability, of true civilization. The central part of the play, which displaces the action to the Forest of Arden where human relationships are taken temporarily into the state of nature (itself presented in conventional terms) and set in contrast to the corrupt sophistication which prevails at Duke Frederick's court, presents a set of variations on the theme of love. When the various amorous combinations have been sorted out, leading into the concluding "dance" of married harmonies which is a reflection of the universal order of things, the reconciliation at which comedy aims is finally consummated.

The last of these great comedies, *Twelfth Night*, deals in its "serious" part with two characters, Orsino and Olivia, whose lives are initially a blend of sentiment and artifice, and who learn, largely through their relationship with the self-reliant Viola, that the compulsive force of their passions is such as to draw them finally beyond themselves, demanding from each the acceptance of a fuller, more natural and spontaneous way of living. The "lesson" is reinforced by the comic underplot, and more particularly by the exposure of Olivia's steward Malvolio, who is – and remains to the last – "imprisoned" in a darkness which reflects his self-infatuation. Feste, too, the most individual thus far of Shakespeare's clowns, stands rather outside the prevailing mood, answering to the constant tendency of Shakespearean comedy to qualify its imaginative harmonies with a profound sense of relativity, of a final uniqueness and autonomy in human experience.

The period which produced these great comedies was followed by a turning of the dramatist's interest towards tragedy. Two plays of obscure intention and uneven execution – *Troilus and Cressida* and *Measure for Measure* – form the background to *Hamlet* in which many of the same issues were raised to the consistent level of tragedy. The play presents a central figure of unique complexity whose motives penetrate the action at every point, seeking clarification through contact with it and illuminating it in turn by his central presence. In pursuing his duty to avenge his father's death, Hamlet brings to light a state of disease in "Denmark" – the "world" of the play – which affects the entire field presented to his consciousness; and, in the various stages through which the ramifications of this infection are exposed, he finds himself exploring progressively the depths of his own disaffection.

In the great tragedies that followed *Hamlet*, the conflicts there presented are polarized, on an ever-increasing scale, into more clearly defined contrasts. In the earliest of them, *Othello*, the heroic figure of the Moor, tragically compounded of nobility and weakness, is exposed to the critical scepticism of Iago which operates upon his simplicity with the effect of an anarchic and sinister dissolvent. "Perplexed" to the last, betrayed by emotions which he has never really understood in their true nature, Othello makes a last attempt to return, through suicide, to his original simplicity of nature. By then, however, the critical acid supplied by Iago has undermined the structure of his greatness.

In his next tragedy, *King Lear*, Shakespeare embarked upon what is probably the most universal of his conceptions. Lear is at once father and king, head of a family and ruler of a state. As father he produces in his daughters contrasted reactions which reflect contradictions in his own nature; as king, his wilful impulses release in society destructive forces which nothing less than their utter exhaustion can contain. In the central storm scenes, the action of the elements becomes a reflection of Lear's own condition. Man and his environment are seen as organically related in the conflicts of a universe poetically conceived. Human relationships are shattered, and the state of "unaccomodated man" is seen in terms of subjection to the beast of prey in his own nature. Through these overwhelming events we are led step by step to Lear's awakening and recognition of his returned daughter Cordelia. This is the central reconciliation, the restoration of the natural "bond" between father and child, which is seen − while it lasts − as the resolution of the ruin caused by passion and egoism in the most intimate of human relationships. It is not, however, lasting. Since we are engaged in an exploration of the human condition under its tragic aspect, not elaborating the supposedly beneficial effects of suffering in promoting moral understanding, the armies of France are defeated by the "Machiavellian" realist Edmund; and though he dies in meeting the challenge of his disguised half-brother Edgar, his death cannot reverse the hanging of Cordelia by his orders. As the play ends, Lear returns with her dead body in his arms and, in a world dominated by returning darkness, the curtain falls.

The next great tragedy, *Macbeth*, deals with the overthrow of harmony not merely in an individual of tragic stature, but in an ordered realm. Macbeth murders, not only a man and a kinsman, but order, sanity, life itself. From the moment of the execution of his deed his character and that of his wife develop on lines of rigid determinism. One crime leads logically, by a dreadful and pre-determined process, to another; and the career that began by following the illusion of "freedom," mastery of circumstance, ends by an inexorable development in a complete enslavement from which defeat and death provide the only conceivable release.

Close in time to the writing of these great tragedies, a series of plays on Roman themes represents Shakespeare's final effort in this kind. The earliest, *Julius Caesar*, is one of his most effective studies of public behaviour. The central character, Brutus, the nearest approach to a truly consistent figure which the play offers, is flawed by the self-consciousness of his determination to be true to his ideals. His need to live up to an acceptable image of himself makes him the victim of those who appeal to him in the name of friendship and devotion to freedom, but who are moved in no small part by resentment and envy. The other principal agent in the tragedy, Mark Antony, combines genuine feeling with the ability to exploit mob emotion, and ends by disclaiming responsibility for the destruction and brutality he has unleashed. Finally, after Caesar's death, the world which survives him is shown separating into its component elements of selfish "realism" and disillusionment.

The next Roman play, *Antony and Cleopatra*, is among Shakespeare's greatest masterpieces. His Cleopatra is at once the Egyptian queen of history and something more: a woman experienced in the ways of a corrupt and cynical world and ready to use her fascination over men in order to survive in it. Antony's love for her is, at least in part, the fascination of a man no longer young, who has chosen to give up his public responsibilities to become the dupe of an emotion that he knows to be unworthy. Side by side with the moral judgment that is unrelentingly pressed throughout the tragedy, the implication remains that the measure of the passion which has led this pair to accept death and ruin may be correspondingly universal in its value. It is the play's achievement to convey that *both* judgments contain a measure of truth, that neither can be suppressed without distorting our sense of the complete human reality which the play offers.

After *Coriolanus*, the disconcerting study of a gauche and inflexible hero whose unnatural desire for revenge upon his city leaves him at the last disoriented and ruined in a world that he is incapable of understanding, the last stage of Shakespeare's development consists of a series of "romances," written from 1607 onwards, which represent an effort to give dramatic form to a new "symbolic" intuition. After two plays − *Pericles* and *Cymbeline* − which can be thought of as experiments, *The Winter's Tale* presents the story of two kings whose life-long friendship is broken up by the jealous conviction of one of them − Leontes − that his friend Polixenes has replaced him in the affection of his wife Hermione. By the end of an action in which the passage of time has an essential part to play, the estranged monarchs are reconciled through the spontaneous love of their children, the divisions introduced by disordered and self-consuming passion into the harmony of life have been healed, and winter has passed through spring into the summer of gracious fulfilment.

The Tempest, which some have seen, perhaps a little over-schematically, as Shakespeare's farewell to the stage, takes us to an island in which the normal laws of nature are magically suspended. Prospero can be seen as a figure of the imaginative artist, bringing together on his island stage the men who, in another world, have wronged him and whom he now subjects to a process of judgment and reconciliation. He is accompanied by his servants Ariel and Caliban, the former of whom may represent the imaginative, creative side of his nature, the latter the passionate instincts which, as a human being, he keeps uneasily under control. By the end of the play, as in *The Winter's Tale*, a measure of reconciliation has been born out of the exposure to tragic experience. Prospero's daughter Miranda marries Ferdinand, the son of his former enemy, whom she first saw in her inexperience as a vision proceeding from a "brave new world," but whom she has learned to love as a man. The "brave new world" is seen as an ennobling vision of love in the light of an enriched experience, and upon it the "gods" are invited to bestow the "crown" which raises a new-born vision of humanity into a symbol of royalty. The "crown" they bestow is a sign of the "second," the redeemed and "reasonable" life which Prospero's action has made accessible. At this point, if anywhere, and always within the limits of the imaginative action which has created a *play*, the design presented by Shakespeare's work is substantially complete.

—Derek A. Traversi

SHIRLEY, James. English. Born in Walbrook, London, 18 September 1596. Educated at Merchant Taylors' School, London, 1608–12; St. John's College, Oxford, 1612, subsequently St. Catharine's College, Cambridge, B.A. c. 1618. Married Elizabeth Gilmet in 1618; three sons and two daughters. Ordained: parish priest in or near St. Albans, and Headmaster at Edward VI Grammar School in St. Albans, 1623 until he was converted to Roman Catholicism and resigned his positions c. 1625; settled in London, 1625, and began writing plays: became a favourite of the court; wrote for Ogilby's theatre in Dublin, after plague closed the London theatres, 1636–40; returned to London and continued to produce plays until Parliament closed the theatres in 1642; fought for the Royalists, under his patron, the Earl of Newcastle, 1642–44, then returned to London: taught school during the Commonwealth. *Died* (buried) *29 October 1666.*

PUBLICATIONS

Collections

Dramatic Works and Poems, edited by William Gifford and Alexander Dyce.   6 vols., 1833.

Plays

The School of Compliment (produced 1625). 1631; as *Love Tricks*, 1667.

The Wedding (produced 1626?). 1629; edited by A. S. Knowland, in *Six Caroline Plays*, 1962.

The Maid's Revenge (produced 1626). 1639.

The Witty Fair One (produced 1628). 1633; edited by Edmund Gosse, in *Plays*, 1888.

The Grateful Servant (produced 1629). 1630.

The Traitor (produced 1631). 1635; edited by J. S. Carter, 1965.

Love's Cruelty (produced 1631). 1640.

The Humorous Courtier (as *The Duke*, produced 1631). 1640.

The Arcadia, from the work by Sidney (produced before 1632). 1640.

Changes; or, Love in a Maze (produced 1632). 1632.

The Ball (produced 1632). 1639; edited by Thomas Marc Parrott, in *Plays and Poems of Chapman*, 1914.

Hyde Park (produced 1632). 1637; edited by Edmund Gosse, in *Plays*, 1888.

The Bird in a Cage (produced 1632–33?). 1633.

A Contention for Honour and Riches. 1633; revised version, as *Honoria and Mammon*, 1658.

The Gamester (produced 1633). 1637.

The Young Admiral (produced 1633). 1637.

The Example (produced 1634). 1637.

The Triumph of Peace (produced 1634). 1634; edited by Edmund Gosse, in *Plays*, 1888.

The Opportunity (produced 1634). 1640.

The Night-Walker; or, The Little Thief, from a play by Fletcher (produced 1634). 1661.

The Lady of Pleasure (produced 1635). 1637; edited by A. S. Knowland, in *Six Caroline Plays*, 1962.

The Coronation (produced 1635). 1640.

Chabot, Admiral of France, from the play by Chapman (produced 1635). 1639; edited by Ezra Lehman, 1906.

The Duke's Mistress (produced 1636). 1638.

The Constant Maid (produced 1636–40?). 1640; as *Love Will Find Out the Way*, 1661.

The Royal Master (produced 1637). 1638; edited by A. W. Ward, in *Representative English Comedies*, 1914.

The Doubtful Heir (produced 1638?). In *Six New Plays*, 1653.

The Country Captain, with William Cavendish (produced 1639?). With *The Variety*, 1649; edited by A. H. Bullen, as *Captain Underwit*, in *Old English Plays 2*, 1883.

St. Patrick of Ireland (produced 1639?). 1640.

The Politician (produced 1639?). 1655.

The Gentleman of Venice (produced 1639). 1655.

The Imposture (produced 1640). In *Six New Plays*, 1653.

The Brothers (produced 1641?). In *Six New Plays*, 1653.

The Cardinal (produced 1641). In *Six New Plays*, 1653; edited by Charles R. Forker, 1964.

The Court Secret (produced 1642). In *Six New Plays*, 1653.

The Sisters (produced 1642). In *Six New Plays*, 1653.

The Contention of Ajax and Ulysses for the Armour of Achilles (produced 1645–58?). With *Honoria and Mammon*, 1658.

The Triumph of Beauty (produced ?). In *Poems*, 1646.

Six New Plays. 1653.

Cupid and Death, music by Matthew Locke (produced 1653). 1653; edited by B. A. Harris, in *A Book of Masques in Honour of Allardyce Nicoll*, 1967.

Verse

Poems. 1646; edited by R. L. Armstrong, 1941; *Narcissus* edited by Elizabeth Story Donno, in *Elizabethan Minor Epics,* 1963.
The Rudiments of Grammar: The Rules Composed in Verse for the Greater Benefit and Delight of Young Beginners. 1656; revised edition, as *Manductio,* 1660.

Other

Via ad Latinam Linguam Complanata, The Way Made Plain to the Latin Tongue. 1649; as *Grammatica Anglo-Latina,* 1651.
The True Impartial History and Wars of the Kingdom of Ireland. 1693.

Bibliography: *Shirley: A Concise Bibliography* by S. A. and D. R. Tannenbaum, 1946; supplement in *Elizabethan Bibliographies Supplements 8* by C. A. Pennel and W. P. Williams, 1968.

Reading List: *The Relation of Shirley's Plays to the Elizabethan Drama* by R. S. Forsythe, 1914; *Shirley, Dramatist: A Biographical and Critical Study* by Arthur H. Nason, 1915; *Shirley: His Catholic Philosophy of Life* by S. J. Radtke, 1929.

*　　*　　*

James Shirley wrote as many plays as Shakespeare, and his work displays a quality and range which make him easily the most important dramatist for more than a decade before the closing of the theatres in 1642. Though never an actor, he was a thorough man of the theatre, and he built very successfully on the main dramatic patterns popular with Stuart playwrights, among whom Beaumont and Fletcher were for him supreme; their work, he declares in an Address to the Reader which he wrote for the 1647 Beaumont and Fletcher folio, is "the greatest monument of the scene that time and humanity have produced."

He is probably at his best in his comedies, which usually employ romantic multiple plots, with thin but dramatically effective characters and, especially when the setting is London, many realistic touches. In *Hyde Park* the high-spirited Mistress Carol (a simplified version of Shakespeare's Beatrice) had rather hear "the tedious tales of Holinshed" than lovers' speeches but is conquered by a suitor cleverer than she; the out-of-door scenes in the same play are enlivened by offstage sounds of racing in the Park and (for both realism and romance) the voices of cuckoo and nightingale to presage lovers' fortunes. Shirley is also capable of good epigrammatic wit, as in *The Lady of Pleasure*, where French is "one of the finest tongues for ladies to show their teeth in."

The tragi-comedies are typically noble and rhetorical, though lightened by occasional comic episodes. In *The Young Admiral*, which owes something to Lope de Vega, the brave hero and his sweetheart are captured by enemy forces who threaten to kill her unless he will lead them against his native Naples, but if he does this his father will be put to death in Naples. The characters are appealing enough to carry the contrived plot, and the skill of the playwright resolves all problems happily at the end.

The tragedies show a starker confrontation of good and evil. In *The Politician* the black-souled Gotharus attempts to usurp power in Norway from a weak king and a virtuous prince; ultimately he is poisoned by his hellish paramour the queen, who then poisons herself and dies with an anguished "forgive, forgive." Shirley's most famous tragedy, *The Cardinal*, which he himself called "the best of my flock," has a relatively simple plot, with an atmosphere of brooding evil which twice breaks into terrifying violence. The language is generally restrained, the blank verse admirably fluent.

Shirley also wrote the showiest of the Stuart masques (*The Triumph of Peace*) and many lyrics which compare well with those of his best contemporaries, to whom they were sometimes misascribed. One of his songs, "The glories of our blood and state," achieves a sombre dignity which has made it better remembered than the rest. It occurs as a dirge at the end of a short piece dramatised from Ovid, *The Contention of Ajax and Ulysses for the Armour of Achilles*, which Shirley perhaps intended, after Parliament had closed the theatres, for production by schoolboys.

—Rhodes Dunlap

TATHAM, John.   English.   Born in England c. 1610. Nothing is known about his background, family, or education. Probably served in the Army under Lord Carnarvon in 1642. Settled in London, and began writing for the stage in 1632; appointed Laureate of the Lord Mayor's Show, and wrote the City pageants, 1657–64. Nothing is known about him after 1664.

PUBLICATIONS

Collections

   Dramatic Works, edited by James Maidment and W. H. Logan.   1879.

Plays

   Love Crowns the End: A Pastoral (produced 1632).   In *The Fancy's Theatre*, 1640.
   The Distracted State (produced 1641–50?).   1651.
   The Scots Figgaries; or, A Knot of Knaves.   1652.
   London's Triumphs (produced 1657).   1657; other pageants produced and published 1658–64.
   The Rump; or, The Mirror of the Late Times (produced 1660).   1660.
   The Royal Oak (produced 1660).   1660.
   Neptune's Address to Charles the Second (produced 1661).   1661.
   Aqua Triumphalis (produced 1662).   1662.

Verse

   The Fancy's Theatre.   1640.
   Ostella; or, The Faction of Love and Beauty Reconciled.   1650.

Reading List: "English Street Theatre 1655–1708" by L. J. Morrissey, in *Costerus 4,* 1972.

*   *   *

John Tatham, one of those minor talents who observes all of the outward forms of the art he would imitate, must have been puzzled when he did not succeed. His two books of poetry, *The Fancies Theatre* and *Ostella*, include most of the poetic types of the 17th century – acrostic odes, epithalamiums, elegies, epigrams, dialogues, as well as a poem of 110 quatrains called "Daphnes" and a poem on "A Wart on a Gentlewomans Arme." His several poems "To a Coy Mistress" touch on conventional themes (time, decay, reversed compliments), and he can write lyrics of sustained personification, as he does in "The Letter." At his best he can rise to a minor metaphysical conceit when he ends "The Nut to Ostella" with "[our hearts] may knit and seem to be/Two Kirnels in one shell." At his worst he sinks to anti-petrarchan bathos when he tells a lady that "Grape or Gooseberry/yield a juyce more savoury" than her breasts. The masque *Love Crownes the End* illustrates the elements that made him a successful writer of pageants for the City of London from 1657 to 1664. In this masque Tatham mixes the low comedy of a country bumpkin, a heavenly messenger, violent action (an attempted murder), and both Christian and overtly sexual language with the usual pastoral romance of the masque. Thus, his masques and pageants have many of the elements of the primitive mummings from which the Jacobean masque evolved. He wrote both Lord Mayors pageants – most, like *The Royal Oake*, "staged" on 29 October 1660, call for loyalty and unity – and the water fete *Aqua Triumphalis* staged by the City to welcome Charles II and his new Queen from Hampton Court to Whitehall in 1662.

Tatham wrote three regular plays. All three were political. Both *The Scots Figgaries*, a comedy partly in Scottish stage dialect, and *The Distracted State*, a tragedy set in Sicily, attack the Scots, religious extremism, and disunity in household and state. *The Distracted State* illustrates Tatham's weakness as a playwright. He cannot find a means of enacting his ideas, and so this "revenge" tragedy is full of scenes of static intrigue followed by outbursts of violence. After two static acts, the third begins with the head of a decapitated man thrown on stage, a man shot, another killed in a sword battle, and a suicide by falling on a sword. Twelve of the nineteen characters die violently on stage in the play, including the heroine Harmonia. The language of the play, which deserves to be memorialized in Fielding's *Tragedy of Tragedies*, is nearly as excessive: "I have a soul as big/with grief as you, that fain would be deliver'd/If reason would turn midwife." Despite its excesses, this play is part of a tradition, which continues into the 18th century, of thinly disguising contemporary politics as remote tragedy. *The Rump*, a broad comedy written after General Monk forced the dissolution of the Rump parliament, is the best of Tatham's plays. It brings real Commonwealth leaders, and their wives, on stage, and ends with the elder Mrs. Cromwell hawking kitchen stuff, Stoneware (Warestone) selling ballads, and Lockwhite (Whitelock) returning to his practice as a cheating lawyer. Again Tatham fails to find an appropriate action for his play, and he can only solve this problem by staging riots of apprentices. The strength of the play lies in its dialogue which is a compendium of cliché language ("trust them no farther than I can fling 'um") and folk sayings ("soft fire makes sweet malt") that reveal the "simplicity" of the Commonwealth leaders. With scenes of the male world balanced by scenes of the female world, it anticipates the witty comedies of Etherege and Congreve, and was revised by Aphra Behn in 1681 as *The Roundheads*.

—L. J. Morrissey

TOURNEUR, Cyril. English.   Born in England c. 1575. Very little is known about his life: served the Cecils, the Veres, and the Earl of Essex at various times during his career, much of which was spent in military or diplomatic service: government courier in 1613; campaign soldier, probably in the Low Countries, 1614; accompanied Sir Edward Cecil, Lord Marshall of the Fleet, on expedition to Spain, 1625–26, having been appointed by Cecil Secretary to the Council of War and Secretary to the Marshall's Court: died from wounds incurred in the expedition. *Died 28 February 1626.*

PUBLICATIONS

Collections

   Works, edited by Allardyce Nicoll.   1930.

Plays

   The Revenger's Tragedy (produced 1606–07?).   1607; edited by R. A. Foakes, 1966.
   The Atheist's Tragedy; or, The Honest Man's Fortune (produced 1607–11?).   1611;
      edited by Brian Morris and Roma Gill, 1974.

Verse

   The Transformed Metamorphosis.   1600.
   A Funeral Poem upon the Death of Sir Francis Vere, Knight.   1609.
   A Grief on the Death of Prince Henry, in *Three Elegies.*   1613.

Bibliography: *Tourneur: A Bibliography* by S. A. and D. R. Tannenbaum, 1937.

Reading List: *A Study of Tourneur* by Peter B. Murray, 1964; *The Language of "The Revenger's Tragedy"* by Daniel J. Jacobson, 1974.

*   *   *

   The name of Cyril Tourneur would be virtually unknown were it not for its association with *The Revenger's Tragedy,* one of the most impressive dramatic productions of the seventeenth century. Yet the association may be no more than conventional, the acceptance of an arbitrary assignment made by Edward Archer in 1656, thirty years after Tourneur died in Ireland, having been put ashore there when he was taken ill on Cecil's unhappy Cadiz expedition.
   Born probably in the decade 1570–1580, Tourneur seems to have spent much of his life in the service of the Vere and Cecil families, and he occasionally celebrated their members in verses that testify more to his sense of duty than to any poetic ability. In 1600 he published a long and obscure satiric poem, *The Transformed Metamorphosis,* which shows the influence of Spenser and Marston but ultimately yields up no very clear meaning. A short spell of dramatic activity is vouched for by the publication of *The Atheist's Tragedy,* said on its title-page to have been "written by Cyril Tourneur." There is also an entry in the Stationers' Register, February 1611/12, for "a Tragecomedy called, the Noble man, written by Cyrill Tourneur," and a letter of 1613 in which Robert Daborne tells Henslowe that he has "given

Cyrill Tourneur an act of yᵉ Arreignment of london to write." These two plays were never printed, but Warburton claimed to have possessed the manuscript of "The Nobleman T. C." by "Cyrill Turnuer," until his cook used it underneath her pies, and burnt it.

The Atheist's Tragedy stands as an epitaph to the revenge tradition, incorporating all the salient features, but not the life. The "atheist" is D'Amville, convinced that "death casts up Our total sum of joy and happiness." He resolves to provide for his posterity (in whom he sees his only immortality) by murdering and robbing those from whom he will inherit. Having killed his brother and reported his nephew, Charlemont, to be dead in the wars, D'Amville secures the marriage of Castabella, Charlemont's betrothed, to his own son Rousard. But the union is not consummated: Rousard confesses that "A general weakness did surprise my health/The very day I married Castabella." To compensate for his son's impotence, D'Amville proposes that he should himself supply Rousard's place, to beget the desired heir. The proposition is made in the churchyard, D'Amville assuring Castabella that "These dead men's bones lie here of purpose to/Invite us to supply the number of/The living." The living, however, are already present in the graveyard. A puritan chaplain and his wench are bent on fornication; Borachio (D'Amville's servant) is intending murder; and his victim is Charlemont, supposed dead but in secret returned from the wars and now brooding over mortality among the tombs. The scene is a hilarious mixture of melancholy and murder, bawdy farce, and the melodrama of attempted incestuous rape. Charlemont kills Borachio and rescues Castabella, then a stage direction (probably authorial) indicates that the two lovers "*lie down with either of them a death's head for a pillow.*" This edifying spectacle, *de contemptu mortis*, is immediately disturbed by the arrival of the puritan, who mistakes the corpse of Borachio for his paramour, kisses with anticipation, then recoils in precise horror: "Now purity defend me from the sin of Sodom."

The scene ends with D'Amville's distracted vision of his brother's ghost (really the chaplain in a sheet) seeking revenge for his murder; and the last act of the play shows how the revenge is exacted with true Senecan excess. D'Amville's own death is comically appropriate. He attends the execution of Charlemont (condemned for his killing of Borachio), and offers his services as headsman; the author's stage direction indicates the course of justice: "*As he raises up the axe [he] strikes out his own brains.*" Charlemont, the most inactive of heroes, pronounces the moral that "patience is the honest man's revenge."

Shifting from solemn philosophizing to melodrama, heightened by supernatural interjections in the thunder, and relieved by the lascivious caperings of a tallow-chandler turned chaplain, *The Atheist's Tragedy* could hardly hope for success in the theatre, where it must bewilder audiences with the instability of its mood. This is the first point of contrast with *The Revenger's Tragedy*, a magnificently sombre play published anonymously. Here, only flashes of the blackest comedy light up skeletal figures, whose personalities reside in their names alone, pursuing a *danse macabre* where gold and lust lead to death and revenge.

For nine years Vindice has waited for the right opportunity to avenge the death of his betrothed lady, Gloriana. She was poisoned by the lustful Duke, a seventeenth-century stereotype of "royal lust ... grey-hair'd adultery." Vindice's constant companion, his "study's ornament," throughout these years has been Gloriana's skull; and now, concealed in a mask but with poison in its mouth, the skull becomes a weapon. Lured by the promise of a "country lady ... [who] has somewhat a grave look with her," the Duke kisses his destruction. Diversifying the action, but not dissipating the mood, are parallel plots of lust and its rewards. The Duchess commits incestuous adultery with Spurio, the Duke's bastard son. Her own youngest son rapes a virtuous lady, while his two brothers plot against Lussurioso, their step-brother and the Duke's heir, to have him disinherited. Their plot fails, and Lussurioso inherits his father's throne – and also Vindice's hatred, which finds a new focus in Lussurioso's attempt on the honour of Castiza, Vindice's sister.

The catastrophe comes in a masque, the traditional vehicle for vengeance ever since *The Spanish Tragedy*: "A masque is treason's licence, that build upon:/'Tis murder's best face, when a vizard's on." Vindice stabs Lussurioso; suspecting a rival for the throne, Ambitioso (the Duchess's son) stabs his brother; he himself is stabbed by the Duke's bastard.

Momentarily Vindice is triumphant, and boasts of his victory. Then he is condemned to death by Antonio, the play's survivor, who cares little for the justice or appropriateness of Vindice's revenge but looks (wisely) to his own safety: "You that would murder him would murder me."

The exaggerations and contrivances of character and plot are supported in *The Revenger's Tragedy* (as they never are in *The Atheist's Tragedy*) by a poetry of distinction and intensity. Sharpened by the verse, the plot develops into a keenly pointed attack on the corruptions of court life, where "lordships [are] sold to maintain ladyships." From being a personal "ornament" to Vindice's study, and the petard with which the Duke's lust is hoist, Gloriana's skull becomes a *memento mori*. The emblematic cliché is brought to new life by the poetry, felt at its most powerful in Vindice's unanswerable rhetoric:

> Does the silkworm expend her yellow labours
> For thee? for thee does she undo herself?
> Are lordships sold to maintain ladyships
> For the poor benefit of a bewitching minute?

The Revenger's Tragedy has been discussed along with the known works of Cyril Tourneur because, as yet, there is no overwhelming evidence to disprove Archer's 1656 attribution. Many critics react instinctively that this cannot be the work of the author of *The Atheist's Tragedy*, and Thomas Middleton continues to be proposed as a strong claimant.

—Roma Gill

WEBSTER, John. English. Born in England, probably in London, c. 1580. Very little is known of his life: he was married and had several children; possibly a member of the Merchant Taylors' Company; clerk of the parish of St. Andrews, Holborn; writer for Henslowe c. 1602. *Died in the 1630's.*

PUBLICATIONS

Collections

   Works, edited by F. L. Lucas. 4 vols., 1927; revised edition, 1966.

Plays

   Sir Thomas Wyatt, with Thomas Heywood and Dekker (produced 1602–07?). 1607; edited by Fredson Bowers, in *Dramatic Works of Dekker,* 1953–61.
   Westward Ho, with Dekker (produced 1604). 1607; edited by Fredson Bowers, in *Dramatic Works of Dekker,* 1953–61.

Northward Ho, with Dekker (produced 1605).   1607; edited by Fredson Bowers, in *Dramatic Works of Dekker,* 1953–61.

Appius and Virginia, with Thomas Heywood (produced 1608?).   1654.

The Devil's Law Case; or, When Women Go to Law the Devil Is Full of Business (produced 1610?).   1623; edited by Elizabeth M. Brennan, 1974.

The White Devil (produced 1612?).   1612; edited by J. R. Mulryne, 1970.

The Duchess of Malfi (produced 1613–14?).   1623; edited by Clive Hart, 1972.

Any Thing for a Quiet Life, with Middleton (produced 1621?).   1662.

Monuments of Honour (produced 1624).   1624; edited by R. T. D. Sayle, in *Lord Mayors' Pageants of the Merchant Taylors' Company,* 1931.

A Cure for a Cuckold, with William Rowley (produced 1624–25?).   1661.

Verse

A Monumental Column, in *Three Elegies on the Most Lamented Death of Prince Henry.*   1613.

Bibliography: *Webster: A Classified Bibliography* by William E. Mahaney, 1973.

Reading List: *Webster: A Critical Study,* 1951, and *Webster: The Duchess of Malfi,* 1963, both by Clifford Leech; *The Tragic Satire of Webster* by Travis Bogard, 1955; *Webster's Borrowings* by Robert W. Dent, 1960; *Webster* by Ian Scott-Kilvert, 1964; *Webster and His Critics 1617–1964* by Don D. Moore, 1966; *A Study of Webster* by Peter B. Murray, 1969; *Webster* edited by Brian Morris, 1970; *The Art of Webster* by Ralph Berry, 1972; *Tragedy and the Jacobean Temper: The Major Plays of Webster* by Richard Bodtke, 1972; *Webster: Politics and Tragedy* by Robert P. Griffin, 1972.

*   *   *

John Webster is among the shadowiest figures of the Elizabethan age; even the dates of his birth and death are not known for certain. We first hear of him in May 1602 when Philip Henslowe records a payment of £5 to Drayton, Webster, Middleton, and others as advance fees on a play called *Caesar's Fall;* the play, however, is lost. In the preface to his play *The Devil's Law Case* Webster himself refers to another of his plays, *The Guise;* this too is lost. In his pageant *Monuments of Honour* he describes himself as "born free of the Merchant Taylers' Company." This may mean that he was the son of John Webster, a freeman of that guild. Webster may also be the actor of that name who toured Germany in 1596.

In 1604 Webster wrote an induction to Marston's *The Malcontent* when the King's Men first performed the play, which was originally written for a boys' company. The induction ingeniously frames the play within a discussion of its merits by the actors about to perform it. In the same year he collaborated with Thomas Dekker in writing *Westward Ho* and the following year they wrote *Northward Ho.* The same pair also contributed verses to a volume illustrating the allegorical arches erected to welcome King James to London. In 1613 Webster published *A Monumental Column* commemorating Prince Henry who had died the year before.

Many plays or parts of plays have been assigned to Webster but only four are generally recognized as being by him alone. Of these *The Devil's Law Case* is the least impressive, being a meagre and loosely structured tragi-comedy. Swinburne wrote that "the author of *Appius and Virginia* would have earned an honourable and enduring place in the history of English letters," and the play, in various adaptations, held the stage for a century or so after Webster's death. But it does not bear sustained comparison with his two great achievements in tragedy, *The White Devil* and *The Duchess of Malfi.*

Both plays are based on actual events in the recent past as transmitted through popular Italian novellas. The appetite for scenes of blood and violence and for lavish spectacle, and the audience's delight in elaborate stage apparatus are amply catered for in both plays. Ghosts, poisoned paintings, disembodied hands as well as murder by strangulation and breaking the victim's neck are a few of the many such occurrences in the plays. Incest, adultery, lycanthropy, to say nothing of mere murder, form the ingredients of both plots. But what gives them their tragic intensity is the atmosphere of brooding darkness which pervades them and the eloquent dignity with which Webster's central figures face their impending death. Vittoria, Flamineo, and the Duchess of Malfi find in their last moments epitaphs for themselves of such compelling power that, in the case of the two former figures at least, we forget how corrupt the course of their lives has been: "My soul like to a ship in a black storm,/Is driven, I know not whither," cries Vittoria, the "White Devil," and her brother responds with "While we look up to heaven we confound/Knowledge with knowledge. Oh, I am in a mist!" The intense melancholy, haunting disillusionment, and pervasive sense of corruption in high places, which are so marked a feature of Jacobean tragedy, found in these two plays their most striking expression. Encountering them we understand, if we cannot altogether share, the feeling which moved Swinburne to write: "Except in Aeschylus, in Dante and in Shakespeare, I at least know not where to seek for passages which in sheer force of tragic and noble horror ... may be set against the subtlest, the deepest, the sublimest passages of Webster."

—Gāmini Salgādo

WILSON, Robert. English. Nothing is known about his background or education. Married; the playwright Robert Wilson, The Younger, is probably his son. Joined the Earl of Leicester's Company at its establishment, 1574, and quickly gained a reputation as a comic actor; chosen as one of twelve actors to form Queen Elizabeth's Company, 1583, and remained with the company until 1588 when he joined Lord Strange's Company, which subsequently became the Lord Chamberlain's Men. *Died* (buried) *20 November 1600.*

PUBLICATIONS

Plays

The Three Ladies of London (produced 1581?).   1584; edited by J. S. Farmer, 1911.
The Three Lords and Three Ladies of London (produced 1589?).   1590; edited by J. S. Farmer, 1912.
The Cobbler's Prophecy (produced 1594?).   1594; edited by A. C. Wood, 1914.

Reading List: "The Two-Wilsons Controversy" by H. S. H. Mithal, in *Notes and Queries,* March 1959.

*   *   *

In his extant plays Robert Wilson is seen adapting the morality play to the changing theatrical taste of the time of Marlowe and the early Shakespeare. *The Three Ladies of London* is centred on social criticism, employing mid-century techniques in a lively manner. Four knaves, Dissimulation, Fraud, Simony, and Usury, seek employment with the three ladies. Refused by Conscience and by Love (who instead engages Simplicity, a clown having a leading role), they are entertained by the already corrupt Lucre, in whose service they do much social harm. Conscience and Love are dispossessed of their house; the former is deluded into being Lucre's bawd and the latter into marrying Dissimulation. Finally all three ladies are arraigned before Judge Nemo who condemns them. Though the play's moral view is pessimistic, its technique is lively, a number of minor characters providing concrete examples of London's corruption, and the clown being frequently involved. Two striking episodes are the unscrupulous Mercatore's abuse of an honest Jew's trust, and the cutting of Hospitality's throat by Usury. There is vivid stage symbolism when corrupt Conscience is given a spotted face and corrupt Love a double one. The style is homely; as for the versification, though some regular "fourteener" passages are found, long irregular couplets predominate.

The sequel, *The Three Lords and Three Ladies of London*, takes an optimistic view. Though the knaves reappear, they vainly solicit the reformed ladies, who are claimed in marriage by the three lords, Policy, Pomp, and Pleasure. Before the wedding, the lords must outbrave Pride, Ambition, and Tyranny, three Spanish lords bent on conquest, and, these defeated, encounter (in a short, abstract, and superfluous episode) three further rival lords of Lincoln. Much use is made of moral-heraldic spectacle. The clown Simplicity is again prominent, having some scenes with the knaves and another with the lords' witty pages. The style is more elevated; the verse is mostly now iambic pentameter, either unrhymed or (occasionally) rhyming in couplets and quatrains; there is also some prose and some use of irregular couplets tighter than those of the earlier play.

In *The Cobbler's Prophecy*, which has more elaborate stage requirements suggesting performance at court, Wilson continues in this later style. Any social criticism is embodied in, and secondary to, a part-mythological allegory whereby the effete Mars's mistress Venus is seduced by Contempt and bears a child Ruina – events which Mercury causes the once-again-prominent clown, this time Ralph Cobbler, to foretell; finally military and civic virtue prevails and disaster is averted.

Wilson's classical pretensions appear in all three plays alongside his English vivacity: there are Latin speeches and mottoes in his second play, and allusions (Nemo, St. Nihil, Brifrons) even in his first.

—T. W. Craik

NOTES ON CONTRIBUTORS

ASHLEY, Leonard R. N. Professor of English, Brooklyn College, City University of New York. Author of *Colley Cibber*, 1965; *19th-Century British Drama*, 1967; *Authorship and Evidence: A Study of Attribution and the Renaissance Drama*, 1968; *History of the Short Story*, 1968; *George Peele: The Man and His Work*, 1970. Editor of the *Enriched Classics* series, several anthologies of fiction and drama, and a number of facsimile editions. **Essays:** Henry Chettle; Nathan Field; Anthony Munday.

BRISSENDEN, Alan. Senior Lecturer in English, University of Adelaide, Australia: Joint General Editor, Tudor and Stuart Text series. Author of *Rolf Boldrewood*, 1972. Editor of *A Chaste Maid in Cheapside* by Thomas Middleton, 1968, *Shakespeare and Some Others*, 1976, and *The Portable Boldrewood*, 1978. **Essay:** William Rowley.

CRAIK, T. W. Professor of English, University of Durham. Author of *The Tudor Interlude*, 1958, and *The Comic Tales of Chaucer*, 1964. Joint General Editor of *The Revels History of Drama in the English Language*, and editor of plays by Massinger, Marlowe, and Shakespeare. **Essays:** George Peele; Thomas Sackville and Thomas Norton; Robert Wilson.

DeMATTEIS, Daniel. Visiting Assistant Professor, Scarborough College, University of Toronto. **Essays:** Henry Glapthorne; Thomas Nabbes.

DRAKAKIS, John. Member of the Department of English Studies, University of Stirling, Scotland. **Essay:** Shakerley Marmion.

DUNLAP, Rhodes. Member of the Department of English, University of Iowa, Iowa City. Editor of *The Poems of Thomas Carew*, 1949. **Essays:** William Cartwright; Thomas Killigrew; Thomas May; James Shirley.

FOREY, Margaret. Examiner and part-time teacher; currently editing a work by William Strode. Formerly Lecturer at the University of Durham. Author of "Cleveland's 'Square Cap': Some Questions of Structure and Date" in *Durham University Journal*, 1974. **Essays:** Jasper Mayne; Thomas Randolph.

GIBBS, A. M. Professor, School of English and Linguistics, Macquarie University, New South Wales. Author of *G. B. Shaw*, 1969. Editor of *The Shorter Poems, and Songs from the Plays and Masques* by Sir William Davenant, 1972. **Essay:** Sir William Davenant.

GILL, Roma. Member of the Department of English, University of Sheffield. Editor of *The Plays of Christopher Marlowe*, 1971, *William Empson: The Man and His Work*, 1974, and of works by Middleton and Tourneur. **Essays:** Sir Aston Cockayne; Christopher Marlowe; Thomas Middleton; Cyril Tourneur.

GORDON, Ian A. Professor of English, University of Wellington, 1936–74; also taught at the University of Leeds and the University of Edinburgh. Author of *John Skelton*, 1943; *The*

Teaching of English, 1947; *Katherine Mansfield*, 1954; *The Movement of English Prose*, 1966; *John Galt*, 1972. Editor of *English Prose Technique*, 1948, and of works by William Shenstone, John Galt, and Katherine Mansfield. **Essays:** Robert Greene; John Lyly.

GURR, Andrew. Professor of English Language and Literature, University of Reading, Berkshire. Author of *The Shakespearean Stage*, 1970. Editor of several plays by Beaumont and Fletcher. **Essay:** Francis Beaumont.

MORRISSEY, L. J. Member of the Department of English, University of Saskatchewan, Saskatoon. Author of articles on English street theatre and the theatrical records of the London Guilds, and of a forthcoming book on Swift. **Essay:** John Tatham.

RUOFF, James E. Associate Professor of English, City College of New York. Author of *Elizabethan Poetry and Prose*, 1972, *Crowell Handbook of Elizabethan and Stuart Literature*, 1973, and *Major Shakespearean Tragedies* (with Edward G. Quinn), 1973. **Essays:** Thomas Dekker; John Fletcher.

SALGÂDO, Gãmini. Professor of English, University of Exeter, Devon. Author of *Eyewitnesses of Shakespeare: Firsthand Accounts of Performances, 1590–1890*, 1975, and *The Elizabethan Underworld*, 1977. Editor of *Sons and Lovers: A Collection of Critical Essays*, 1969, *Cony Catchers and Bawdy Baskets*, 1973, works by D. H. Lawrence and Shakespeare, and collections of Jacobean and Restoration plays. **Essays:** Richard Brome; John Ford; Ben Jonson; Thomas Kyd; Philip Massinger; John Webster.

SHADY, Raymond C. Member of the English Department, St. John Fisher College, Rochester, New York. Editor of *Love's Mistress* by Thomas Heywood, 1977. **Essays:** John Day; John Marston.

STAGG, Louis Charles. Professor of English, Memphis State University, Tennessee; Member of the Executive Committee, Tennessee Philological Association. Author of *Index to Poe's Critical Vocabulary*, 1966; *Index to the Figurative Language in the Tragedies of Webster, Jonson, Heywood, Chapman, Marston, Tourneur*, and *Middleton*, 7 vols., 1967–70, revised edition, as *Index to the Figurative Language of the Tragedies of Shakespeare's Chief 17th-Century Contemporaries*, 1977. **Essay:** Thomas Heywood.

TRAVERSI, Derek A. Professor of English Literature, Swarthmore College, Pennsylvania. Author of *An Approach to Shakespeare*, 1938 (revised, 1968); *Shakespeare: The Last Phase*, 1954; *Shakespeare: From Richard II to Henry V*, 1957; *Shakespeare: The Roman Plays*, 1963; *T. S. Eliot: The Longer Poems*, 1976. **Essay:** William Shakespeare.

WADDINGTON, Raymond B. Professor of English, University of Wisconsin, Madison; Member of the editorial boards of *Sixteenth Century Journal* and *Literary Monographs*. Author of *The Mind's Empire: Myth and Form in George Chapman's Narrative Poems*, 1974, and of articles on Shakespeare, Chapman, Milton, and others. Co-Editor of *The Rhetoric of Renaissance Poetry*, 1974. **Essay:** George Chapman.